Understanding and Preventing Campus Violence

Edited by Michele A. Paludi

Westport, Connecticut
London

Library of Congress Cataloging-in-Publication Data

Understanding and preventing campus violence / edited by Michele A. Paludi.
    p. cm.
  Includes bibliographical references and index.
  ISBN-13: 978-0-313-34828-0 (alk. paper)
  1. Campus violence. 2. Campus violence–Prevention. I. Paludi, Michele
Antoinette.
  LB2345.U68 2008
  371.7′82—dc22   2008008783

British Library Cataloguing in Publication Data is available.

Library of Congress Catalog Card Number: 2008008783
ISBN-13: 978-0-313-34828-0

First published in 2008

Praeger Publishers, 88 Post Road West, Westport, CT 06881
An imprint of Greenwood Publishing Group, Inc.
www.praeger.com

Printed in the United States of America

The paper used in this book complies with the
Permanent Paper Standard issued by the National
Information Standards Organization (Z39.48–1984).

10 9 8 7 6 5 4 3 2 1

In memory of victims of campus violence

Contents

Acknowledgments

I thank Jeff Olson at Praeger for his encouragement of me to edit this book. It is an honor to work with Jeff and his colleagues at Praeger.

The following family, friends, and colleagues have been supportive during the preparation of this book: Rosalie Paludi, Lucille Paludi, Carmen Paludi, Jr., and Tony Deliberti.

I also thank the contributors to this volume for their commitment to preventing campus violence at their own institutions. Their personal stories have strengthened this book.

I extend my appreciation again to my mother, Antoinette Rose Peccichio Paludi, who offered me great advice when I was 10 years old and announced I wanted to be a nun. She told me that I would never be able to keep the vow of silence; that she noticed that whenever I see injustice I have to speak out. She told me to help others by being their voice and to help make institutions do the right thing for students and employees. I know she is smiling down on me now because this book does exactly what she wanted me to do.

Introduction

Michele A. Paludi

The secret in education lies in respecting the student.
                                        Ralph Waldo Emerson

The day the murders took place at Virginia Tech's campus, I received several phone calls and e-mail messages from students in my graduate course on human resource management, in which they asked me whether class was going to be held that evening and whether our classroom was safe. I did teach that night, but before the planned topic I decided to spend time listening to their fears and anxieties about campus violence. I also told them what we would do should there be a similar incident to what happened at Virginia Tech at our campus, in the building in which our class meets, and in our classroom. I provided them with definitions of various forms of campus violence, including stalking, hazing, hate crimes, sexual assault, and sexual harassment and discussed our college's policies and procedures on these issues.

Teaching about campus violence is not new for me. I have taught about it at the undergraduate and graduate levels since 1980 in courses such as Psychology of Women, Educational Psychology, Introduction to Women's Studies, and Gender and Power in the Workplace. But discussing it in a course on human resource management? I do teach about workplace violence in this course but I was concerned that some students would think I was overreacting and taking unnecessary precautions by discussing campus violence. But students thanked me for not keeping the issue of campus and workplace violence silent, as so many of their professors had done. They knew I was editing this book on campus violence and several asked if they could be part of this project. They wanted to help out to educate students, administrators, and faculty about campus violence. I am proud that their work is included in this text.

There are times when silence has the loudest voice.

Leroy Brownlow

LABELING CAMPUS VIOLENCE

The silence surrounding campus violence identified by these students is not something unique to them or their college. I have frequently used the following exercise in my courses on the psychology of women and gender as well as in my consulting with campuses about violence (see Paludi, 2002):

> *For the next few minutes jot down the behaviors in which you engage as you leave campus at night to go to your dorm or apartment.*

I first ask women in the class to generate a list of their responses to this question. The following behaviors have been identified each time I have used this exercise:

- *Take out my can of mace.*
- *Look behind me and across the street as I walk home.*
- *Look in the backseat of my car before I get into it.*
- *Call my roommate to tell her I'm on my way back to the dorm.*
- *Call for a campus escort to help me get home.*
- *Be sure the lock on my door hasn't been tampered with.*

(Paludi, 2002, p. 336)

I ask men in the class the same question; however similar responses are not generated. When I ask students to provide a label to these behaviors, they frequently respond "phobias" or "life." When I inform them that these behaviors are rape-avoidance strategies, the classroom is silent. It is difficult for women to use this label to describe their behavior, yet many of them have indicated they spend a good part of every day avoiding rape or other forms of sexual victimization both on and off campus.

Rape

While labeling experiences as campus violence is low, the incidence of all forms of campus violence is high (Bachar & Koss, 2001; Fisher, Cullen, & Turner, 2000; Koss, 2006; LaVant, 2001; Nicoletti, Spencer-Thomas, & Bollinger, 2001; Paludi, Nydegger, DeSouza, Nydegger, & Allen Dicker, 2006; Pezza & Bellotti, 1995). For example, Finn (1995) described rape as the most common violent crime on college/university campuses. Humphrey and Kahn (2000) noted that women between the ages of 16 to 24 are raped at rates four times higher than the assault rate of all women. Fisher, Cullen, and Turner (2000) reported that college women are at risk for rape more than women who are not attending college.

Rape is legally defined as nonconsensual oral, anal, or vaginal pene-tration obtained by force, by threat of bodily harm, or when the victim is incapable of giving consent. Based on data from the Harvard School of Public Health's Center for Alcohol Studies, Mohler-Kuo, Dowdall, Koss, and Wechsler (2004) reported that one in every 20 woman college student is raped each year. The study also found that approximately 70% of college women are raped when they are too intoxicated to give consent. Fisher, Cullen, and Turner (2000) reported that among college women, within the past seven months, 5% had someone expose their genitals to them; 3% were observed naked.

Stranger rape of college women is not as common as acquaintance rape (Fisher, Cullen, & Turner, 2000). Rape involving a victim who is familiar with the rapist is referred to as acquaintance rape. On college campuses, acquaintance rape is frequently referred to as date rape (Warshaw, 1988). Fisher, Cullen, and Turner (2000) reported that 90% of college women who were raped knew the assailant. The rapist is typically a classmate, friend, or current or ex-boyfriend. Women are significantly more likely to be raped than men. Rozee (1999) has referred to the United States as a "rape-prone" culture.

Sexual Harassment

The incidence of sexual harassment among undergraduate students by their peers ranges between 20–80% each year (Dziech, 2003; Paludi, Nydegger, DeSouza, Nydegger, & Allen Dicker, 2006; Sandler & Shoop, 1997). These behaviors include:

- Sexual comments, gestures, and jokes
- Being touched, pinched, or grabbed in a sexual way
- Forced to kiss someone
- Intentionally being brushed up against in a sexual way

Research has indicated that one of the most serious forms of peer sex-ual harassment involves groups of men, including:

- Intimidating a woman student by surrounding her, demanding that she expose her breasts, and refusing to allow her to leave until she complies.
- Creating a disturbance outside of women's residence halls.
- Yelling, shouting, and whistling obscenities at women who walk by frater-nity houses or other campus sites.

Sexual harassment of college students by professors ranges from 30–50%, ranging from sexual come-ons to coercing students into a sexual relationship by threatening to lower their grades or threatening to not write a letter of recommendation for a job or graduate school, and requests for sexual activity by promising a higher grade, an internship, or a scholarship (DeSouza, 2007; Dziech, 2003; Dziech & Hawkins, 1998; Dziech & Weiner, 1984; Fitzgerald & Omerod, 1993; Hill & Silva, 2005).

DeSouza and Solberg (2003) reviewed incidence rates of sexual harassment of college students in several countries: Australia, Brazil, China, Italy, Israel, Pakistan, Puerto Rico, Sweden, and Turkey. Their review indicated that incidence rates of sexual harassment are relatively high in all countries surveyed. Mecca and Rubin (1999) reported that African American women college students report they frequently experience sexual touching. Uhari and colleagues (1994) studied medical students in Finland's experiences with sexual harassment. They found that most incidents of sexual harassment were of a sex discrimination nature: women students were denied career opportunities because of their sex.

For certain students, the incidence of sexual harassment is higher than for others (Barickman, Paludi, & Rabinowitz, 1992; DeFour, 1996; DeFour, David, Diaz, & Thompkins, 2003; Dziech, 2003):

- Women of color
- Students in small colleges or small academic departments where the number of faculty available to students is small
- Women students in male-populated fields, e.g., engineering
- Lesbians
- Economically disadvantaged students
- Physically or emotionally disabled students
- Women students who work in residence halls or dormitories
- Socially isolated women

Battering

In addition to rape and sexual harassment, other forms of campus violence are equally egregious. For example, battering in dating relationships affects between 20–33% of United States college/university students (Bookwala, Frieze, Smith, & Ryan, 1992; Ward & Lundberg-Love, 2006; Smith, 2003; White & Koss, 1991). Ryan, Hanson Frieze, and Sinclair (1999) reported that in dating relationships women experience being pushed, grabbed, or shoved by their male dates. Women further report being slapped and having objects thrown at them. They may also be stalked by a former lover who refused to accept the end of their relationship (DeKeseredy & Kelly, 1993). In fact, 90% of the women killed by mates or dating partners reported being stalked prior to being murdered.

Stalking

Fisher, Cullen, and Turner's (2000) research with 4,446 college women at 223 campuses found that 13% of the women had been stalked since the academic year began. In addition, 80.3% of the women who were stalked reported knowing their stalker: 42.9% were current or ex-boyfriends, 29% were classmates, 10.4% were acquaintances. Stalking incidents lasted on average two months. Fisher, Cullen, and Turner also reported that in 10.3% of stalking incidents, women stated that the stalker forced or attempted sexual contact. Furthermore, in 15.3% of stalking incidents, women reported that the stalker threatened or attempted to harm them. The research also found that American Indian/Alaska Native women were more likely to be stalked than women of other racial identities.

Abrams and Robinson (1998) and Mullen, Pathe, Purcell, and Stuart (1999) reported that similar to other forms of campus violence, most victims of stalking are women; most offenders are men. They also noted that most stalking occurs in the aftermath of a failed intimate relationship, with the stalker exhibiting obsessional love or erotomania (Ward & Lundberg-Love, 2006).

IMPACT OF CAMPUS VIOLENCE ON VICTIMS

The impact of each of these forms of campus violence must be underscored. The outcomes of the victimization process can be examined from the following main perspectives: (1) education-work related; (2) psychological or emotional; and (3) physiological or health-related (Dansky & Kilpatrick, 1997; Fitzgerald, Gold, & Brock, 1990; Lundberg-Love & Marmion, 2003, 2006). For example, sexual harassment victims frequently change career goals; are absent from classes; and have decreased morale, decreased satisfaction with their studies, and damage to interpersonal relationships at school (Lundberg-Love & Marmion, 2003; Sandler & Shoop, 1997). In addition, college women who have experienced sexual harassment have reported fear, guilt, anger, anxiety, powerlessness, fear of rape, fear of crime in general, decreased self-esteem, withdrawal from social settings, depression, and a fear of meeting new people (Dziech, 2003).

Ramos's (2000) study with Spanish college women attending the University of Puerto Rico identified that sexual harassment had a negative impact on students' health, academic performance, and psychological well-being. Students reported more physical symptoms, poorer mental health, greater academic withdrawal, lower self-esteem, and lower life satisfaction than women who had not been sexually harassed.

Sexual harassment victims also report headaches, sleep disturbances, disordered eating, gastrointestinal disorders, nausea, and crying spells. They also exhibit a post-abuse syndrome characterized by shock, emotional numbing, constriction of affect, flashbacks, and other signs of anxiety and depression (Lundberg-Love & Marmion, 2003; Quina, 1996). All of these responses become more pronounced the longer the victim endures the harassment.

Research has indicated that rape victims, including date rape victims, exhibit high distress levels within the first week (Koss, 1993; Rozee, 1999). This distress peaks in severity three weeks following the victimization, continues at a high level for one month and then starts to improve three months post-rape. One-fourth of women who were raped continue to experience negative effects several years post-victimization. Common symptoms include depression, substance abuse and dependence, generalized anxiety, and posttraumatic stress disorder (Hanson, 1990; Koss, Heise, & Russo, 1994). In addition, symptoms reported by rape victims include headaches, gastrointestinal disorders, premenstrual symptoms, general pain, pelvic pain, and psychogenic seizures (Koss, 1988).

Injuries sustained by college students involved in battering include bruises, cuts, concussions, black eyes, broken bones, scars from burns, loss of hearing and/or vision, knife wounds, and joint damage (Ryan, Frieze, & Sinclair, 1999). Reactions to battering include confusion, psychological numbing, substance abuse, disturbed sleep, eating disorders, and fear (Bogal-Allbritten & Allbritten, 1985; Renzetti, 1992).

PEOPLE, NOT STATISTICS

The statistics of campus violence are indeed startling. They translate into thousands of students each year who are physically and psychologically harmed. The following cases that received national attention further highlight the alarming nature of campus violence:

- August 15, 1996: Frederick Davidson, a graduate student in engineering at San Diego State University killed three of his professors as he was defending his thesis before a faculty committee.
- January 16, 2002: Peter Odignizuwa killed the dean, a professor, and student at Virginia's Appalachian School of Law after he was dismissed from the school. This attack also wounded three students.
- October 28, 2002: Robert Flores entered his instructor's office at the University of Arizona's Nursing College and killed her. Shortly thereafter, armed with five guns, Flores entered one of his classrooms and killed two more of his professors before killing himself.
- April 16, 2007: Thirty-two students and employees were killed in a dorm and classroom at Virginia Tech by student Seung-Hui Cho, who later took his own life.

Personal accounts from student victims of campus violence further inform us of the responsibility campuses have to prevent violence:

I felt as if my whole world had been kicked out from under me and I had been left to drift all alone in the darkness. I had horrible nightmares in which I relived the rape, and others which were even worse. I was terrified of being with people and terrified of being alone. I couldn't concentrate on anything and began failing several classes. Deciding what to wear was enough to make me panic and cry uncontrollably. I was convinced I was going crazy, and I'm still convinced I almost did.

I didn't tell anyone. In fact, I wouldn't even admit to it myself until four months later when the guilt and fear that had been eating at me became too much to hide and I came very close to a complete nervous breakdown.

I tried to kill myself, but fortunately I chickened out at the last minute. (Rape victims' words, quoted in Warshaw, 1988, p. 67)

Of all the women I am close to I would say there are only one or two who haven't experienced sexual harassment—from either a series of winks that make it uncomfortable to go to class to actual seduction. This student said that when she was in her sophomore year at college, her academic advisor invited her to his house for dinner. She stated he told her how "lovable" she was, grabbed her, pulled up her shirt, and tried to kiss her. As she stated: "I dashed out, absolutely in shock.... It just grossed me out." (Reported in Carmody, 1989)

There is a guy in all my classes who consistently touches me in a sexual way that I really don't appreciate.

People who lived in the same hall as me in the dorms started spreading rumors about my sex life, which were not even close to true. They also spread condoms around my room.

Phone harassment calling me derogatory homosexual names and leaving messages. (Quoted in Hill and Silva, 2005, p. 20)

RESPONSIBILITIES OF CAMPUSES

I decided it's better to scream.... Silence is the real crime against humanity.
                                                                    Nadezhda Mandelstam

Despite the high incidence of campus violence, there is no relationship between incidence and reporting. For example, rape is one of the most underreported of all serious crimes (Koss, 1993). The majority of women refuse to report rape to the authorities on campus. Fisher, Cullen, and Turner (2000) indicated that fewer than 5% of college women who are raped report the assault to the police. However, approximately 65% of rape victims tell someone, usually a friend but not a campus administrator (Benson, Charton, & Goodhart, 1992). Research indicates that women may have a sense of shame, guilt, or self-blame about their role in the rape, stemming from stereotypes about women's sexuality and their control of men's sexuality (Koss, 1993; Paludi, 2002; Rozee, 1999). Additional reasons for not reporting rape include fear of publicity, fear of reprisal from assailant, self-blame for drinking, self-blame for being alone with the assailant, and mistrust of the campus investigative system (Bohmer & Parrot, 1993).

Very often when women do report being raped they are met with degrading and humiliating experiences (Rozee, 1999). Schwartz and

DeKeserdy (1997) reported that women did not identify their rape experiences when it happened between dating partners and when they had previously consented to sexual behavior with this man. Similarly, sexual harassment victims fear being blamed for the harassment or not being believed (Paludi & Barickman, 1998).

Colleges and universities must be prepared to address campus violence including preventative procedures and campus postvention services in the aftermath of campus violence. Attention must be paid to international students' concerns, legal responsibilities of campuses, and the impact of campus violence on individuals' emotional and physical health and well-being. The finding that students do not report campus violence to campus administrators necessitates campuses establishing and maintaining safe reporting procedures. Campuses have a legal responsibility to educate students about risks of campus violence and provide them with reasonable protection (see Howard, this volume).

Recently, the results of the investigative report from the Virginia Tech Review Panel (2007) about the Virginia Tech murders indicated the following:

> During Cho's junior year at Virginia Tech, numerous incidents occurred that were clear warnings of mental instability. Although various individuals and departments within the university knew about each of these incidents, the university did not intervene effectively. No one knew all the information and no one connected all the dots.
>
> Senior university administrators, acting as the emergency Policy Group, failed to issue an all-campus notification about the WAJ killings until almost 2 hours had elapsed. University practice may have conflicted with written policies.
>
> The VRPD erred in not requesting that the Policy Group issue a campus-wide notification that two persons had been killed and that all students and staff should be cautious and alert.

UNDERSTANDING AND PREVENTING CAMPUS VIOLENCE

This book offers suggestions for campus administrators, educators, and parents on how to prevent and deal with all forms of campus violence, taking into account the recommendations from Virginia Tech and other campuses. Part One describes empirical research on campus violence. We also address the impact of campus violence on college students, including the impact on their physical and emotional well-being. Part One also includes a chapter dealing with international students' concerns about campus violence.

Using this research summarized in Part One, we offer recommendations and strategies for educating students, faculty, and administrators. Part Two thus provides a variety of pedagogical techniques for teaching students about campus violence.

In Part Three, we offer recommendations for dealing with and preventing campus violence in the form of laws, policies, procedures, and training programs for all members of the campus community. Attention is paid to stalking, hate crimes, sexual harassment, sexual assault, and other forms of campus violence. We have included workplace violence as a form of campus violence since in addition to students, employees, faculty, and administrators are also involved in violence. Examples of campus-wide educational programs for students and employees are also offered. We also provide information from Security on Campus, Inc., an organization whose mission is to prevent campus violence as well as to assist victims of these crimes.

Campus violence is a complex issue and demands complex solutions whereby individuals from all parts of the campus and surrounding community work in concert to help with its prevention and dealing with its aftermath. All contributors to this book are internationally recognized social scientists, human resource specialists, attorneys, management consultants, educators, and Title IX compliance officers who have worked in various aspects of campus violence. I am honored they wanted to join me in contributing to this book to assist campuses in keeping students, faculty, employees, and administrators safe.

The goal of this book is to break the silence that very often surrounds campus violence. In my own consulting, I have noted that campus violence confronts individuals, including victims, with perceptions that are often invalidated by those around them. Victims' experiences frequently get relabeled as anything but campus violence. Consequently, victims of sexual harassment, rape, stalking, battering, or other forms of campus violence doubt their experiences.

Never be bullied into silence. Never allow yourself to be made a victim. Accept no one's definition of your life, but define yourself.

Harvey Fierstein

In the last several years I have been describing colleges' response to violence against a backdrop of a classic experiment by Solomon Asch on social influence or conformity, how individuals alter the thoughts, feelings, and behavior of others in order to adhere to social norms (see Paludi, 1999). In the Asch experiment, an individual would enter a laboratory room with six people and be told the experiment concerns visual discrimination. The task for the individuals was relatively simple. They were shown two cards. On the first card appeared a single line. On the second card, three lines were drawn and numbered 1, 2, and 3. One of the lines on the second card was the same length as the line on the first card. Participants in this study were asked to call out one at a time the number of the line on card 2 that was identical in length to the line on card 1.

One of the seven individuals was the real research participant; the remainder were confederates of the experimenter. The confederates had been previously told to say an incorrect response. For example, five of the confederates would say "1" when the correct answer was "3." When confronted with five individuals responding with the objectively incorrect answer, Asch looked to see if the research participant would conform to the erroneous group judgment or not conform. His research indicated that individuals doubted their judgments: their discomfort was caused by the pressure to conform. Seventy-five percent of the participants went along with the crowd rather than assert what they knew to be the right answer.

This experiment has implications far beyond the research laboratory. It illustrates how campus violence can confront individuals with perceptions that are often invalidated by those around them. Similar to the research participants in the Asch study, victims of campus violence doubt what they see with their own eyes and conform to their mate's, professor's, or campus administrator's perspectives.

It is my hope that this book will support victims in their perceptions of their experiences and assist faculty and administrators in creating safer havens on their campuses so that all members of the campus community may reach their full potential (see Hill and Silva, 2005). This book also calls for what Martin (2000) referred to as a "global campaign for a woman-friendly academy" (p. 182). As Cooper and Eddy (2007) noted:

> A woman-friendly academy would not only embrace the needs of women students, faculty members, staff, and administrators today, but also create a future filled with greater possibilities for women and men in higher education today. (p. 631)

REFERENCES

Abrams, K., & Robinson, G. (1998). Stalking: Part I: An overview of the problem. *Canadian Journal of Psychiatry, 43,* 473–476.

Bachar, K., & Koss, M. (2001). From prevalence to prevention: Closing the gap between what we know about rape and what we do. In C. Renzetti, J. Edleson, & R. Bergen (Eds.), *Sourcebook on violence against women* (pp. 117–142). Thousand Oaks, CA: Sage.

Barickman, R., Paludi, M., & Rabinowitz, V. (1992). Sexual harassment of students: Victims of the college experience. In E. Viano (Ed.), *Victimology: An international perspective.* New York: Springer.

Benson, D., Charton, C., & Goodhart, F. (1992). Acquaintance rape on campus: A literature review. *Journal of American College Health, 40,* 157–165.

Bogal-Allbritten, R., & Allbritten, W. (1985). The hidden victims: Courtship violence among college students. *Journal of College Student Personnel, 26,* 201–204.

Bohmer, C., & Parrot, A. (1993). *Sexual assault on campus: The problem and the solution*. New York: Lexington Books.

Bookwala, J., Frieze, J., Smith, C., & Ryan, K. (1992). Predictors of dating violence: A multivariate analysis. *Violence and Victims, 7*, 297–311.

Carmody, D. (1989). Education: Sexual harassment on campus: A growing issue. *New York Times*.

Cooper, J., & Eddy, P. (2007). Improving gender equity in postsecondary education. In S. Klein (Ed.), *Handbook for achieving gender equity through education* (pp. 631–653). Mahwah, NJ: Erlbaum.

Dansky, B., & Kilpatrick, D. (1997). Effects of sexual harassment. In W. O'Donohue (Ed.), *Sexual harassment: Theory, research and practice* (pp. 152–174). Boston: Allyn & Bacon.

DeFour, D. (1996). The interface of racism and sexism in sexual harassment. In M. Paludi (Ed.), *Sexual harassment on college campuses: Abusing the ivory power* (pp. 49–55). Albany, NY: State University of New York Press.

DeFour, D., David, G., Diaz, F., & Thompkins, S. (2003). The interface of race, sex, sexual orientation, and ethnicity in understanding sexual harassment. In M. Paludi & C. Paludi (Eds.), *Academic and workplace sexual harassment: A handbook of cultural, social science, management and legal perspectives* (pp. 31–45). Westport, CT: Praeger.

DeKeseredy, W., & Kelly, K. (1993). The incidence and prevalence of woman abuse in Canadian university and college daring relationships. *Canadian Journal of Sociology, 18*, 137–159.

DeSouza, E. (2007, August). *Same-sex sexual harassment: Research findings and implications for policymakers*. Invited Presentation, Conference of the International Coalition Against Sexual Harassment, New York, NY.

DeSouza, E., & Solberg, J. (2003). Incidence and dimensions of sexual harassment across cultures. In M. Paludi & C. Paludi (Eds.), *Academic and workplace sexual harassment: A handbook of cultural, social science, management and legal perspectives*. Westport, CT: Praeger.

Dziech, B. (2003). Sexual harassment on college campuses. In M. Paludi & C. Paludi (Eds.), *Academic and workplace sexual harassment: A handbook of cultural, social science, management and legal perspectives* (pp. 147–171). Westport, CT: Praeger.

Dziech, B., & Hawkins, M. (1998). *Sexual harassment in higher education*. New York: Garland Press.

Dziech, B., & Weiner, L. (1984). *The lecherous professor*. Boston: Beacon Press.

Finn, P. (1995). *Preventing alcohol-related problems on campus: Acquaintance rape- a guide for program coordinators* Newton, MA: Higher Education Center for Alcohol and Other Drug Prevention.

Fisher, B., Cullen, F., & Turner, M. (2000). *The sexual victimization of college women*. Washington, DC: U.S. Department of Justice, National Institute of Justice and Bureau of Justice Statistics.

Fitzgerald, L., Gold, Y., & Brock, K. (1990). Responses to victimization: Validation of an objective policy. *Journal of College Student Personnel, 27*, 34–39.

Fitzgerald, L., & Omerod, A. (1993). Sexual harassment in academia and the workplace. In F. Denmark & M. Paludi (Eds.), *Psychology of women: Handbook of issues and theories* (pp. 553–581). Westport, CT: Greenwood Press.

Hanson, R. (1990). The psychological impact of sexual assault on women and children: A review. *Annals of Sex Research, 3,* 187–232.

Hill, C., & Silva, E. (2005). *Drawing the line: Sexual harassment on campus.* Washington, DC: American Association of University Women Educational Foundation.

Humphrey, S. E., & Kahn, A. S. (2000). Fraternities, athletic teams, and rape: Importance of identification with a risky group. *Journal of Interpersonal Violence, 1,* 1313–1322.

Koss, M. (1988). Hidden rape: Sexual aggression and victimization in a national sample of students in higher education. In A. Burgess (Ed.), *Rape and sexual assault* (pp. 3–25). New York: Garland.

Koss, M. (1993). Rape: Scope, impact, interventions and public policy. *American Psychologist, 48,* 1062–1069.

Koss, M. (2006). Restoring rape survivors: Justice, advocacy, and a call to action. In F. Denmark, H. Krauss, E. Halpern, & J. Sechzer (Eds.), *Violence and exploitation against women and girls* (pp. 206–234). Boston, MA: Blackwell Publishing.

Koss, M., Heise, L., & Russo, N. (1994). The global health burden of rape. *Psychology of Women Quarterly, 18,* 509–537.

LaVant, B. (2001). Understanding violence on the college campuses and strategies for prevention. In D. Sandhu (Ed.), *Faces of violence: Psychological correlates, concepts, and intervention strategies* (pp. 73–86). Hauppauge, NY: Nova Science Publishers.

Lundberg-Love, P., & Marmion, S. (2003). Sexual harassment in the private section. In M. Paludi & C. Paludi (Eds.), *Academic and workplace sexual harassment: A handbook of cultural, social science, management and legal perspectives* (pp. 77–101). Westport, CT: Praeger.

Martin, J. R. (2000). *Coming of age in academe.* New York: Routledge.

Mecca, S., & Rubin, L. (1999). Definitional research on African American students and sexual harassment. *Psychology of Women Quarterly, 23,* 813–817.

Mohler-Kuo, M., Dowdall, G., Koss, M., & Wechsler, A. (2004). Correlates of rape while intoxicated in a national sample of college women. *Journal of Studies on Alcohol, 65,* 37–45.

Mullen, P. E., Pathe, M., Purcell, R., & Stuart, G.W. (1999). A study of stalkers. *American Journal of Psychiatry, 156,* 1244–1249.

Nicoletti, J., Spencer-Thomas, S., & Bollinger, C. (2001). *Violence goes to college: The authoritative guide to prevention and intervention.* New York: Thomas.

Paludi, M. (Ed.) (1999). *The psychology of sexual victimization: A handbook.* Westport, CT: Greenwood Press.

Paludi, M. (2002). *The psychology of women.* Upper Saddle River, NJ: Prentice Hall.

Paludi, M., & Barickman, R. (1998). *Sexual harassment, work, and education: A resource manual for prevention.* Albany, NY: State University of New York Press.

Paludi, M., Nydegger, R., DeSouza, E., Nydegger, L., & Allen Dicker, K. (2006). International perspectives on sexual harassment of college students: The sounds of silence. In F. L. Denmark, H. Krauss, E. Halpern, & J. Sechzer (Eds.), *Violence and exploitation against women and girls* (pp. 103–120). Boston: Blackwell Publishing

Pezza, P. E., & Bellotti, A. (1995). College campus violence: Origins, impacts, and responses. *Educational Psychology Review*, 7, 105–123.

Quina, K. (1996). Sexual harassment and rape: A continuum of exploitation. In M. Paludi (Ed.), *Ivory power: Sexual harassment on campus* (pp. 183–197). Albany, NY: State University of New York Press.

Ramos, A. (2000). Sexual harassment at the University of Puerto Rico. *Dissertation Abstracts Inernational, 60,* 5839.

Renzetti, C. (1992). *Violent betrayal: Partner abuse in lesbian relationships.* Newbury Park, CA: Sage.

Rozee, P. (1999). Cultural issues in rape. In M. Paludi (Ed.), *The psychology of sexual victimization: A handbook* (pp. 97–115). Westport, CT: Greenwood Press.

Ryan, K., Frieze, I., & Sinclair, H. (1999). Physical violence in dating relationships. In M. Paludi (Ed.), *The psychology of sexual victimization: A handbook* (pp. 33–54). Westport, CT: Greenwood Press.

Sandler, B., & Shoop, R. (1997). *Sexual harassment on campus: A guide for administrators, faculty and students.* Boston: Allyn and Bacon.

Schwartz, M., & DeKeserdy, W. (1997). *Sexual assault on the college campus: The role of male peer support.* Newbury Park, CA: Sage.

Uhari, M., Kokkone, J., Nuutinen, J., Vainiopaa, L., Rantala, H., Lautala, P., & V'yrynen, M. (1994). Medical student abuse: An international phenomenon. *Journal of the American Medical Association, 271,* 1049–1051.

Virginia Tech Review Panel (2007). *The Virginia Tech review panel report.* Arlington, VA.

Ward, C., & Lundberg-Love, P. (2006). Sexual abuse of women. In P. Lundberg-Love & S. Marmion (Eds.), *Intimate violence against women: When spouses, partners or lovers attack* (pp. 47–68). Westport, CT: Praeger.

Warshaw, R. (1988). *I never called it rape.* New York: Harper & Row.

White, J., & Koss, M. (1991). Courtship violence: Incidence in a national sample of higher education students. *Violence and Victims, 6,* 247–256.

PART I

Empirical Research on Campus Violence

Chapter 1

Gendered Violence on Campus: Unpacking Bullying, Harassment, and Stalking

Jennifer L. Martin

Violence on college campuses is an issue that is of growing relevance in today's media, in the popular culture, and in the minds of the general public. With the media intensifying our concerns about school shootings, such as the Virginia Tech massacre and the Nickel Mines, Pennsylvania, Amish schoolhouse shootings, there is a heightened fear of gun violence on campuses and a heightened belief that the safety of students is at risk because of unstable students or intruders. However, what the popular media fails to recognize, in large part, is that many of these shootings are manifestations of gendered violence.

Because many of these shooters seem to fit the profile of the loner who has been bullied and ignored by fellow classmates (or feels as though this is the case), schools and campuses across the country are concerning themselves with the effects of bullying and allotting funds to bullying prevention programs. Bullying is an important issue, and its effects are devastating, but it should not be the only concern here. Other issues affecting today's college students and society in general often get lumped under the umbrella of bullying, such as relationship violence, sexual harassment, and stalking. These phenomena have different causes and effects, but they all represent real dangers to students, particularly to women and LGBTTIQQ (lesbian, gay, bisexual, transgender, transsexual, intersex, queer, and questioning) individuals; these dangers are often ignored because they have been eclipsed under the banner of bullying.

Research suggests that women on college campuses are at a higher risk for certain types of violence than women in other groups (Fisher, Cullen, & Turner, 2000); college women experience phenomena such as sexual harassment, stalking, and relationship violence in far greater numbers than men. Often, these crimes escalate to murder—which is the leading cause of death for women in the American workplace (Gross, 1994). Ninety percent of the women killed by former or current intimates were stalked prior to being murdered (Gross, 1994). Thus, schools and society in general must take violence against women seriously and understand that this is the root cause of much campus violence; in other words, much campus violence is gendered violence, but it is masked by other names, such as bullying, or its role is hidden by more serious crimes such as homicide (Gross, 1994).

BULLYING

Research on child and adolescent bullying began in Scandinavia in the 1970s. Currently, research is being conducted on the subject in Scandinavia, the United Kingdom, and the United States. Many early adolescents who are bullied by peers have been found to suffer psychological trauma, including a decrease in self-esteem, depression, loneliness, and anxiety (Olweus, 1993). Bullying has also been associated with absenteeism and decreased academic performance (Casey-Cannon, Hayward, & Gowen, 2001). Olweus (1993), a leading expert in the field of childhood and adolescent bullying, defines bullying as aggression that intends to harm, that occurs repeatedly, and that contains an imbalance of power (where a more powerful person or group attacks a less powerful individual or group).

Studies of bullying at the college level are lacking (Chapell et al., 2004). However, research does indicate that bullying occurs in the workplace and thus with adults (Chapell et al., 2004). Chapell et al. (2004) studied the phenomenon of bullying in college by surveying over 1,000 college students. Of these students, 60% reported witnessing a student bullying another student; and over 44% reported witnessing a teacher bully a student at the college level. Furthermore, 6% of students reported being bullied by another student, and approximately 5% reported being bullied by a teacher. Additionally, 5% reported bullying other students. The researchers also found that male college students bully verbally and physically more so than female college students (Chapell et al., 2006). Gruber and Fineran (2007) found a higher prevalence of bullying for gender minorities (such as LGBTTIQQ individuals) and non-white adolescents. It is not known whether this finding extends to college campuses.

Bullying does not occur in a vacuum (O'Connell, Pepler, & Craig, 1999). It occurs within a broader social context, involving a delicate balance of power. Peer behavior in support of victims may do much to shift the balance of power away from the bully, although peer behavior most often reinforces bullying behavior. Research suggests that peers can serve as catalysts for change within the bully/victim dynamic (O'Connell, Pepler, & Craig, 1999; Salmivalli, 1999; Stevens, Van Oost, & de Bourdeaudhuij, 2000). It is logical to suggest that peers and bystanders may be a prime target for interventions. If interventions focus on the role of the peer group and reinforce the importance of reporting witnessed acts of bullying or voicing disapproval when they occur, bullying may be reduced. In other words, if the culture of the school refuses to tolerate bullying, inappropriate behaviors may change. Effective interventions should focus on altering student attitudes and group norms and give strategies to deal effectively with bullies (Stevens, Van Oost, & de Bourdeaudhuij, 2000). Successful interventions should also target bullying behavior, give examples of appropriate behavior, and provide suggestions on how to deal with inappropriate behavior.

The notion of diffusion of responsibility or the bystander effect, where individuals in a group do not assist in an emergency situation because they believe others will (Darley & Latané, 1968), has much to do with the bully/victim dynamic. Bullying *may* be reduced by reaching bystanders (Salmivalli, 2001). However, O'Connell et al. (1999) found that 54% of the time peers reinforced bullying behavior by passively observing the scenario and not attempting to assist the victim. Many of these same peers will also insist that they are guilty of nothing. Successful interventions should reinforce the notion that inaction can in fact imply guilt. Interventions must also target the peer group, the bystanders, to empathize with the victim instead of tacitly reinforcing bullying behavior by doing nothing.

Salmivalli (1999) found that although the majority of students' attitudes were found to be anti-bullying, the majority of their behaviors did not correspond to their attitudes (Stevens, Van Oost, & de Bourdeaudhuij, 2000, echo this finding). Many non-involved parties are motivated by either the notion that they will lose social influence if they challenge the bully, or that they will be bullied themselves (Stevens, Van Oost, & de Bourdeaudhuij, 2000). Salmivalli argues that the group dynamic influences behaviors through conformity, pressuring students to act in certain ways that reinforce bullying. Salmivalli also argues that interventions created to combat bullying should be directed to target the whole group; successful interventions should include awareness raising, self-reflection, possibilities to role-play positive peer behavior, and assertiveness training (which includes how to resist group pressure). Trained peer supporters should be used to assist in combating bullying behavior and in the creation of a more positive school culture (Salmivalli, 1999).

Interventions designed to combat bullying should involve students in the creation of policies intended to alter the school climate with regard to bullying for the promotion of positive interaction between students, which will heighten inclusion and empowerment for all students (Casey-Cannon, Hayward, & Gowen, 2001). Interventions should also send a clear message that bullying will not be tolerated, and involve all stakeholders, such as students, faculty, staff, and administrators.

In conclusion, it is important that interventions to combat bullying identify clear definitions of bullying behaviors and clear consequences for bullying behaviors. Students should be encouraged to stand up for victims and to report bullying incidents that they witness. Clear procedures for reporting incidents of bullying should also be made clear for all students. Staff, faculty, and administrators should not only be trained in the bully/victim dynamic (including what bullying is, what behaviors constitute bullying, and the effects of bullying on victims), but also they should be expected to intervene when they witness bullying.

It is dangerous for schools to combine sexual harassment with bullying, or in other words, to lump sexual harassment with bullying as opposed to viewing it as a type of gendered violence. The effects of bullying are not as harmful as are the effects of sexual harassment on victims (Gruber & Fineran, 2007). Additionally, a major difference between the two phenomena is that sexual harassment is illegal. There are federal laws protecting individuals from sexual harassment (Title VII and Title IX), but there are no federal laws that protect against bullying. Thus, if an act of sexual harassment is defined as bullying, the victim will not have as much recourse as if it were deemed sexual harassment, for schools are legally mandated to address incidents of sexual harassment. As Gruber and Fineran (2007) state, "as long as sexual bullying continues to be viewed as bullying and not identified as sexual harassment, problems of victimization that stem from gender or sexuality will be interpreted as private or interpersonal troubles experienced by unfortunate students who are caught up in difficult situations" (p. 6). As long as incidents of sexual harassment are defined as bullying in our schools and colleges, they will be perceived as individual problems or interpreted as personality conflicts as opposed to institutional or systemic misogyny, gender bias, or hate crimes.

SEXUAL HARASSMENT

Sexual harassment is a complex phenomenon involving various interrelated factors such as gender, patriarchal norms (most specifically, hegemonic masculinity), and issues of power; thus, sexual harassment possesses many accepted definitions. Brandenburg (1997) defines sexual harassment as "unwanted sexual attention that would be offensive to a reasonable person and that negatively affects the work or school environment" (p. 1). Sexual harassment is defined by the American Association of University Women as "*unwanted* and *unwelcome* sexual behavior that interferes with your life. Sexual harassment is *not* behaviors that you *like* or *want* (for example wanted kissing, touching, or flirting)" (2001/1993, p. 2). The literature on sexual harassment suggests that over 90% of the time, males are the perpetrators of sexual harassment against females (Fineran & Bennett, 1999).

Ignoring claims of sexual harassment or viewing them as "normal" behavior will not alleviate the problems it causes. In fact, to *not* deal with the issue of sexual harassment in a proactive manner only serves to create an environment that is more hostile where students do not feel safe. Schools, on an institutional level, must be proactive in dealing with sexual harassment; if they are not, traditional gender roles (Stein, 1996b), hegemonic masculinity, and compulsory heterosexuality will be reinforced whether implicitly or explicitly. Ignoring claims of sexual harassment on the part of women and LGBTTIQQ individuals and the reinforcement of traditional gender roles translates to these populations that their places in society are secondary, their voices are not valued, and there is nothing much they can do about it (Brown & Gilligan, 1992; van Roosmalen, 2000).

Schools that do not intervene in incidents of sexual harassment may be doing more than reinforcing the traditional hierarchy and devaluing the voices of certain populations—they may also be implicitly encouraging a pattern of male violence. As Stein (1996b) states, "If school authorities do not intervene and sanction students who sexually harass, the schools may be encouraging a continued pattern of violence in relationships: schools may be training grounds for the insidious cycle of domestic violence" (p. 22). In essence, a lack of intervention on the part of schools can adversely affect both the victim and the perpetrator. If students who harass do not receive consequences for their actions and information on how to interact with others, their problems with harassment and victimization may grow steadily worse (Stein, 1996b).

MacKinnon (1979) argues that sexual harassment affects women differently than men, no matter if the harasser is male or female. According to MacKinnon, these harms suffered by women justify considering sexual harassment sex discrimination. Bartky (1990) provides insight into why women are the most frequent victims of sexual harassment and also why sexual harassment was considered to be normal behavior until the recent past. As Bartky argues, "Sexual objectification occurs when a woman's sexual parts or sexual functions are separated out from her person, reduced to the status of mere instruments, or else regarded as if they were capable of representing her" (p. 35). In other words, women are often thought of in terms of the body, in terms of sexuality, and thus they are often reduced to just that: sexual beings that are not on an equal plane with men. As Bartky suggests, "Clearly, sexual objectification is a form of fragmentation and thus an impover-ishment of the objectified individual; it involves too the implicit denial to those who suffer it that they have capacities which transcend the merely sexual" (pp. 35–36). In sum, Bartky's sexual objectification theory not only explains why women often are not viewed as possess-ing capacities that transcend the body, but also how women internalize these negative societal perceptions of their sex and therefore fail to reach their maximum potential.

Objectification theory suggests that sexual harassment may cause a higher self-consciousness about one's body (Fredrickson & Roberts, 1997). Moreover, sexual harassment has been linked to problems with body image for adolescent girls and college women (Murnen & Smo-lak, 2000). In other words, objectification theory posits that the female body is objectified in American society through history, tradition, the media, and so on. Because women are thought of largely in terms of their bodies, they are more susceptible to sexual harassment. As alluded to previously, objectification itself, as well as its repercussions (namely sexual harassment), have damaging consequences for women.

Sexual terrorism theory (Sheffield, 1989) suggests that violence against women, such as sexual harassment, instills fear in women. Thus, females may show more distress when experiencing sexual har-assment than do males because of the unequal power afforded to them by traditional gender roles. Also, sexual terrorism maintains traditional patriarchal power and reinforces hegemonic masculinity. As Sheffield (1989) states:

> Sexual terrorism is a system that functions to maintain male supremacy through actual and implied violence. Violence against the female body (rape, battery, incest, and harassment) and the perpetuation of fear and violence form the basis of patriarchal power. Both violence and fear are functional. If men did not have the power to intimidate and to punish, their domination of women in all spheres of society—political, social, and economic—could not exist. (p. 17)

In other words, sexual harassment is merely one facet of sexual terror-ism that serves to keep women in positions of fear and powerlessness. Sexual terrorism theory suggests that sexual harassment functions as a tool to maintain the status quo where men enjoy the lion's share of power, autonomy, and economic opportunity.

Murrell and Dietz-Uhler (1993) found that direct experience with sexual harassment desensitized male respondents to the phenomenon. In other words, those males who reported having direct experience with sexual harassment also reported having more tolerance for sexual harassment. Direct experience with sexual harassment did not predict female attitudes toward sexual harassment, however. Murrell and Dietz-Uhler (1993) suggest that intervention programs take these findings into account and that it may be fruitful to examine traditional notions of gender to put an end to adversarial gender relations.

Co-victimization occurs when witnesses or bystanders of violence experience negative psychological outcomes (Glomb et al., 1997). Indirect exposure to sexual harassment can have similar effects as to its direct victims; this phenomenon is also known as ambient sexual harassment (Glomb et al., 1997). The effects of sexual harassment may be more serious and pervasive than previous research has indicated (Glomb et al., 1997). Organizational tolerance of sexual harassment relates to an increase in reported incidents of sexual harassment and to ambient sexual harassment (Glomb et al., 1997).

Campus culture is shaped by the behavior and practices of students, teachers, and administrators. If the awareness of students is raised as to what constitutes sexual harassment, the effects of sexual harassment, and strategies to deal with sexual harassment, then this awareness may translate into action. If students refuse to tolerate sexually harassing behavior when they experience it or witness it, then this may cause the perpetrators to alter their behavior. Simply telling a harasser to stop may be an effective strategy in certain cases (Schwartz, 2000), but it does not always work (De Becker, 1997). Thus, campuses must have policies in place to deal with sexual harassment. Additionally, campuses should present an attitude of institutional intolerance toward sexual harassment, create policies including reporting and investigative procedures and consequences for perpetrators that are widely accessible, and provide/publicize services for victims.

VICTIMIZATION PREDICTORS

According to Humphrey and White (2000), 69.8% of college women experience at least one instance of sexual violence from the age of 14 to their fourth year in college. Additionally, women who were sexually assaulted in high school were more likely to be sexually assaulted in college (Hall Smith, White, & Holland, 2003). National sexual assault data indicate that half of all female sexual assault victims are between the ages of 12 and 24, and that most rapes occur prior to age 24 (Hall Smith, White, & Holland, 2003). According to Hall Smith, White, and Holland (2003), women who were physically assaulted as adolescents are more likely to be revictimized during their freshman year in college. Adolescent victimization is a better predictor than childhood victimization for victimization in college (Hall Smith et al., 2003).

In a study of undergraduate students, Banyard (2007) found that women reported higher rates of unwanted sexual experiences than did men. Further analyses indicated that both women and men experience negative consequences because of these experiences and have low disclosure rates.

Tjaden, Thoennes, and Allison (2002) found that younger and more educated women "are more likely to define assaultive behaviors as inappropriate and worthy of sanction" (p. 22). Hall Smith et al. (2003) argue that interventions to prevent dating violence are needed in high schools and colleges and that additional research is needed on factors affecting revictimization.

Because gendered violence is so prevalent on college campuses, it is important to examine its risk factors so that effective interventions can be created. In addition to the aforementioned factors, women at risk of further victimization include women who were abused as children, or women who witnessed domestic violence as children. Additionally, as Spitzberg and Rhea (1999) state, "jealousy, possessiveness, and insecure attachment styles can work as predictors of both perpetration and victimization, because they all indicate a tendency to cling to a partner, even if the relationship is destructive" (p. 15). In sum, women who are at risk for revictimization should be made aware of the risk factors for abusive partners. Interventions should focus on these and other warning signs of relationship violence. Additional research is necessary in the area of males who are at risk for relational victimization.

RELATIONSHIP VIOLENCE

Intimate violence is considered to be a leading health risk for women according to the National Institutes of Justice and the National Institutes of Health (Sinclair & Frieze, 2005). White and Koss found that 32% of women experienced violence in dating relationships between the ages of 14 through college. According to Marshall and Rose (1988), 75% of all college students may have experienced intimate violence (as cited in Logan, Leukefeld, & Walker, 2002). Additionally, physical violence occurs in approximately 20% of college students' current relationships (Arias, Samios, & O'Leart, 1987; Riggs, O'Leary, & Breslin, 1990, as cited in Logan, Leukefeld, & Walker, 2002). Adolescence is the time when women are most vulnerable to physical dating violence (Hall Smith, White, & Holland, 2003). Thus, adolescence is a crucial time for intervention. Psychological abuse in the early stages of a relationship is a predictor of future physical violence (Logan, Leukefeld, & Walker, 2002). Additionally, researchers have found a link between alcohol and intimate partner violence (Logan, Leukefeld, & Walker, 2002); alcohol on college campuses is very common. Approximately 50% of sexual assaults are associated with the use of alcohol— either on the part of the perpetrator, on the part of the victim, or both. In cases of sexual assault, alcohol is involved in approximately one-half of the cases (Abbey, Clinton-Sherrod, McAuslan, Zawacki, & Buck, 2003). Alcohol consumption is also associated with increased aggression (Abbey, Clinton-Sherrod, McAuslan, Zawacki, & Buck, 2003). The use of alcohol on college campuses must be monitored with sanctions for underage drinking. In addition, sexual assault and dating violence interventions on campus should include the effects of alcohol and drugs.

Research indicates that stalking behaviors can occur prior to the development of relationships (Sinclair & Frieze, 2002). This may be a common occurrence (Sinclair & Frieze, 2002; Williams & Frieze, 2005). Men feel that women "play hard to get" more so than women feel this is the case (Sinclair & Frieze, 2005). Women sometimes may feel powerless to dissuade a pursuer because their attempts to reject their pursuers are often ineffective (Sinclair & Frieze, 2005). To complicate matters, the accepted communication styles of women and men (which are a result of societal convention and gender socialization) differ such that the message sent by a woman may be diametrically opposed to the message received by a man. As Gross (1994) states, "Typically, women don't communicate their desires directly. Even as girls, they tend to express preferences as suggestions rather than commands. Uncomfortable situations are discussed or alluded to rather than disputed" (p. 76). Furthermore, if a woman chooses to end a relationship, her desire to do so may not be respected by a man who views his role as primary. As Gross argues, "In domestic situations, for example, men used to calling the shots feel compelled to react when the woman decides to leave. By refusing to let go when they've been rejected, they're not only asserting male power, they're protecting their own identities, which are bound up in the masculine myth" (p. 57). Men often misperceive women's intentions; for example, a woman may just be being friendly and a man may perceive this as showing romantic interest. Extreme cases of these misperceptions can lead to sexual assault (Abbey, McAuslan, Zawacki, Clinton, & Buck, 2001).

Williams and Frieze (2005) examined persistence or prestalking behaviors during early courtship in relation to future relationship violence. They found that in relationships, persistence behaviors and behaviors of violence are related. Additionally, mild aggression performed at the beginning of a relationship is associated with a greater likelihood of further violence during the course of the relationship. These behaviors include surveillance, intimidation, hurting the self, verbal aggression, and physical violence (Williams & Frieze, 2005). The researchers argue that during the beginning of the relationship, a pattern for acceptance of violence or tendencies toward violence may be set into motion. In other words, the early stages of a relationship may serve as a time of "grooming," where one party tests the waters to see what behaviors can be gotten away with. On the other hand, some may view the use of violence—such as jealousy and possessiveness—as a sign of caring. Such mild forms of violence may be viewed by the intimate partner as "normal" occurrences, and thus heighten the intimacy of the pair (Williams & Frieze, 2005). As Bancroft (2002) states, "The longer you have been living with his cycles of intermittent abuse and kind, loving treatment, the *more* attached you are likely to feel to him, through a process known as *traumatic bonding*" (p. 134). Traumatic bonding enables abusive partners to cultivate a deep bond with intimate partners very quickly through the cycle of terror and romance, anger and caring, emotional blackmail and emotional bonding. The result is that the victim feels de-stabled, powerless, and fearful, while simultaneously feeling closer to the abusive partner.

In Western culture, persistence is a value that is rewarded (Williams & Frieze, 2005). The same can be said of relationship persistence. The media portrays images of men pursuing and eventually breaking down the resistance of women in film (*There's Something About Mary, The Graduate*, etc.). These films portray stalking behaviors as necessary to reach the eventual reward: the desired woman. Many men follow these patterns of mild violence in their own relationships.

In a longitudinal study of university women, Hall Smith, White, and Holland (2003) examined dating violence in adolescent and college women over a period of four years. Regarding the issue of sexual victimization, research indicates that the most common form for adolescent females is verbally coercive sexual assault at 15.1%; this figure increases to 21.1% by the end of college. Attempted rape was reported at 7.4% in adolescence and 11.8% at the end of college. Forcible rape was reported at 13% in adolescence and 21.1% by the end of college (Hall Smith, White, & Holland, 2003). At the study's end, Hall Smith, White, and Holland (2003) found that 74.8% of white women and 81.5% of black women reported being sexually victimized, and 76.6% of white women and 81.1% of black women had been physically assaulted. The group of women most likely to be victimized was women who had reported a history of childhood or adolescent victimization.

Spitzberg and Rhea (1999) studied sexual coercion and found that the sexual double standard still has much to do with sexual assault and gendered violence. More specifically, the sexual double standard rewards men for sexual persistence and women for resistance, penalizing women for expressing sexual interest overtly. This essentializing system results in a web of mixed messages where silence can become consent, and where no does not necessarily mean no. As Spitzberg and Rhea (1999) state, "Undue reliance on nonverbal communication in sexual pursuit can lead to a lack of communicative resources for negotiating appropriate conduct" (p. 5). Additionally, males may not trust or adhere to the resistance messages of females because of this (Spitzberg & Rhea, 1999). According to Bancroft (2002), an expert in abusive relationships, abusers have a distorted sense of right and wrong, "Their value system is unhealthy, not their psychology" (p. 38). An abusive person justifies his actions by his sense of entitlement. He believes that he deserves rights and privileges that others do not (Bancroft, 2002). Bancroft typically uses the masculine pronoun in his discussion of the abusive personality because, in his experience, most abusive persons who terrorize their partners physically, psychologically, or both, are males, who learn these behaviors from a variety of sources, "including key male role models, peers, and pervasive cultural messages" (p. 113).

The warning signs of an abusive person are as follows: he speaks disrespectfully about former partners, he claims that former partners have accused him of abuse, he is controlling and possessive, he exhibits over-the-top generosity, he avoids responsibility for his own actions, he is self-centered, he abuses drugs and alcohol, he pressures for sex, he gets serious too quickly, he uses intimidation when angry, he possesses double standards, he has negative attitudes toward women, he treats his partner differently around others, he is attracted to vulnerability, etc. (Bancroft, 2002). The abuser's goal is to control and to divide and conquer. As Bancroft states, "The abusive man's charm makes his partner reluctant to reach out for support or assistance because she feels that people will find her revelations hard to believe or will blame her. ... One of the most important challenges facing a counselor of abusive men is to resist being drawn in by the men's charming persona" (p. 69). An abusive person uses isolation through manipulation as a control tactic. Once a partner is isolated from family and friends, she becomes more dependent upon the abusive partner.

Bancroft (2002) indicates that intervention programs for abusive men are highly ineffective because "[a]n abuser who does not relinquish his core entitlements will not remain nonabusive" (p. 345). The abuser's cycle of power and control is maintained through manipulation. The manipulation signs of abusers include the following according to Bancroft:

> Changing his moods abruptly and frequently, denying the obvious about what he is doing or feeling, convincing you that what *he* wants you to do is what is best for you, getting you to feel sorry for him, getting you to blame yourself, or blame other people, for what he does, using confusion tactics in arguments, lying or misleading you about his actions, his desires, or his reasons for doing certain things, getting you and the people you care about turned against each other. (pp. 66–67)

Such manipulation signs should be made clear to persons involved in relationship violence prevention programs.

In terms of relationship violence prevention, interventions should take place during the courtship when levels of persistence are high, but prior to the occurrence of high levels of intimacy (Williams & Frieze, 2005). Because the rate of abusive relationships is so high on college campuses, services should be provided where partners can gain information, participate in support groups, and get assistance when needed.

STALKING

Stalking is often a prevalent problem on college campuses because most students are in a period of partner seeking. Contributing to this is a culture where the romantic heterosexual prototype (reinforced by the media) is the reluctant or resisting female (often playing hard to get) and the persistent, pursuing male (Finn, 2004). "Negativeness blindness" is a phenomenon where individuals do not hear or see negative reactions to their romantic pursuits or advances (Malamuth & Brown, 1994). This phenomenon is common among stalkers.

Stalking is a form of gendered violence, but prior to the passage of the Violence Against Women Act in 1994, police departments, and the legal system in general, typically overlooked cases of stalking (Gross, 1994). It is estimated that 90% of women who are murdered by former intimates were stalked prior to their deaths (Bjerregaard, 2002). More disturbing is the fact that 90% of these women had contacted the police prior to their deaths (Bjerregaard, 2002). According to Mechanic (2002), "Stalking has been described in the literature as intense, pursuit-oriented behavior targeted toward an individual, often a love object or former intimate, who experiences such behaviors as intrusive, invasive, and even threatening" (p. 31). Stalking lasts an average of 60 days (Fisher, Cullen, & Turner, 2000).

Stalking affects approximately 1 million women and 400,000 men per year (Sinclair & Frieze, 2005). Typically, these victims are stalked by current or former intimates (Sinclair & Frieze, 2005). Over 8 million women have been stalked at some point in their lives (Merschman, 2001). The overwhelming majority of stalkers are male (Merschman, 2001). Approximately four out of five stalking victims are women (Merschman, 2001).

In a nationally representative study of stalking, researchers found that 8% of women and 2% of men have been stalked (Tjaden & Thoennes, 1997). Most cases of stalking occur within the context of past relationships, or with current or former intimates (Tjaden & Thoennes, 1997). Stalking is used to achieve and maintain power and control in relationships (Morewitz, 2003). Sexual harassment can overlap with stalking (McCann, 2001), for stalking may or may not have sexual undertones.

Stalking is also sometimes known as obsessive relational intrusion (ORI) and is defined by Cupach and Spitzberg (1998) as "the repeated and unwanted pursuit and invasion of one's sense of physical or symbolic privacy by another person, either stranger or acquaintance, who desires and/or presumes an intimate relationship" (pp. 234–235).

A National Violence Against Women (NVAW) survey has estimated that over 1 million women per year are stalked. The survey also found that approximately 300,000 women are victims of attempted or completed rape (Merschman, 2001). One out of every 12 women, and one in 45 men, will be stalked at some time in their lives (Merschman, 2001; Logan, Leukefeld, & Walker, 2002). The NVAW results indicate that most victims are acquainted with their stalkers (Morewitz, 2003). Stalkers may not be mentally ill, as is commonly thought (Merschman, 2001). In essence, stalking is a more pervasive behavior than was believed just decades ago.

Stalking behaviors include incessant phone calls, sending continual gifts/letters, professing love to the target, following the target, stealing the target's mail, spying on the target, standing outside the target's home or workplace, vandalizing the target's property, killing or threatening to kill the victim's pet, etc. (Merschman, 2001). According to Merschman (2001), there are three types of stalkers: intimate or former intimate stalkers, acquaintance stalkers, and stranger stalkers. It is estimated that violence occurs in 25–35% of stalking situations, especially when the stalker has had an intimate relationship with the target (Merschman, 2001).

The reported effects of stalking on its victims include anxiety, depression, fear and other forms of emotional distress, sleep disturbances, losing time from work, changing jobs when stalked at work, feeling compelled to change appearance and/or lifestyle, moving to a new place of residence, changing schools, feelings of powerlessness, digestive problems, headaches, appetite and weight changes, fatigue, self-medication, seeking psychological counseling, post-traumatic stress disorder, etc. (McCann, 2001). Additionally, one in four stalking victims considers suicide (Mechanic, 2002; Merschman, 2001; Morewitz, 2003). Women reported feeling fear as a result of being stalked more than did men (Mechanic, 2002). Victims of stalking become more cautious as a result of this victimization; they also can become more paranoid, and more easily frightened. They may tend to alter their own behavior, and sometimes become more aggressive themselves (Wolbert Burgess & Baker, 2002).

Stalking is exacerbated by a society that condones, encourages, and celebrates male stalking behaviors in the media. Media images on TV, in print ads, and in films still present the male as pursuer, the man as in control. Women are often not shown as possessing the capacity to resist. As Gross states, "The social conditioning that most American men receive feeds this distorted view of relationships as ownership, and love as a predestined occurrence that can't be denied. Even when they have targeted a woman who doesn't return their affection, the socially accepted notion that men choose women, rather than the other way around, feeds their sense of righteousness" (p. 7).

Sinclair and Frieze (2002) found that in terms of stalking behaviors in general, men perform more acts of approach (attempts at direct contact) whereas women perform more acts of surveillance. Stalkers tend to be male, with above average intelligence; they also tend to be readers with the ability to do research and access information. Finally, they lack a core identity, which means they attach to another person to validate their sense of self-worth (Gross, 1994).

Stalking is common among college-aged populations (Spitzberg & Rhea, 1999). Stalking occurs at a slightly higher level with the college population than it does in the general population for a variety of reasons: college is a time of exploration, not only in terms of intellectual development, but also in terms of developing and sustaining relationships; students live in close proximity to one another; and dating patterns are in flux (McCann, 2001). According to a study by Gallagher, Harmon, and Lingenfelter (1994), 34.5% of chief student affairs administrators had to intervene in at least one stalking case in the previous year of the study (as cited in McCann, 2001). Responses for these administrators to cases of stalking varied. According to Gallagher et al., a warning was sufficient in 15% of cases, while a warning and mandated counseling sufficed in another 21% of cases. Other measures to be taken were: denying access to residence halls (18%), board sanctions (31%), suspension or dismissal from school (15%).

While few studies have examined stalking among college students using a random sample, Bjerregaard (2002) did so and found that 96% of female stalking victims are stalked by males. Almost one-third of male stalking victims reported being stalked by members of the same sex. In terms of race, 67% of females and 81.5% of males reported that their stalkers were white (Bjerregaard, 2002). Among women, receiving a threat of violence increases the chances of violence occurring (Bjerregaard, 2002). Of the women, 24.7% reported being stalked at least once in their lives, whereas 10.9% of the men reported this. Of those surveyed, 6% were current stalking victims (Bjerregaard, 2002). Victims of stalking and ORI are commonly also victimized by sexual coercion and often by the same person (Spitzberg & Rhea, 1999).

Tjaden, Thoennes, and Allison (2002) analyzed the results of the National Violence Against Women (NVAW) survey that was conducted from November 1995 to May 1996 via telephone interviews. They found that the prevalence of stalking increases when respondents can self-define stalking. According to Tjaden, Thoennes, and Allison (2002), "Further analysis showed that over 60% of these respondents did not fit the legal definition of a stalking victim because they failed to meet the fear requirement: Either they did not report feeling frightened by their assailant's behavior or they did not think they or someone close to them would be seriously harmed or killed" (p. 19).

Men are more likely to be stalked by strangers and acquaintances as opposed to former intimates (Tjaden, Thoennes, & Allison, 2002), but not much is known about men who are stalked. According to Logan, Leukefeld, and Walker (2002), "male victims of stalking ... have fewer options available to them than women and ... the psychological consequences for males are unclear" (p. 279).

According to Logan, Leukefeld, and Walker (2002), "Stalking should be addressed in violence prevention programs, as well as counseling. It is possible that young males and females are not even aware of stalking and how it might be dangerous" (p. 283). Explicit and direct approaches to dealing with prestalking behaviors are more effective than attempting to let a stalker "down easy" (De Becker, 1997; Sinclair & Frieze, 2005). Definitions of stalking and stalking behaviors, effects on victims, warning signs, and services for victims should be part of college campus anti-violence prevention programs and student handbooks.

STALKING LEGISLATION

Stalking was criminalized in 1990 when California passed the first anti-stalking law (largely because of cases involving celebrities) (Tjaden, 2003). By 1995, all 50 states instituted anti-stalking legislation. But stalking was criminalized before most people knew anything about it. For example, the National Institute of Justice and the Centers for Disease Control and Prevention commissioned the Center for Policy Research to conduct the National Violence Against Women survey (previously mentioned), which was created to determine information about stalking.

Stalking laws vary from state to state, but most contain three common elements: (1) a pattern of conduct that is directed at a specific person; (2) conduct that is intended to place victims in fear for their safety; and (3) conduct that actually places the intended victims in fear for their safety (Beatty, 2003).

Some stalking statutes focus on the effect stalking has on the victim (Merschman, 2001). The limitations of many stalking statutes, such as those in Massachusetts, are that in order for law enforcement to become involved in a case, a credible threat must be proven (Merschman, 2001). Such threats are often difficult to prove. Such an emphasis on the stalker's behavior ignores the effect stalking has on its victims. Additionally, physical violence is not the only form of violence stalking can take, but often it is the only form prosecuted because it is immediately quantifiable. Some stalking laws require prosecutions to prove intent—specifically, that a stalker intends harm upon the victim. This is difficult if the stalker "intends" a love relationship, for in the mind of the stalker this is not harmful. Eighteen states possess stalking statutes that include implicit threats: Alabama, Arizona, California, Colorado, Delaware, Illinois, Indiana, Iowa, Kansas, Kentucky, Maine, Michigan, New Hampshire, New Jersey, Pennsylvania, South Dakota, Utah, and Washington (Beatty, 2003).

Defendants in stalking cases often use as a defense that stalking statutes are overly vague (Merschman, 2001). According to Merschman

(2001), the most effective type of stalking statute is the one that is broad enough to criminalize as many threatening behaviors as possible and simultaneously narrow enough to avoid constitutional protections.

Cyberstalking

Cyberstalking has become a major problem on college campuses in the past decade, but there are few academic studies on the subject (Bocij, 2004). According to D'Ovidio and Doyle (2003), "Cyberstalking is defined as the repeated use of the Internet, e-mail, or related digital electronic communication devices to annoy, alarm, or threaten a specific individual or group of individuals" (p. 10). Cyberstalking can be just as dangerous as traditional stalking and can have similar effects such as anxiety, mental distress, and physical harm (Finn, 2004). Bocij (2004) defines cyberstalking as:

> A group of behaviors in which an individual, group of individuals, or organization uses information and communications technology to harass another individual, group of individuals, or organization. Such behaviors may include, but are not limited to, the transmission of threats and false accusations, identity theft, damage to data or equipment, computer monitoring, solicitation of minors for sexual purposes, and any form of aggression. Harassment is defined as a course of action that a reasonable person, in possession of the same information, would think causes another reasonable person to suffer emotional distress. (p. 14)

Bocij (2004) also found seven fallacies about cyberstalking: (1) cyberstalking is an extension of offline stalking, (2) cyberstalkers are "obsessional," (3) cyberstalkers know their victims, (4) cyberstalking is less harmful than offline stalking, (5) cyberstalkers do not attempt to elicit others to participate in the online stalking of their target, (6) cyberstalkers do not pose a credible threat, and (7) cyberstalkers possess the same motivations as offline stalkers.

Reno (1999) reported on the major similarities and differences between cyberstalking and traditional (or offline) stalking. The major similarities include: most victims are women, the primary motivation of the stalker is to control the target, and the majority of cases involve former intimates. The major differences include: threats are more easily made through online communications where the stalker need not directly confront the target, online stalking can occur between people in different geographic locations, and cyberstalking makes it easy for third parties to get involved in stalking the target.

It is estimated that organizations dealing with cyberstalking field approximately 30,000 complaints per year (Goldsborough, 2004). Internet interactions can intensify more quickly than person-to-person interactions (which can lead to stalking behaviors) because of the effects of the anonymity factor inherent with the Internet, such as a lack of social clues, likelihood for uninhibited behavior, etc.

Cyberstalkers or cyberbullies can be disruptive to the learning environment in K–12 education and at the college level; they can disrupt the learning process by posting an attack on a class discussion board before the instructor has a chance to deal with it (Reigle, 2007). Cyberstalkers make posts to online discussion boards about the victim or send instant messages to the victim in an attempt to intimidate or offend. The intention can also include attempting to ruin the reputation of the victim. Reigle (2007), in her Web survey of randomly selected higher education instructors across the country, found that 44.9% of instructors in higher education reported frequent encounters with students who post inflammatory comments intended to incite negative reactions in classmates. According to Reigle (2007), 86.1% of respondents reported that their institutions do not have policy manuals to deal with online bullying, or actions to be taken when faced with online bullying.

Some states provide protection against cyber-harassment in their stalking statutes. Also, Title 18, Section 875, U. S. Code criminalizes threatening messages sent over the Internet in interstate or foreign commerce. However, with cyberstalking, offenders are finding new ways of bypassing these laws (Merschman, 2001). Compounded with the lack of knowledge on cyberstalking by law enforcement officials and judges, cyberstalkers are getting away with their behaviors (Merschman, 2001). Victims of cyberstalking/bullying may be more likely to skip school, see a decline in academic performance, and experience depression (Stover, 2006).

In her research on college students, Alexy (2005) found that male students were more likely than female students to experience cyberstalking. Additionally, the most likely perpetrator was a former intimate partner. D'Ovidio and Doyle (2003) found that males were more likely than females to commit cyber-harassment. Reno (1999) found that among college women, 25% of stalking cases could be classified as cyberstalking.

E-mail harassment was more likely for self-identified LGBTTIQQ individuals than for other students (Finn, 2004). LGBTTIQQ students were also twice as likely to experience e-mail harassment from a stranger (Finn, 2004). In a study of online harassment of college students, Finn (2004) found that males were as likely as females to be harassed via e-mail.

In order to protect students on campus from online harassment, it is important to develop a culture that supports positive online interaction with expectations and consequences outlined and discussed prior to problems arising (and what behaviors constitute online harassment). It is also important for instructors and policy makers to work directly with the administration on these matters (Reigle, 2007).

When problems do arise, there are Internet safety organizations that can assist with cyberstalking and other Internet related crimes, such as Working to Halt Online Abuse (WHO@), and CyberAngels; these groups can provide helpful information and resources to cyberstalking targets. Other strategies individuals can use to protect themselves from cyberstalking include refraining from the following: completing personal profile information, divulging personal information online, sending photos to strangers, engaging in arguments in chat rooms, and meeting strangers in person. Using a gender-neutral screen name is also a useful strategy. Colleges must include online harassment in their policies regarding Internet use and in the student handbook. Consequences for perpetrators should be included as well.

SOLUTIONS

McNulty, Heller, and Binet (1997) argue that education is the most effective strategy in combating abusive behavior when it makes clear that violence is *not* a normal or integral part of interpersonal relationships. There are many factors that contribute to gendered violence: the element of male dominance, the perception of females as objects, the negation of acquaintance rape as sexual assault, the tolerance of violence in our culture, and so on. These factors also serve to contribute to notions of victim blame. As Cowan (2000) states, "To the extent that women believe in rape and sexual harassment myths that serve the function of blaming the victim and exonerating the perpetrator, women indirectly participate in the maintenance of a rape culture" (p. 238). It seems that possessing beliefs associated with victim blame serves to separate the holder of these beliefs from victims. That is, by holding such beliefs, women can distance themselves from the thought that this very well may happen to them. As Cowan states:

> Devaluation of women as a class may influence women to see themselves as exceptions to their group, and they may come to believe that other women provoke rape and sexual harassment. Women's hostility toward women also may prevent women from bonding together in action against sexual violence. (p. 239)

Victim blaming is said to be an attribution error, in other words, that individuals attribute their failures to external forces and their successes to internal characteristics (Johnson, Mullick, & Mulford, 2002). People assess others in the exact opposite manner; thus, victim blaming results. Additionally, people who believe that the world is an inherently "just place," where good things happen to good people and bad things happen to bad people, are more likely to possess victim blaming attitudes (Johnson, Mullick, & Mulford, 2002).

Working with students on the realities of violence against women and the consequences of traditional (and limiting) expectations of gender that often put women and LGBTTIQQ individuals at a disadvantage may help in reducing students' implicit participation in the rape culture of which sexual harassment, stalking, and relationship violence are directly related. It is also important to discuss the implicit messages that are derived from the different societal expectations for males and females. To a certain degree females are still taught to be deferential to males when they are being pursued. As De Becker (1997) states, "It isn't news that men and women often speak different languages, but when the stakes are the highest, it's important to remember that men are nice when they pursue, and women are nice when they reject. Naturally this leads to confusion ..." (p. 237).

There are many things that college campuses can do to reduce gendered violence. First, it is important to raise awareness of the problem of gendered violence. Student organizations and school administrations can team with domestic violence and sexual assault prevention organizations to help spread the word about the effect of violence against women (and gendered violence in general) and violence against LGBTTIQQ individuals, and to let victims know how they can get the support and services they need. Campus campaigns to illuminate violence and harassment on campus can begin with such partnerships. White ribbon campaigns, where men pledge "never to commit, condone, nor remain silent about violence against women" (Katz, 2006), could be a great way to elicit men's cooperation with the campaign, to explicitly address the issue of violence against women on campus, and to contribute to the creation of a campus culture that does not tolerate violence.

Campuses also must widely publicize anti-harassment policies, including definitions of bullying, sexual harassment, stalking, cyberstalking, and so on, as well as examples of said behaviors. These policies should be provided to faculty, staff, students, and others in the campus culture, and should include complaint and investigative procedures, and consequences/disciplinary actions for perpetrators. Campuses should make reporting procedures public and easily accessible for all, and provide counseling for victims or for people with questions and/or those in need of support; such services should also be widely publicized.

Campuses should provide ongoing and up-to-date training for faculty, staff, and students to recognize and deal with violence and harassment. A more comprehensive anti-stalking and harassment handbook for college campuses should be made available to all students, faculty, and staff and should include online policies and procedures, including: definitions, examples of behaviors, effects of stalking and harassment on victims, a list of campus support services and how to access them, local community law enforcement information, and mental health information.

Because of the link between alcohol consumption and various forms of gendered violence, which are exacerbated by peer support for these types of violence and traditional and essentialist gender role expectations, campus Greek organizations and sports teams (where alcohol consumption tends to be heightened) should participate in gender sensitivity training and alcohol/drug awareness programs. As Abbey, McAuslan, Zawacki, Clinton, and Buck (2001) argue:

> Men need to know that their own intoxication does not provide a moral or legal justification for forced sex and that having sex with a woman too intoxicated to give consent is illegal. College is an excellent intervention point because students are being exposed to new ideas, norms, and social groups. (p. 804)

Women, also, must be made aware that they experience motor impairments with alcohol consumption, such that their efforts to thwart an attack may be ineffective; this absolutely does not decrease the culpability on the part of the male, however. Silence or intoxication does not imply consent, and everyone, men and women, must be made aware of this. All students should have access to sexual assault and dating violence prevention/awareness programs. Campuses should also make the entire student population aware of the effects of alcohol and drugs and how consumption can heighten incidents of dangerous, risky, and criminal behavior. Campuses should also provide serious sanctions for underage drinking.

Finally, campuses should elicit assistance from their Women's Studies or Women and Gender Studies programs in their campaigns to raise awareness of gendered violence.

REFERENCES

Abbey, A., Clinton-Sherrod, A. M., McAuslan, P., Zawacki, T., & Buck, P. O. (2003). The relationship between the quantity of alcohol consumed and the severity of sexual assaults committed by college men. *Journal of Interpersonal Violence, 18*(7), 813–233.

Abbey, A., McAuslan, P., Zawacki, T., Clinton, A. M., & Buck, P. O. (2001). Attitudinal, experiential, and situational predictors of sexual assault perpetration. *Journal of Interpersonal Violence, 16*(8), 784–807.

Alexy, E. M. (2005). Perceptions of cyberstalking among college students. *Brief Treatment and Crisis Intervention, 5*(3), 279–289.

American Association of University Women Educational Foundation (2001/1993). *Hostile hallways: Bullying, teasing, and sexual harassment in school.* Washington, DC: The American Association of University Women Educational Foundation.

Bancroft, L. (2002). *Why does he do that? Inside the minds of angry and controlling men.* New York: Berkley.

Banyard, V. L. (2007). Unwanted sexual contact on campus: A comparison of women's and men's experiences. *Violence and Victims, 22*(1), 57–70.

Bartky, S. L. (1990). *Femininity and domination.* New York: Routledge.

Beatty, D. (2003). Stalking legislation in the United States. In M. P. Brewster (Ed.), *Stalking: Psychology, risk factors, interventions and law* (pp. 2.1-2.21). Kingston, NJ: Civic Research Institute.

Beauvais, K. (1986). Workshops to combat sexual harassment: A case study of changing attitudes. *Signs, 12*(1), 130–145.

Bjerregaard, B. (2002). An empirical study of stalking victimization. In K. E. Davis, I. H. Frieze, & R. D. Maiuro (Eds.), *Stalking: Perspectives on victims and perpetrators* (pp. 112–137). New York: Springer Publishing Company.

Bocij, P. (2004). *Cyberstalking: Harassment in the Internet age and how to protect your family.* Westport, CT: Praeger Publishers.

Bonate, D. L., & Jessell, J. C. (1996). The effects of educational interventions on perceptions of sexual harassment. *Sex Roles, 35*(11/12), 751–764.

Brandenburg, J. B. (1997). *Confronting sexual harassment: What schools and colleges can do.* New York: Teachers College Press.

Brown, L. M., & Gilligan, C. (1992). *Meeting at the crossroads: Women's psychology and girls' development.* New York: Ballantine Books.

Cantu, N. V., & Heumann, J. E. (2000). *Memorandum on harassment based on disability.* Washington, DC: United States Department of Education.

Casey-Cannon, S., Hayward, C., & Gowen, K. (2001). Middle-school girls' reports of peer victimization: Concerns, consequences, and implications. *Professional School Counseling, 5*(2), 138–147.

Chapell, M., Casey, D., De la Cruz, C., Ferrell, J., Forman, J., Lipkin, R., Newsham, M., Sterling, M., & Whittaker, S. (2004). Bullying in college by students and teachers. *Adolescence, 39*(153), 53–64.

Chapell, M. S., Hasselman, S. L., Kitchin, T., Lomon, S. N., MacIver, K. W., & Sarullo, P. L. (2006). Bullying in elementary school, high school, and college. *Adolescence, 41*(164), 633–648.

Cowan, G. (2000). Women's hostility toward women and rape and sexual harassment myths. *Violence Against Women, 6*(3), 238–246.

Cupach, W. R., & Spitzberg, B. H. (1999). Obsessive relational intrusion and stalking. In B. H. Spitzberg & W. R. Cupach (Eds.), *The dark side of close relationships* (pp. 233–296). Hillsdale, NJ: Erlbaum.

Darley, J., & Latané, B. (1968). Bystander intervention in emergencies: Diffusion of responsibility. *Journal of Personality and Social Psychology, 8,* 377–383.

De Becker, G. (1997). *The gift of fear and other survival signals that protect us from violence.* New York: Dell Publishing.

D'Ovidio, R., & Doyle, J. (2003). A study on cyberstalking: Understanding investigative hurdles. *FBI Law Enforcement Bulletin, 72*(3), 10–17.

Durham, M. G. (1999). Girls, media, and the negotiation of sexuality: A study of race, class, gender in adolescent peer groups. *Journalism & Mass Communication Quarterly, 76*(2), 193–216.

Farley, L. (1978). *Sexual shakedown: The sexual harassment of women on the job.* New York: McGraw-Hill Book Company.

Fineran, S., & Bennett, L. (1999). Gender and power issues of peer sexual harassment among teenagers. *Journal of Interpersonal Violence, 14*(6), 626–641.

Finn, J. (2004). A survey of online harassment at a university campus. *Journal of Interpersonal Violence, 19*(4), 468–483.

Fisher, B. S., Cullen, F. T., & Turner, M. G. (2000). *The sexual victimization of college women.* Washington, DC: U.S. Department of Justice. (NCJ 182369).

Flanagan, M. (2000). Navigating the narrative in space: Gender and spatiality in virtual worlds. *Art Journal, 59*(3), 74–85.

Fredrickson, B., & Roberts, T. (1997). Objectification theory: Toward understanding women's lived experiences and mental health risks. *Psychology of Women Quarterly, 21*(2), 173–206.

Glomb, T. M., Richman, W. L., Hulin, C. L., Drasgow, F., Schneider, K. T., & Fitzgerald, L. F. (1997). Ambient sexual harassment: An integrated model of antecedents and consequences. *Organizational Behavior and Human Decision Processes 71*(3), 309–328.

Gross, L. (1994). *Surviving a stalker: Everything you need to know to keep yourself safe.* New York: Marlowe & Company.

Gruber, J. E., & Fineran, S. (2007). *Teens and trouble: A comparison of health and school related effects of bullying and sexual harassment among middle and high school students.* Paper presented at the International Coalition Against Sexual Harassment Conference, New York, NY.

Guldry, L. L. (2005). Review of stalking and psychological obsession: Psychological perspectives for prevention, policing, and treatment. *Psychiatric Services 56*(8), 1029–1030.

Hall Smith, P., White, J. W., & Holland, L. J. (2003). A longitudinal perspective on dating violence among adolescent and college-age women. *Research and Practice, 93*(7), 1104–1109.

Hartmann, H. (1977). Capitalism, patriarchy, and job segregation by sex. In N. Glazer & H. Y. Waehaer (Eds.), *Woman in a man-made world* (pp. 71–84). Chicago, IL: Rand McNally.

Humphrey, J. A., & White, J. W. (2000). Women's vulnerability to sexual assault from adolescence to young adulthood. *Journal of Adolescent Health, 27,* 419–424.

Hunter, S. C., & Boyle, J. M. E. (2002). Perceptions of control in the victims of school bullying: The importance of early intervention. *Educational Research, 44*(3), 323–336.

Johnson, L. M., Mullick, R., & Mulford, C. L. (2002). General versus specific victim blaming. *The Journal of Social Psychology, 142*(2), 249–263.

Katz, J. (2006). Coverage of "school shootings" avoids the central issue. Retrieved September 28, 2007, from http://www.commondreams.org/cgi-bin/print.cgi?file=/views06/1011-36.htm

Logan, T. K., Leukefeld, C., & Walker, B. (2002). Stalking as a variant of intimate violence: Implications from a young adult sample. In K. E. Davis, I. H. Frieze, & R. D. Maiuro (Eds.), *Stalking: Perspectives on victims and perpetrators* (pp. 265–291). New York: Springer Publishing Company.

Lucks, B. D. (2004). Cyberstalking: Identifying and examining electronic crime in cyberspace. *Dissertation Abstracts International, 65* (02B). (UMI No: 99016–300).

MacKinnon, C. A. (1979). *Sexual harassment of working women: A case of sex discrimination.* New Haven, CT: Yale University Press.

Malamuth, M. B., & Brown, L. M. (1994). Sexually aggressive men's perceptions of women's communications: Testing three explanations. *Journal of Personality and Social Psychology, 67,* 699–712.

McCann, J. T. (1998). Subtypes of stalking (obsessional following) in adolescents. *Journal of Adolescence, 21*, 667–675.

McCann, J. (2001). *Stalking in children and adults: The primitive bond.* Washington, DC: American Psychological Association.

McMahon, P. P. (1995). Stemming harassment among middle school students through peer mediation exercises. (Doctoral practicum paper, Nova Southeastern University, 1995). (ERIC Document Reproduction Service No. ED393027).

McNulty, R. J., Heller, D., & Binet, T. (1997). Confronting dating violence. *Educational Leadership, 55*(2), 26–28.

Mechanic, M. B. (2002). Stalking victimization: Clinical implications for assessment and intervention. In K. E. Davis, I. H. Frieze, & R. D. Maiuro (Eds.), *Stalking: Perspectives on victims and perpetrators* (pp. 31–61). New York: Springer Publishing Company.

Merschman, J. C. (2001). The dark side of the web: Cyberstalking and the need for contemporary legislation. *Harvard Women's Law Journal, 24*, 255–292.

Morewitz, S. J. (2003). *Stalking and violence: New patterns of trauma and obsession.* New York: Kluwer Academic/ Plenum Publishers.

Murnen, S. K., & Smolak, L. (2000). The experience of sexual harassment among grade-school students: Early socialization of female subordination? *Sex Roles, 43*(1/2), 1–17.

Murrell, A. J., & Dietz-Uhler, B. L. (1993). Gender identity and adversarial sexual beliefs as predictors of attitudes toward sexual harassment. *Psychology of Women Quarterly, 17*(2), 169–175.

Naylor, P., & Cowie, H. (1999). The effectiveness of peer support systems in challenging school bullying: The perspectives and experiences of teachers and pupils. *Journal of Adolescence, 22*, 467–479.

O'Connell, P., Pepler, D., & Craig, W. (1999). Peer involvement in bullying: Insights and challenges for intervention. *Journal of Adolescence, 22*, 437–452.

Olweus, D. (1993). *Bullying at school: What we know and what we can do.* Oxford, UK: Blackwell.

Olweus, D. (2003). A profile of bullying. *Educational Leadership, 60*(6), 12–17.

Reigle, R. R. (2007). *The online bully in higher education.* Online. (ERIC Document Reproduction Service No. ED495686).

Reno, J. (1999). Cyberstalking: A new challenge for law enforcement and industry. Retrieved September 11, 2007, from http://www.usdoj.gov/criminal/cybercrime /cyberstalking.htm

Salmivalli, C. (1999). Participant role approach to school bullying: Implications for interventions. *Journal of Adolescence, 22*, 453–459.

Salmivalli, C. (2001). Peer-led intervention campaign against school bullying: Who considered it useful, who benefited? *Educational Research, 43*(3), 263–278.

Schwartz, W. (2000). *Preventing student sexual harassment* (Report No. EDO-UD-00-9). Washington, DC: Office of Educational Research and Improvement. (ERIC Document Reproduction Service No. ED448248).

Sheffield, C. J. (1989). Sexual terrorism. In J. Freeman (Ed.), *Women: A feminist perspective* (4th ed.) (pp. 3–19). Mountain View, CA: Mayfield Publishing Company.

Sinclair, H. C., & Frieze, I. H. (2002). Initial courtship behavior and stalking: How should we draw the line? In K. E. Davis & I. H. Frieze (Eds.),

Stalking: Perspectives on victims and perpetrators (pp. 186–211). New York: Springer.

Sinclair, H. C., & Frieze, I. H. (2005). When courtship persistence becomes intrusive pursuit: Comparing rejecter and pursuer perspectives on unrequited attraction. *Sex Roles, 52*(11/12), 839–851.

Smith, P. H. (2003). A longitudinal perspective on dating violence among adolescent and college-age women. *American Journal of Public Health, 93*(7), 1104–1109.

Spitzberg, B. H. (2002). Cyberstalking and the technologies of interpersonal terrorism. *New Media & Society, 4*(1), 71–92.

Spitzberg, B. H., & Rhea, J. (1999). Obsessive relational intrusion and sexual coercion victimization. *Journal of Interpersonal Violence, 14*(1), 3–20.

Stein, N. (1996a). Slippery justice. *Educational Leadership, 53*(8), 64–68.

Stein, N. (1996b). From the margins to the mainstream: Sexual harassment in K-12 schools. *Initiatives, 57*(3), 19–26.

Stein, N. (2002). Bullying as sexual harassment in elementary schools. In *The Jossey-Bass reader on gender in education* (pp. 409–428). San Francisco, CA: Jossey-Bass.

Stephens, G. (1995). Crime in cyberspace: The digital underworld. *The Futurist, 29*, 24–28.

Stevens, V., Van Oost, P., & de Bourdeaudhuij, I. (2000). The effects of an anti-bullying programme on peers' attitudes and behaviour. *Journal of Adolescence, 23*, 21–34.

Stover, D. (2006). Treating cyberbullying as a school violence issue. *The Education Digest, 72*(4), 40–42.

Tjaden, P. (2003). Prevalence and characteristics of stalking. In M. P. Brewster (Ed.), *Stalking: Psychology, risk factors, interventions and law* (pp. 1.1-1.16). Kingston, NJ: Civic Research Institute.

Tjaden, P., & Thoeness, N. (1997). *Stalking in America: Findings from the National Violence Against Women Survey* (N. I. J. Grant No. 93-IJ-CX-0012). Washington, DC: National Institutes of Justice/Centers for Disease Control.

Tjaden, P., Thoennes, N., & Allison, C. J. (2002). Comparing stalking victimization from legal and victim perspectives. In K. E. Davis, I. H. Frieze, & R. D. Maiuro (Eds.), *Stalking: Perspectives on victims and perpetrators* (pp. 9–30). New York: Springer Publishing Company.

van Roosmalen, E. (2000). Forces of patriarchy: Adolescent experiences of sexuality and conceptions of relationships. *Youth & Society, 32*(2), 202–227.

White, J. W., & Koss, M. P. (1991). Courtship violence: Incidence and prevalence in a national sample of higher education students. *Violence and Victims, 6*, 247–256.

Williams, S. L., & Frieze, I. H. (2005). Courtship behaviors, relationship violence, and breakup persistence in college men and women. *Psychology of Women Quarterly, 29*, 248–257.

Wolbert Burgess, A., & Baker, T. (2002). Cyberstalking. In J. Boon, & L. Sheridan (Eds.), *Stalking and psychological obsession: Psychological perspectives for prevention, policing and treatment* (pp. 201–220). West Sussex, UK: John Wiley & Sons, Ltd.

Zorza, J. (2003). Stalking controversies and emerging issues. In Brewster, M. P. (Ed.), *Stalking: Psychology, risk factors, interventions, and law,* (pp. 515–521). Kingston, NJ: Civic Research Institute.

Chapter 2

Bullying and Hazing: A Form of Campus Harassment

Florence L. Denmark
Maria D. Klara
Erika M. Baron

The problem of bullying has come to the forefront and into the attention of the American public due to recent episodes of school shootings, beginning with Columbine in 1999 and more recently in the case of the Virginia Tech shootings (Anderson et al., 2001). In the center of many of these tragedies are solitary figures who frequently were the subject of taunts and harassment by fellow classmates. Although never condoning the method in which these individuals chose to retaliate, these stories do articulate and exemplify the necessity to understand bullying and prevent such extreme repercussions.

Bullying in schools is common throughout the world (Smith et al., 1999). When the term *bullying* is brought up, younger children most likely come to mind. Although bullying is often experienced in this age bracket, harassment in other age groups should not be discounted. Today there are approximately 18 million teenagers in college campuses across the country (U.S. Department of Education, 2007). College campuses bring thousands of teenagers together in a small area, where many areas of their lives intersect on a myriad of levels. Students constantly interact with each other in academic, work, and social settings, making it likely that there will be social conditions optimal for bullying. It is not only possible, but common for students to see each other frequently on and off campus, know of each other through mutual friends and acquaintances, and have little choice but to associate with them in some way due to class schedules and extracurricular activities. One could argue that a person would have less chance of being harassed and bullied on a college campus, but depending on the activities one is engaged with, it is more evident than expected.

Despite the growing amount of information on bullying in primary and secondary schools, literature and research on the composition and consequences of bullying in college is lacking (Chapell et al., 2004). Most information includes background information as well as prevention, and intervention methods are solely focused on the younger age group. However, it is important to target colleges as an environment where bullying can occur as well.

BULLYING: DEFINITIONS AND TYPOLOGIES

McLaughlin, Laux, and Pescara-Kovach (2006) assert that it is challenging to find one definition of bullying that is appropriate in every situation. There are various definitions of bullying in a college environment and generally they include verbal abuse; conduct that is degrading, insulting, or intimidating; and/or professional or social ostracism (Gray, 2003). Camodeca and Goossens (2005) define bullying as behavior of negative actions toward a peer with the intention of inflicting harm. In most situations, this type of violence is about power that is misused.

The reasons why people bully in college are similar to reasons for younger students. Bullying is about power that is misguided and about perpetrators using this power in an unacceptable way (Gray, 2003); namely, power is used to relieve frustrations, assert authority, or maintain social status. In essence, one achieves elevated social status by degrading another student and therefore placing him or her in a position of less power.

However, the presentation of bullying within the college setting can present itself in novel ways, which distinguishes it from bullying in other age brackets. The first is bullying that occurs between teachers or coaches toward students. One study conducted by Chapell et al. (2006) sought to examine the nature of bullying by teachers and coaches on verbal (attacking a person verbally using harmful words, names, or threats), physical (attacking a person physically), and social (intentionally isolating or excluding a person from a social group) dimensions. They found that verbal bullying of students was the most common form used by both college teachers and coaches. Twenty-two percent of the participants ($N = 119$) indicated that they had been verbally bullied by instructors, and 6.7% said they had experienced social bullying. In addition, 5.1% stated they had been verbally bullied by coaches, 3.4% reported social bullying by coaches, and 1.7% reported physical bullying.

It is important to understand that bullying does not only occur only in educational settings but in other settings also. Studies have indicated that bullying frequently occurs with adults in the workplace (Glendenning, 2001; Quine, 2001). Therefore it stands to reason that this would be the same for younger persons as well. Places of employment have similar characteristics that can breed bullying. Namely, they are places where many young people can work at the same time, and where an atmosphere of desire for social acceptance can be found. In addition, many young people work to earn extra money and therefore employment is very important to them.

HAZING

For the purpose of this chapter, a specific type of bullying, hazing, will be discussed. Hazing is a form of bullying that is especially common in colleges and universities since it by definition involves a college lifestyle and institutions. *Hazing* is defined as any action that inflicts or intends to cause physical or mental harm or anxieties and which may demean, degrade, or disgrace any person, regardless of location, intent, or consent of participants. Hazing can also be defined as any action or situation that intentionally or unintentionally endangers a student for admission into or affiliation with any student organization (www.angelfire.com/ky/collegepopularity/hazing.html). Keating et al. (2005) offer another definition of hazing and divide hazing into several further subdivisions. First, hazing involves initiation activities that include physical challenge or pain; social deviance; embarrassment or humiliation.

Most universities have express policies that define hazing. For instance, Bridgewater State University has defined hazing as such:

> The term "hazing" should mean any conduct or method of initiation into any student organization, whether on public or private property, which willfully or recklessly endangers the physical or mental health of any student or other person. Such conduct may include whipping, beating, branding, forced calisthenics, exposure to the weather, forced consumption (or deprivation) of any food, liquor, beverage, drug, or other substance or any other brutal treatment or forced physical activity which is likely to adversely affect the physical health or safety of any such student or other person or which subjects such student or other person to extreme mental stress, including extended deprivation of sleep or rest or extended isolation (www.bridgew.edu/Handbook/PoliciesProcedures/Hazing.htm).

However, many agree that definitions and policies about hazing are not explicit enough, leaving students loopholes with which to argue that certain behaviors are not under the hazing umbrella (Campo, Poulos, & Sipple, 2005). Additionally, many students believe that hazing includes only dangerous activities such as being tied up, beaten, or hurt in some way. From the above definition, it is evident that there are many other actions or behaviors that can be categorized as hazing apart from these more extreme forms. However, students can frequently find ways to bypass the definitions by stating that they did not believe they were doing anything to endanger the welfare of another student.

Hazing has been more prevalent in the media in recent years, as many dangerous consequences have caught the public's attention. For instance, in 2000, the University of Vermont men's ice hockey season was terminated after a legal complaint was filed by one of its players who was forced to undergo hazing (CBS News, 2000). The hazing activities included an atmosphere that allegedly brought about civil rights violations, assault, and battery. Additionally, several high-profile hazing incidents like the 1997 alcohol-related death of MIT student, Scott Kruger, have prompted wide recognition of the dangers of hazing by sports teams and fraternities (www.cbsnews.com/stories/2000/04/02/national/main179106.shtml).

PREVALENCE AND SETTING OF HAZING EVENTS

"It's been a tremendous problem since 1970, where either in a hazing or pledging related incident, we've had a death a year since 1970," claimed Hank Nuwer, a hazing expert (www.cbsnews.com/stories/2000/04/02/national/main179106.shtml). Most experts believe that hazing deaths are underreported as accidental deaths (Nuwer, 1990) and therefore it is difficult to get an accurate figure of how many injuries or deaths there were in hazing-related activities. What is known, however, is that in 2000, 23 students died of hazing; 24 in 2001 died; and in 2002, 42 students died to hazing related activities (http://hazing.hanknuwer.com).

Hazing more frequently occurs on campus since it is closely associated with fraternities and sororities and also with college sports teams. Hazing is often conducted in secret, and although the campus may be aware that "something" occurs, not many people outside these organizations know or are willing to share exactly what occurs. In one study, 36% of college students sampled participated in hazing in at least one instance (Campo, Poulos, & Sipple, 2005). The study also found that those who participate in Greek life, and those who are males, leaders, varsity athletes, and upperclassmen were more likely to participate in hazing. Another recent study found that 60% of hazed university athletes stated that they would not report hazing (Hoover, 1999).

An investigation of initiation rites and athletics for NCAA sports teams across the nation was conducted in which over 325,000 athletes at more than 1,000 National Collegiate Athletic Association schools participated. Results indicated that more than a quarter of a million athletes experienced some form of hazing after joining an athletic team. One out of five athletes was subjected to potentially illegal hazing (i.e., kidnapping, physical violence, being forced to commit crimes, etc.). Half of the athletes were required to engage in alcohol-related hazing, while two-thirds of the participants were subjected to humiliation hazing (i.e., being yelled at, forced to wear embarrassing clothes, depriving oneself of hygiene, etc.). Analyses focusing on differences between genders as well as regions of the country revealed that women were more likely to be involved in alcohol-related hazing than in other forms; football players were at more risk for dangerous and potentially illegal hazing; Eastern and Western campuses had the most alcohol-related hazing; and that Southern and Midwestern campuses had the greatest incidence of potentially illegal hazing (Hoover, 1999).

In college, hazing most often involves a group of students performing some task as a rite of initiation into some other, larger group, whose membership is comprised of people who had to endure similar rites of passage at some earlier time. There is therefore a cycle, where those who have endured hazing in turn inflict this onto others. This is somewhat different from types of bullying that occur with younger children. Although those who are bullied are more likely to bully others in return (Chapell et al., 2006), the type of bullying in primary and secondary schools is not conducted to bring people into a social network but rather to separate others from a social network. Hazing therefore is abuse but cloaked in the need for social acceptance.

The age of those in college also plays an important role. College students are in a new setting with novel environmental stressors, and are separated from parental structure and support (Roark, 1987). They also may experience peer pressure, and may feel that they are invincible; they also may have identities that are not yet formed or ones that can resist alluring group pressure.

ACTIVITIES OF HAZING

The following is a list of activities that illustrate hazing. Additional information may be obtained from Nuwer (1990).

- Paddling an individual
- Coerced consumption of alcohol
- Branding
- Making individuals ingest vile substances
- Preventing bathing, brushing teeth, etc.
- Degrading an individual
- Preventing/restricting sleep
- Required eating of raw or spoiled foods
- Making prank calls

- Coerced shaving of heads and/or other body parts
- Burning skin
- Locking up individuals
- Making individuals simulate sex acts

Other activities include being kidnapped, transported, and abandoned; participating in drinking contests; being deprived of sleep; engaging in or simulating sexual acts; being physically assaulted; carrying unnecessary objects; and being required to remain silent. More recently, alcohol-free hazing has been practiced across campuses due to the misconception that it protects victims from harm or death. Hazing expert Hank Nuwer states that being forced to drink large amounts of non-alcoholic liquids (i.e., water, milk, etc.) can be equally as dangerous and has led to fatal brain swelling (Campo, Poulos, & Sipple, 2005).

Hoover (1999, pp. 9–10) differentiates between acceptable, questionable, and unacceptable forms of hazing.

Acceptable Initiation Activities

Attending pre-season training

Testing for skill, endurance, or performance in a sport

Keeping a specific GPA

Dressing up for team functions (besides uniforms)

Attending a skit night or team roast

Doing volunteer community service

Completing a ropes course or team trip

Taking an oath or signing a contract of standards

Questionable Initiation Activities

Being yelled, cursed, or sworn at

Being forced to wear embarrassing clothes

Tattooing, piercing, head shaving, or branding

Consuming extremely spicy/disgusting concoctions

Acting as a personal servant to another

Being forced to deprive oneself of food, sleep, or hygiene

Associating with specific people, not others

Unacceptable Initiation Activities

Making prank calls or harassing others

Engaging in or simulating sexual acts

Destroying or stealing property

Being tied up, taped, or confined in a small space

Being paddled, whipped, beaten, or kicked

Beating others

Being kidnapped or transported and abandoned

SOCIAL PSYCHOLOGICAL UNDERPINNINGS OF HAZING

Understanding the reasoning behind hazing activities is critical in the attempt to develop intervention programs and prevention efforts. Critical to this endeavor is to explore the psychological and sociological perspectives on why perpetrators as well as victims willingly engage in such behavior. The following is an investigation of various hypotheses purported to explain hazing.

Severity-Attraction Hypothesis

Aronson and Mills developed one of the foundational theories of hazing, namely, the severity-attraction hypothesis. This states that the more effort an individual exerts toward reaching a goal or object, the more the individual will rationalize the goal or object as being worthy of such effort (Aronson, Wilson, & Akert, 2002). It is hypothesized that victims utilize rationalization to reduce cognitive dissonance, allowing them to value the group that they essentially suffer for. Cognitive dissonance occurs when an individual's actions are incongruent with feelings and thoughts. More specifically, strict initiation practices often violate concepts of self, and so arouse dissonance within the individuals who engage in the activities. In order to lesson one's conflicting feelings, one must diminish the negativity of the initiation or overvalue the group. Ultimately, this allows victims to endure the mental and physical efforts during the hazing process, and for perpetrators to defend their potentially harmful actions.

Social Dependency

The sociological factors that are behind the actions of the perpetrator and victim are numerous. Initiations often function to promote cognitive, behavioral, and affective forms of social dependency (Moreland & Levine, 1989). More recently, attachment theory, or the process by which individuals create bonds with their caregivers, has been applied to the development of relationships between individuals and groups. Smith, Coats, and Murphy (2001) proposed that a unique aspect of the attachment system, maltreatment effects, applies to the attachment development between humans and groups, shedding light on how group initiations function to promote dependency. Specifically, individuals who undergo mental, emotional, and physical duress can be more stimulated to create a social bond between themselves and the individual who is carrying out the maltreatment. In the case of hazing, the victims might identify with the perpetrators and develop the belief that subjecting themselves to mistreatment will bring them closer to the defined group.

Affective Social Bonds

Another prevalent view is that hazing rituals produce a discomfort that compels individuals to develop emotional bonds with others involved in the shared, secretive rite of passage. From an interpersonal perspective, anxiety that arises from the mistreatment readies an individual to seek protection from potential comrades. When the agents of the abuse are the only available channels, affiliative responses may be directed toward them (Hoover & Milner, 1998). The desire for love and belongingness also has much to do with an individual's desire for a singular and/or collaborative identity. Individuals who are experiencing the initiation process often ponder the extent to which they perceive the group to be invested in their unique belonging as well as the extent to which they are psychologically invested in belonging to the group. Ultimately, acceptance of the mistreatment may indicate that both subjective ratings are high. By enduring the distress, individuals state that the group is important to them, that they are critical to the group, and that exclusivity, of which the mistreatment is a part, makes them distinct from individuals who are not of the group. Furthermore, the angst and discomfort that one tolerates is symbolic of remaking the self, which is projected to emphasize one's connection to another within a group context (Keating et al., 2005).

Conformity and Hierarchy

Several studies have successfully linked induced discomfort to increased conformity (Van Duuren & Di Giacomo, 1997). Conforming to become like many other individuals can make the victim feel like a loyal member of a committed, integrated group. In addition to emphasizing dedication and cohesion, initiation practices are meant to emphasize the group's hierarchical structure. Inherent in hazing is a power differential whereby the perpetrator is the authority figure, while the victim is the submissive figure. Getting recruits to comply is an exercise in social control whereby the victims demonstrate their ability to understand, abide by, and respect the group's structure (Keating et al., 2005).

PSYCHOLOGICAL EFFECTS OF HAZING

Victim

According to Rigby (2005), the effects of bullying can greatly impact victims' sense of well-being, their ability to cope, and the sense of control they have over their lives. Emotional sequelae include exhaustion, duress from humiliation, depression, anxiety, and even re-traumatization of a past abuse. The physical results span a continuum ranging from stress-related illness and accidental injuries to serious inflicted injuries, medical emergencies, and even death. Some researchers acknowledge the socio-emotional benefits of hazing, citing that the process helps an individual learn about oneself, provides a sense of accomplishment, challenges one to develop coping skills, develops healthy interdependency, prepares one for the emotional challenges of life, and promotes self-discipline (Cornell University, 2006).

Perpetrator

Positive and negative effects on the perpetrator have also been explored. The costs of hazing to the executor can include discomfort playing a role that is inconsistent with one's values, guilt arising from actions, conflict developed with groups members who hold different views, potential rejection by prospective group members, and the risk of judicial, criminal, or civil consequences. Cited benefits to the agent of the maltreatment include a sense of pride for continuing traditions, promotion of bonding with other members who are hazing, and diminishing anger regarding personal hazing incidents. Overall, it is important to determine if the benefits to the victim and perpetrator outweigh the costs; most often, they do not (Cornell University, 2006).

Anecdotes

The following anecdotes provide descriptive accounts of various hazing activities and highlight the effect that such practices had on the victim as well as the perpetrator.

- A Rider University male student was reportedly forced to drink more than a half-bottle of vodka in just 15 minutes while partying at a fraternity house. Rescue personnel found the student in cardiac arrest and utilized CPR to revive him before transporting him to the hospital. He was pronounced dead the following day. Two Rider University officials (including the dean of students and the director of Greek life) and three members of the fraternity were indicted in the student's death. If convicted, all individuals will face a maximum penalty of 18 months in prison and individual fines of up to $10,000. The fraternity was permanently closed down (Newmarker, 2007).

- A Chico State University male student was reportedly ordered into the fraternity basement and told to do calisthenics in raw sewage that had leaked on the concrete floor. For hours, he was interrogated, taunted, and forced to drink from a five-gallon jug of water that was repeatedly refilled. While he urinated and vomited on himself, icy air from an air conditioner was blasted onto his body. Ultimately, the student collapsed and began to seizure. He died from water intoxication due to the swelling of his brain and lungs. Four members of the fraternity were found guilty and sent to jail, and the fraternity was permanently closed down (Korry, 2007).

- Two female students at California State University, who reportedly told the sorority that they were unable to swim, were forced into the ocean, and were blindfolded with their hands tied during a pledging incident. Police officers were sent to the beach when sorority members reported that their friends were "swept into the ocean and hadn't come out." They were pulled out of the ocean and pronounced dead at the scene. The families reportedly filed a $100 million wrongful death suit against the sorority and five of its members (Zahn, 2002).

PREVENTION AND INTERVENTION EFFORTS

Although several states have laws that outlaw hazing and denote legal penalties, it is critical to address the practice on a campus-wide level. Research yields the common finding that participation by students, professors, coaches, administrators, parents, and law enforcement in creating as well as implementing an anti-hazing intervention maximizes its effectiveness. Nuwer (2000) states that:

> Hazers ... are nothing more or less than addicts in an addictive system. For hazing to continue to survive within the education system, as it has for thousands of years, requires dependence and tolerance—the two common characteristics of addiction ... on the parts not only of the hazers but also of those who supervise them. (pp. 114–115)

This quote speaks to the primary role of the university administrator in initiating and implementing a multifaceted policy to not only prevent hazing but penalize those who participate in activities deemed as unacceptable.

Hollmann (2002) recommends that administrators should examine their institutional policies and regulations, student codes of conduct, and relationship or recognition statements for student organizations. This should be done to assure that the university has a well-developed and consistent policy that addresses various forms of hazing. Development of a written anti-hazing policy for university students with clear definitions and consequences is most often suggested. In doing so, it is important to utilize clear and concise language when discussing the repercussions when a person or group engages in specific prohibited behaviors. Embedded in the policy should be anonymous reporting and grievance procedures. Some universities suggest that a no-tolerance policy be utilized, citing that it is critical to legally protect all students from harm (Taylor, 2001).

In addition to these components, the policy should be published and disseminated to students, parents, faculty, coaches, and so on. Many universities request that students as well as parents sign a contract acknowledging that they have read and promise to abide by the policy. In addition to communicating about hazing via printed declarations, educational programs that expose students to the policy should be introduced early in the individual's academic career. For example, the University of Michigan conducts an interactive program at orientation during which students learn about the types of hazing, the consequences, and their role in prevention as well as intervention. Individuals watch pre-constructed videos, participate in role-plays, and answer "what-if" questions with the hopes that they will be prepared to combat hazing in the event that they are exposed to it (Hoover, 1999).

Educating the administration as well as coaching staff is a critical piece of the puzzle. It will be necessary for university employees to learn how to effectively monitor campus activities. They should be aware of what student groups are doing by staying in touch with student groups, asking about initiation activities, and being visible at campus events. Furthermore, administration can cooperate with the campus police to get arrest and incident records, allowing for follow-up on suspicious persons or occurrences (Hollmann, 2002). More specifically, athletic coaches or fraternity/sorority leaders can meet personally with each student during recruitment efforts, require individual screenings for academic as well as behavioral problems prior to group acceptance, and make behaviors on campus as well as off campus part of a person's evaluation (Rutledge, 1998).

Creating the ability for students to anonymously report hazing incidents will likely increase the frequency with which incidents are reported. A safe place or person should be designated and counseling services should be available for individuals who report as well as experience hazing. Furthermore, any report of hazing should be thoroughly investigated in a systematic, unbiased way. University administrators and local law enforcement officials should become involved immediately and attempt to protect the privacy of those who are involved. As with any complaint or serious issue in the university, it is extremely important to document every step of the investigation. Reviewing documented incidents might also elucidate a pattern of hazing activities among certain groups that can be addressed utilizing a more focused intervention (Taylor, 2001).

Disciplining individuals (students as well as faculty) who practice, condone, or overlook hazing is essential in preventing future hazing activities. As stated previously, consequences should be well defined and consistently implemented so as to send an important message to members of the university about the university's stance on hazing. Individuals who are punished for engaging or pardoning such maltreatment can be forced to speak to students about hazing and help changes in current policies to be more effective (Campo, Gretchen, Poulus, & Sipple, 2005).

Introducing and facilitating alternative team-building initiation activities might encourage groups to replace hazing with safer practices.

Trained leaders and adults can assist in this process by requiring groups to attend organized initiation events that emphasize loyalty, commitment, and cohesiveness. Additionally, these same individuals can remind group members about the goals of initiation practices and encourage them to develop their own list of activities that are not considered hazing but will achieve the same psychological and sociological goals (Nuwer, 2000).

A specific example of a successful campus anti-hazing program is entitled "Crossing the Line." It was designed to help administrators and students talk openly about hazing within student organizations. Students from Greek life, athletics, and clubs join together in a full-day course that explores various topics related to hazing. The program goals are as follows:

- To provide a safe atmosphere for students and administrators to discuss hazing
- To provide a setting in which to explore perceptions and evaluate how they impact the community's ability to be effective
- To provide resources and a starting point for campus community members to work together within their organizations as well as the larger community to stop hazing

After completing the program, participants will be able to differentiate between acceptable and unacceptable initiation practices, understand the long- and short-term effects of hazing, have brainstormed a list of activities that can replace hazing, and leave with a plan of action for implementing and developing cooperation and cohesiveness on a personal, organizational, and community level (Campus Speak, 2005).

CONCLUSION

Bullying and hazing on college campuses has increased significantly since 1970. Information about what hazing entails and what methods of prevention are available will help to combat this form of harassment. It is important to arm not only institutions of higher learning with more information, but young adults as well. Through prevention and intervention programs that widen awareness of this problem, victimization of college students due to hazing can decrease.

REFERENCES

Anderson, M., Kaufman, J., Simon, T. R., Barrios, L., Paulozzi, L., Ryan, G., Hammond, R., Modzeleski, W., Feucht, T., Potter, L., & The School-Associated Violent Deaths Study Group (2001). School-associated violent deaths in the United States, 1994–1999. *Journal of the American Medical Association, 286,* 2695–2702.

Aronson, E., Wilson, T. D., & Akert, R. M. (2002). *Social psychology (4th ed.)* Upper Saddle River, NJ: Prentice Hall/Pearson Education.

Campo, S., Poulos, G., & Sipple, J. W. (2005). Prevalence and profiling: Hazing among college students and points of intervention. *American Journal of Health Behavior, 29,* 137–149.

Campus Speak (2005). Retrieved on October 30, 2007, from http://www.campusspeak.com/programs/cap/CTL_Campus_Information.pdf.

CBS News (2000). Retrieved on August 12, 2007, from www.cbsnews.com/stories/2000/04/02/national/main179106.shtml.

Chapell, M., Casey, D., De la Cruz, C., Ferrell, J., Forman, J., Lipkin, A. R., Newsham, M., Sterling, M., & Whittaker, S. (2004). Bullying in college by students and teachers. *Adolescence, 39,* 53–64.

Chapell, M., Hasselman, S. L., Kitchin, T., Lomon, S. N., MacIver, K. W., & Sarullo, P. L. (2006). Bullying in elementary school, high school, and college. *Adolescence, 41,* 633–648.

Cornell University (2006). Retrieved September 20, 2007, from http://www.hazing.cornell.edu/issues/arguments.html.

Glendenning, P. M. (2001). Workplace bullying: Curing the cancer of American workplace. *Public Personnel Management, 30,* 269–286.

Gray, D. (2003). College bullying. Retrieved August 12, 2007, from http://www.jcu.edu.au.

Hazing. Retrieved August 12, 2007, from www.angelfire.com/ky/collegepopularity/hazing.html.

Hazing – Student Handbook – Bridgewater State University. Retrieved August 12, 2007, from www.bridgew.edu/Handbook/PoliciesProcedures/Hazing.htm.

Hollman, B. B. (2002). Hazing: Hidden campus crime. *New Directions for Student Services, 99,* 11–23.

Hoover, J., & Milner, C. (1998). Are hazing and bullying related to love and belongingness? *Reclaiming Children and Youth, 7*(3), 128–141.

Hoover, N. C. (1999). Initiation rites and athletics: A national survey of NCAA sports teams. Available: http://www.alfred.edu/news/html. Retrieved August 12, 2007.

Jones, R. L. (2000). The historical significance of sacrificial ritual: Understanding violence in the modern black fraternity pledge process. *Western Journal of Black Studies, 24,* 112–124.

Keating, C. F., Pomerantz, J., Pommer, S. D., Ritt, S. J., Miller, L. M., & McCormick, J. (2005). Going to college and unpacking hazing: A functional approach to decrypting initiation practices among undergraduates. *Group Dynamics: Theory, Research, and Practice, 9,* 104–126.

Korry, C. (2007). Retrieved November 3, 2007, http://www.npr.org/templates/story/story.php?storyId=5012154.

Moreland, R. L., & Levine, J. M. (1989). Newcomers and oldtimers in small groups. In P. Paulus (Ed.), *Psychology of group influence* (pp. 143–231). Hillsdale, NJ: Erlbaum.

Newmaker, C. (2007). Retrieved November 1, 2007 http://www.boston.com/news/nation/articles/2007/08/03/5_indicted_in_nj_drinking_death/?rss_id=Boston.com+%2F+News.

Nuwer, H. Unofficial clearinghouse for hazing and related risks in the news (online). Available: http://hazing.hanknuwer.com. Retrieved August 14, 2007.

Nuwer, H. (1990). *Broken pledges: The deadly rite of hazing.* Atlanta: Longstreet Press.

Nuwer, H. (2001). *Wrongs of passage: Fraternities, sororities, hazing, and binge drinking.* Bloomington: Indiana University Press.

Quine, L. (2001). Workplace bullying in nurses. *Journal of Health Psychology, 6,* 73–84.

Roark, M. L. (1987). Preventing violence on college campuses. *Journal of Counseling and Development, 65,* 367–371.

Rutledge, G. E. (1998). Hell night hath no fury like a pledge scorned ... and injured: Hazing litigation in U.S. colleges and universities. *Journal of College and University Law, 25*(2), 361–398.

Smith, E. R., Coats, S., & Murphy, J. (2001). The self and attachment to relationship partners and groups: Theoretical parallels and new insights. In C. Sedikides & M. B. Brewer (Eds.), *Individual self, relational self, collective self* (pp. 109–122). New York: Psychology Press.

Smith, P. K., Morrita, Y., Junger-Tas, J., Olweus, D., & Dornbusch, S. M. (1991). Authoritative parenting and adolescent adjustment across varied ecological niches. *Journal of Research on Adolescence, 1,* 19–36.

Taylor, K. R. (2001). Is hazing harmless horseplay? *Principal Leadership, 1,* 25–30.

U.S. Department of Education. Institute of Education Sciences: Projections and education statistics to 2015. Available: http://nces.ed.gov/programs/projections/tables/table_10.asp. Retrieved November 1, 2007.

Van Duuren, F. R., & Di Giacomo, J. P. (1997). Degrading situations, affiliation, and social dependency. *European Journal of Social Psychology, 27,* 495–510.

Zahn, P. (2002). Retrieved October 15, 2007, from, http://transcripts.cnn.com/TRANSCRIPTS/0209/25/ltm.10.html.

Chapter 3

Shots Heard Round the World: Campus Violence and International Student Concerns

Presha E. Neidermeyer
Siri Terjesen

Over 2.5 million students around the world are currently studying outside of their home country of origin, with approximately 560,000 international students pursuing degrees at American universities. The international education and exchange of students increase cross-national cultural understanding and constitute important components of academic life. Study-abroad programs promote lifelong changes in an individual's beliefs and perceptions about the world and its residents. Since September 11, 2001, enrollments of international students in U.S. institutions of higher learning have declined (IIE, 2005; Smith, 2007). While the causes of this decrease are varied, many U.S. educators have expressed fear that the tragic events of April 16, 2007, at Virginia Tech may lead to a continued decrease in international enrollments at universities across the United States. (At Virginia Polytechnic Institute and State University, Virginia Tech, 7% of the 28,500 students are international students, and as many as 60% of graduate students in some departments are international.)

This chapter explores the impact of campus violence on international study in the United States and is organized as follows. First, we provide a brief overview of the phenomena of international study in the United States and around the world. Next, we briefly review relevant statistics about campus violence in the United States and elsewhere.

Based on primary and secondary research, we then explore the immediate and long-term reactions of international students (and other international stakeholders, including parents and governments). We conclude with implications for practice.

PHENOMENON: INTERNATIONAL STUDENT STUDY

The United States is the leader (21.6% market share) in international student education—with over 540,000 students coming to its shores in 2006. While this is a considerable number, the post-2001 trend is downward (market share was 25.3% in 2000) and has been attributed to increased difficulty in obtaining student visas for the United States and increasing numbers of overseas opportunities (IIE, 2006). The future trends are uncertain, however last year's student visa applications were up 15% (IIE, 2006).

There is a great diversity of international study-abroad possibilities. The next most popular destinations for international students are the United Kingdom (300,000 students), Germany (250,000 students), and Australia (200,000 students) (IIE, 2005). The top 10 countries sending students to the United States are (in descending order): India, China, South Korea, Japan, Canada, Taiwan, Mexico, Turkey, Germany, and Thailand (IIE, 2006). Most international students rely on personal or family funds to pay for their U.S. educational and living expenses (over 60%), with the next largest source of funds being the U.S. institution itself (25%) (IIE, 2006). Given the importance of family resources in financing international education, it is likely that families have a great deal of influence on institution selection. Along with quality of education, safety is undoubtedly an important consideration in the decision-making process.

Here are the characteristics of the top five countries sending students to the United States for international study.

- *Indian Students in America*: Over 76,000 Indian students are currently pursuing degrees at U.S. institutions, and the number of graduate degree applicants from India has increased 32% recently (IIE, 2005). The trend by graduate schools in the United States to accept non-European, three-year higher education degrees is expected to increase the number of Indian scholars (Schukoske, 2006). Indian students are particularly drawn to international universities' graduate programs, as the Indian graduate education market is comparatively underdeveloped (Gravois, 2006). Furthermore, an additional factor promoting international study to the United States may be that India has the third highest number of international professors and researchers working at U.S. universities (8,836) (Open Doors, 2006).

- *Chinese Students in America*: Over 62,000 Chinese students are currently pursuing degrees at U.S. institutions (IIE, 2005). This number has rebounded in the past two years after declining significantly as a result of the post–September 11 visa restrictions. Since most Chinese students depend on family members' financial support and scholarships to pursue their education, they frequently consult their friends for advice on international study. (In 2007, the Chinese government provided 10,000 scholarships to Chinese students for study abroad, and 12,000 scholarships to foreigners for study in China.) There are many Web sites designed to facilitate Chinese students' transition to American college life. Many Web sites address safety issues; however, we could not find a Web site that specifically addressed campus violence. (See for example www.china-nafsa.aief-usa.org/health/personal.htm.)

- *South Korean, Japanese, and Canadian Students in America*: The historical relationships between the United States and South Korea, Japan, and Canada are well-founded and promote the exchange of students internationally. Trends indicate that while South Korea has dramatically increased the number of students educated in the United States (up 10.3%), Japan's enrollments decreased by 8.3% while Canada's increased slightly (up by 0.2%) (IIE, 2006). IIE researchers attributed the decline in the number of Japanese students both to the strong Japanese economy and to demographic changes, particularly the shrinking number of college-age Japanese.

U.S. INITIATIVES TO INCREASE INTERNATIONAL STUDENTS

Post September 11, the United States has been criticized for long waits for student visas, but now processes the majority in one to two days. According to U.S. Secretary of State, Condoleezza Rice, the United States is "never more eager" to attract international students and to send American students abroad for studies. The secretary outlined four principles to guide U.S. efforts to increase educational exchanges:

- Expand exchange efforts such as the Fulbright and Gilman International Scholarship programs;
- Cultivate new relationships for education exchange with countries playing an increasingly important international role;
- Make U.S. universities more accessible to talented but underprivileged students and to students of diverse backgrounds; and
- Continue to improve visa policies (US DOS, 2006).

Since 1946, the Fulbright Scholarship program has brought over 250,000 international students to the United States and is the flagship academic exchange effort of the U.S. government on behalf of the United States Department of State, Bureau of Educational and Cultural Affairs (www.cies.org). The future will no doubt hold increased fundraising efforts in an attempt to facilitate educational opportunities for those international scholars with lesser means, acceptance of various types of international undergraduate degrees, and an improvement in the number of student visas available as well as the length of time in processing the visas.

Other universities have taken action in their own hands to increase international study at their university, or to establish satellite campuses in other countries. Indeed over 150 institutions are currently offering degree programs at the present time in China, as Peggy Blumenthal states, "20, 30 or 100 times the number of students who cannot come to the U.S. are interested in U.S. education. It makes a whole lot more sense to bring the product to them rather than to wait for them to come to here" (NPR).

OTHER COUNTRIES' INITIATIVES TO INCREASE INTERNATIONAL STUDENTS

International students constitute the bulk of the market in other countries. In Britain, 300,000 of the estimated 2 million university students are not U.K. residents, and plans were recently announced to increase this number by 100,000 over the next five years. In Germany, the percentage of international students has grown between 2000 and 2002 (IIE, 2005). The adoption of the Bologna agreement to harmonize European education is expected to increase intra-European study.

CAMPUS VIOLENCE STATISTICS

Sixteen million students are enrolled in 4,200 colleges and universities in the United States (US DOE, 2002). Each year, approximately 479,000 students are victims of a violent crime—defined as robbery, simple assault, aggravated assault, or rape/sexual assault (Baum & Klaus, 2005). Approximately 93% of violent crimes occur off-campus, and approximately 58% of all violent crimes are committed by strangers (Baum & Klaus, 2005). Male students are more than twice as likely as female students to be victims of violence (Baum & Klaus, 2005). Another set of worrying statistics is the prevalence of guns on campus. Research by Miller and colleagues reveals that, across the United States, 8% of men and 1% of women have a working firearm at college (Miller, Hemenway, & Wechsler, 2002). International students, particularly those of minority-status ethnicity, religion, or other background, are more likely to be the victims of hate crimes than other students. Hate crimes are directed at those of different race (57%), Jews (18%), and those of different sexual orientation (16%) (Wessler & Moss, 2001).

RESEARCH METHODOLOGY

Our study employed an e-mailed survey to discern international students' perceptions of violence within the United States. The survey queried 40 students from 15 countries. The students' home countries included Austria, China, Germany, India, Italy, Oman, Spain, Canada, South Korea, Nigeria, and Kuwait. The students reported that they have studied in Canada, China, the United Kingdom, and United States.

ANALYSIS

The data-processing strategies used were drawn from those used in grounded theorizing, by searching each set of student responses for meaningful unique bits of data worthy of attention due to the stream of data present in the response. Each type of response was coded and assigned to a broader category representing themes of answers. We then incorporated sub-codes as they emerged from the responses and modified the initial supposition if required. The sub-codes (i.e., labels) were derived from the student responses ensuring that the codes were "grounded" in the data itself. When included in the chapter, the quotations may have been slightly edited for readability.

CAMPUS VIOLENCE REACTIONS: IMMEDIATE

At the time this chapter was being written, the most serious incident of violence on a college campus to date occurred at Virginia Tech University, where a South Korean international student killed 32 people on campus, including 27 students and five faculty, prior to committing suicide. Reuters spoke to Jiyoun Yoo, a 24-year-old Korean student at Virginia Tech, just after the tragedy: "I'm from South Korea, so I am a little bit scared ... maybe it will affect all South Korean students ... It is big news in South Korea. Yesterday they were worried if I'm safe, now they are worried there might be a risk that I'm South Korean" (Hopkins, 2007). The Reuters story also quoted a South Korean Foreign Ministry official, "We are working closely with our diplomatic missions and local Korean residents' associations in anticipation of any situation that might arise" (Hopkins, 2007). Condolences for members of the Virginia Tech community came immediately, from all around the world.

When queried, all international students in the current analysis stated that they had never directly experienced campus violence. (Although one international student reported that he and a companion had been assaulted while traveling abroad in Israel.) Most reported that they became aware of campus violence either via e-mail from campus security or from the news media, in the case of the Virginia Tech killings.

- I never experienced any violence there (at the international institution). I only learned about some violence on campus through campus safety e-mails.

- The whole college community is informed about crime happening on campus. In the last month, four crimes were reported. One was very severe. The recommendation was made from campus security that no one should walk alone at night and instead should take the safe ride shuttles whenever possible.

- Personally I do not remember ever considering campus violence in my choice of colleges.

CAMPUS VIOLENCE REACTIONS: LATENT

A reporter for the *Christian Science Monitor* interviewed Nikhil Mantrawadi, a 28-year-old Indian student interested in applying to Virginia Tech. Nikhil was keen to apply to Virginia Tech and said, "that was an isolated incident ... The massacre was committed by a student, not a terrorist. It could have happened anywhere" (Ford, 2007). Given the high levels of media coverage of Virginia Tech and other tragedies, one might have the mistaken impression that campus violence happens only inside America. In fact, campus violence occurs around the world. In India, student-government elections are often a stepping stone to state and national politics, and are fraught with violence, as well as corruption and intimidation. In the last 25 years, in the state of Kerala alone, over 50 students have died as a result of campus politics violence (Neelakantan, 2004). In 1989, Marc Lépine killed 14 women, including 12 of his fellow engineering students, at the École Polytechnique in Montreal, Canada. Another college in Montreal, Dawson, was the site of a gun rampage leaving one student dead and a dozen students and faculty injured.

Virtually all of the respondents felt similarly that incidents of violence could take place anywhere in the world and that such types of incidents are not limited to the United States. Several respondents mentioned a case of campus violence in Germany that had taken place during their course of study in high school, where a former pupil killed 17 students prior to killing himself (BBC News, 2002).

- I think that it is not only a problem of the university. That tragedy could have happened anywhere. The police can't control every single student. It is not the fault of the university.

- Such tragedies could happen everywhere in the world.

- Incidents such as the one at Virginia Tech are very rare and have nothing to do with regular U.S. campus life.

CAMPUS VIOLENCE PERCEPTIONS

According to Paul Green, assistant dean of Boston University, "Market research has shown a widespread feeling among Middle

Eastern families that students will not be safe if they come to study in the United States" (Bollag, 2006). The international students had different views on whether the United States was as safe, safer, or less safe than their home country. Those respondents coming from Europe largely viewed the United States as not as safe as their home country while those from Africa and India viewed the United States as safer than their home country. No respondents said that they believed campus violence to be a reason not to attend college in the United States, nor did any report to having any training while in their home country about ways to mitigate campus violence while studying abroad. Several students mentioned that campus security within the United States was much greater than in their home countries, and many stated that there were no campus security forces within their home countries.

- I think the safety situation in U.S. campuses is still okay. It would not be a reason for me not to come there and study.
- Although there have been terrible events such as the Virginia Tech and Delaware shootings, the general perception is that the USA is still a safe place to study. According to me, American universities are among the safest educational institutions in the world.

INTERNATIONAL STUDENTS' PERCEPTIONS OF THE TRIGGERS OF VIOLENCE

A number of students offered insights into their perceptions of the triggers of campus violence. The vast majority of students cited gun control as a major problem within the borders of the United States, which may be a cause for campus violence.

- There is a perception that America as a whole is riddled with violence aggravated by easy access to guns.
- Friends and family worry about my safety in the U.S. Pre–September 11th, people would remark on how easy it was to procure weapons/guns in the U.S. Their fears were compounded during the aftermath of September 11th.
- The big deal in this case (re: Virginia Tech) is far from the quality of universities; instead, U.S. inhabitants can have weapons in their houses. That is crazy. How can a psychopath be controlled with a personal weapon in his/her hands?
- In my opinion the excessive spread of weapons in the U.S. increases the incidence of tragedies; however this type of occurrence could happen anywhere in the world.

Many international students also felt that competition and an estrangement from the community was at the heart of campus violence.

- Until some time ago, I attributed this violence to lacking gun control in the U.S. But in my country [Germany] we have very tight gun control and we also have had shootings at schools, for example Erfurt in 2002. The committer of this crime was addicted to video games and as with the shooter in Virginia, a loner. I imagine that no student commits such acts without any kind of "announcement"; the problem is that the announcement might not be taken seriously.

- The University system is highly competitive. This, combined with the ability to carry guns and the commercialization of the University experience (where professors no longer care about the students), lead to campus violence.

- The very hard competition and social and mental pressure and their consequences to mental balance lead to tragedies like the one at Virginia Tech. My own personal impression is that the fundamental distinction between the value of human life as absolute criterion and the value of human life as measured by personal success tends to disappear (on a college campus and in these tragedies). The inviolability of human life (as in Kant's philosophy and the charter of the human rights in the EU) in a well-balanced society counterbalances the value of the human life as proportional to success so that failure in working or academic life should not result in an absolute failure and in a refusal of the individual within society. Students may incorrectly perceive failure within an academic setting as a life's complete failure.

- You are very anonymous at University, and the competition is quite difficult. This may lead to increased campus violence.

INTERNATIONAL STUDENTS' SELECTION PROCESS FOR A STUDY-ABROAD VENUE

The most popular reasons for selecting an international venue for foreign study included: reputation of the institution, 97% of students surveyed; geography, 90% of students surveyed; climate, 70% of students surveyed; interesting classes (including desired language delivery), 50% of students surveyed; and cost (including time of study), 40% of students surveyed.

CONCLUSION

With 7.2 million international students projected by 2025 (Boehm et al., 2002), the perception of national education environments is a key concern for those wishing to attract or retain students. Overall, the students reported that campus violence was not a major factor influencing their decision to study abroad in a university setting. Given the pervasiveness of media coverage, and the importance of the extended family as a result of financial considerations with potentially different decision criteria, U.S. institutions need to be vigilant about continuing to reduce the impact of campus violence on their populations or they risk the potential loss of international students.

REFERENCES

Baum, K., & Klaus, P. (2005). *Violent victimization of college students, 1995–2002.* NCJ Publication No. 206386. Washington, DC: Department of Justice, Office of Justice Programs, Bureau of Justice Statistics.

Boehm, A., Davis, T., Meares, D., & Pearce, D. (2002). *Global student mobility 2025: Forecasts of the global demand for international higher education.* Sydney, Australia: IDP Education.

Bollag, B. (2006). America's hot new export: Higher education. *The Chronicle of Higher Education, 52*(24), A44.

Ford, P. (2007). U.S. universities still a top draw for international students. *Christian Science Monitor.* http://www.csmonitor.com/2007/0419/p11s02-wogn.html.

Gravois, J. (2006). First days in the U.S.A. *The Chronicle of Higher Education, 3*(3), A6.

Greenberger, R.S., & Johnson, I. (1997, November 3). Chinese who studied in U.S. undercut dogmas at home. *The Wall Street Journal,* p. 1.

Hopkins, A. (2007, April 17). Asians fear backlash after Virginia Tech shooting. Reuters.

Institute for International Education (IIE) (2005). *Open doors: Report on international student exchange.* New York: IIE.

Institute for International Education (IIE) (2006). *Open doors: Report on international student exchange.* New York: IIE.

Miller, H., Hemenway, D., & Wechsler, H. (2002). Guns and gun threats at college. *Journal of American College Health, 51*(2), 57–66.

Neelakantan, S. (2004). Corruption, mayhem and murder on India's campuses. *The Chronicle of Higher Education, 41*(15), A38.

Smith, L. (2007). Graduate applications from foreigners rise. *The Chronicle of Higher Education, 53*(35), A56.

U.S. Department of Education (2002, Spring). Integrated postsecondary education data system (IPEDS) enrollment survey. National Center for Education Statistics.

U.S. Department of State (2006). http://usinfo.state.gov/scv/Archive/2006/Jan/06-818145.html.

Wessler, S., & Moss, M. (2001). *Hate crimes on campus: The problems and efforts to confront it.* NCJ Publication No. 187249. Washington, DC: U.S. Department of Justice, Bureau of Justice Assistance.

Chapter 4

The Impact of Campus Violence on College Students

Bethany L. Waits
Paula Lundberg-Love

It is safe to assume that violence impacts individuals throughout the world. Through media coverage and advancing technology, people are exposed to violent acts at the local, national, and international level. While such acts often elicit feelings of shock, anger, and sadness among the general public, these immediate reactions tend to abate with the passage of time. However, for the victim, the impact of violence and associated sequelae are not short-lived. According to the World Health Organization, violence typically results in injury, psychological and physical impairment, maldevelopment, and deprivation (Carr, 2007). Indeed, the degradation of an individual's well-being is often the result of a violent act. In order to understand better the impact of violence, researchers often conduct prevalence studies among certain subgroups within the population. Until the last 30 years, the prevalence of violence was often overlooked amid one group, namely college students. As a result, increasing research has been conducted to better understand the incidence of violence on college campuses. One study found that approximately 479,000 acts of violence are committed against college students every year (Carr, 2007). Additional research has documented that college students experience a wide variety of violence including sexual assault, stalking, hazing, celebratory violence, sexual harassment, dating violence, racial and ethnic violence, and homicide (Carr, 2007). Thus, one must consider how violent acts perpetrated upon college students will impact their health.

Generally, student victims often undergo several initial reactions to campus violence, regardless of the type. Students often withdraw from classes, take a temporary leave of absence, move back home, or transfer to a different university to recover from the victimization. If students remain at the university, several problems are likely to develop. For instance, students often report a decline in their abilities to concentrate and to study. Students frequently pass up academic and social activities in order to avoid potential contact with their perpetrator (Carr, 2007). Indeed, a powerful fear of encountering the perpetrator may induce feelings of powerlessness and frustration toward campus life (Pezza & Bellotti, 1995). As these feelings increase, academic freedom, policy enforcement, and the overall welfare of the students are likely to diminish (Carr, 2007). Furthermore, violence that affects the entire campus may alter the educational atmosphere and have negative consequences for the university. Recruitment and retention of students, as well as support from alumni, donors, and legislators, may be jeopardized if the university lacks the ability to cope with campus violence (Pezza & Bellotti, 1995).

Understanding students' initial reactions to campus violence is imperative. Depending on the type of violence committed against the individual, such reactions often evolve into more serious psychological and physical disturbances. A review of the research indicates that there are five types of campus violence (sexual assault, sexual harassment, stalking violence, dating violence, and homicide), that impact student victims. Each of these types of violence will be addressed in this chapter.

SEXUAL ASSAULT VIOLENCE

Sexual assault exists on a continuum from unwanted petting to rape (Goodman, Koss, & Russo, 1993). Victims of sexual assault report significantly higher rates of physical and mental health problems than nonvictims (Kaltman, Krupnick, Stockton, Hooper, & Green, 2005). Indeed, one victim described sexual assault as, "the most horrific event in my life. It broke my spirit and weakened my sense of worth and self-value" (Norment, 2002, p. 152). The prevalence of sexual assault on college campuses is overwhelming. Research suggests that approximately one in four students will be sexually assaulted before they graduate (Norment, 2002). Undergraduate victims often report diminished feelings of respect and acceptance on campus (Cortina, Swan, Fitzgerald, & Waldo, 1998). The most common form of sexual assault among college students is rape. For instance, one study found that 20–25% of college women experience attempted or completed rape while in school (Carr, 2007). Unfortunately, only 57% of college women, whose experience met the legal definition of rape, referred to themselves as rape victims (Koss, 1990). Since 80% of campus sexual assaults are perpetrated by an acquaintance, perhaps these victims feel that they were somehow responsible for the attack (Goodman et al., 1993).

The initial impact of sexual assault and the subsequent reaction to such victimization have been labeled *rape trauma syndrome*. Before discussing other various psychological impacts of sexual assault, it is important to understand the progression of symptomatology that occurs as a result of such abuse. The majority of researchers agree that rape trauma syndrome consists of two phases: an acute phase and a long-term reorganization phase (Frampton, 1998). The acute phase of rape trauma syndrome is rather brief, beginning a few days after the victimization (Frampton, 1998; Lenox & Gannon, 1983). During this phase, victims experience high levels of fear, anxiety, and disorganization (Lenox & Gannon, 1983). Common psychological symptoms involve flashbacks, shock, denial, and hypervigilance (Frampton, 1998). According to Lenox and Gannon (1983), the victim progresses into the long-term reorganization phase when he or she is able to return to normal daily activities.

The long-term reorganization phase typically begins three months postassault and can be characterized by overwhelming feelings of anger (Frampton, 1998). The victim may feel the need repeatedly to recount the details of the assault, which may lead to problems with family and friends. In order to escape from the pain of the trauma, victims may engage in a drastic lifestyle change, such as dropping out of school or moving (Lenox & Gannon, 1983). In addition, the risk of suicide drastically increases as victims become emotionally distant from others. Psychological symptoms such as hopelessness, shame, despair, isolation, loss of control, loss of autonomy, and a diminished ability to enjoy life are reported during this phase (Frampton, 1998). While the development of the concept of a rape trauma syndrome has allowed practitioners to better understand the aftermath of sexual assault, a variety of psychological disorders are often associated with such abuse. These include: anxiety, depression, posttraumatic stress disorder, sexual dysfunction, social adjustment disturbances, and negative self-esteem. Each possible consequence will be considered individually.

Fear and anxiety are the most common psychological symptoms following sexual assault (Bohn & Holz, 1996; Resick, 1993). Three days postassault, 86% of victims reported intense fear of their perpetrator and anxiety concerning personal safety (Koss et al., 1994). Specifically, victims often fear that the perpetrator will return and do further harm (Goodman et al., 1993). Victims tend to feel anxious about other people's reaction to the assault (i.e., disclosure anxiety). In general, fear and anxiety peak in severity three weeks after the assault and may continue, at a lower level, for several years (Koss et al., 1994). Prolonged exposure to anxiety can lead to the development of specific phobias and panic disorder in some victims (Resick, 1993). Such phobias commonly involve a fear of people or crowds, a fear of the dark, and a fear of trauma-related objects or symbols. Recurrent nightmares, changes in lifestyle, and difficulty carrying out normal routines have also been linked with anxiety (Bohn & Holz, 1996). The lifetime prevalence of anxiety disorders among victims is unknown. However, one study found that a majority of victims were still experiencing elevated levels of anxiety one year postassault (Kilpatrick, Resick, & Veronen, 1981).

According to Koss and colleagues (1994), victims frequently experience moderate depressive symptoms within a few hours or days following the attack. After several weeks, full-blown depression is often observed. When the Beck Depression Inventory was administered to 34 rape victims two weeks after the victimization, 75% of the sample reported mild to severe depression (Resick, 1993). Depressive symptoms such as sad feelings about the assault, apathetic feelings about life, suicidal ideation, chronic fatigue, despondency, crying spells, dysphoria, appetite disturbance, decreased concentration, nightmares, catastrophic fantasies, feelings of alienation and isolation, social withdrawal, and immobility are frequently reported (Bohn & Holz, 1996; Goodman et al., 1993; Koss et al., 1994). The most problematic symptom, suicidal ideation, is reported by 33–50% of victims (Koss et al., 1994). In one study, 50% of a sample of sexual assault victims had considered suicide (Resick, 1993). Typically, the depression associated with victimization lasts at least three months. However, the lifetime prevalence of major depression among victims is 13%, compared to 5% of nonvictims (Koss et al., 1994).

Victims of sexual assault are considered the largest single group that suffers from posttraumatic stress disorder, or PTSD. In a study of hospital-referred rape victims, 94% met the diagnostic criteria for PTSD 12 days after the assault and 46% continued to meet those criteria three months later (Koss et al., 1994). The most common symptoms of rape-related PTSD involve intrusive recollections of the traumatic event (i.e., flashbacks), repetitive dreams and nightmares, psychological numbing, anxiety, irritability, insomnia, hypersensitivity, anger, and hypervigilance (Bohn & Holz, 1996; Resick, 1993). The lifetime prevalence of PTSD among a national sample of sexual assault victims was 31% (Koss et al., 1994). Further, Resick (1993) reported that approximately 4 million American women have had rape-related PTSD at some point in their lives.

Sexual dysfunction is the most enduring psychological disorder among victims (Resick, 1993). Typically, victims experience less sexual satisfaction and more sexual problems than nonvictims. Immediately following the attack, the majority of victims report a disruption in sexual functioning and an avoidance of sexual activities (Koss et al., 1994). One study found that 43% of victims were no longer intimate with their partners one month after victimization (Resick, 1993). Sexual dysfunction is characterized by a diminished sex drive, fear of sex, and difficulty becoming aroused (Koss et al., 1994; Resick, 1993). As mentioned, sexual dysfunction is long-lasting. For instance, 30% of rape victims still did not feel that their sexual functioning had returned to normal levels six years after the assault occurred (Koss et al., 1994).

Often, victims experience a period of social adjustment following the assault; yet, most of these difficulties are temporary. Social and leisure activities are normally disrupted for the first two months after the incident. The greatest disturbance involves work performance, which persists for approximately eight months (Koss et al., 1994). Since work performance is comparable to academic performance in college students, perhaps academics are affected for the longest period of time after the attack; however, no research has been conducted that supports this assumption. Additional disturbances such as difficulties within intimate relationships, proneness to revictimization, isolation, inappropriate limit-setting, and an inability to trust others are repeatedly observed (Bohn & Holz, 1996). Victims who report their assault to the police have significantly fewer social adjustment problems compared to those that do not disclose the trauma for an extended period of time (Cohen & Roth, 1987).

According to Resick (1993), a major problem among victims involves self-esteem. Indeed, victims often report lower levels of self-esteem for at least one year after the attack. Self-esteem issues are likely caused by victim blaming among the general population. When victims seek help from family, friends, and even the police, they are often led to believe that they are somehow responsible for the assault (e.g., you shouldn't have been walking alone so late). Research suggests that victim blaming reinforces shame and guilt, which in turn leads to a diminished sense of self-worth and lowered self-esteem (Bohn & Holz, 1996).

While the incidence of anxiety, depression, PTSD, sexual dysfunction, social adjustment, and lowered self-esteem is significant among victims, amelioration of symptoms may not occur for a long period of time. Approximately 25% of women victims continue to experience negative psychological sequelae several years after their assault (Koss & Kilpatrick, 2001). Burgess and Holmstrom conducted a study concerning the long-term effect of sexual assault. Rape victims were interviewed four to six years after the attack and asked if they felt "back to normal." The results indicated that 37% felt recovered within months, 37% felt recovered but said that the process had taken several years, and 26% still did not feel recovered at the time of the study (Koss et al., 1994). Among victims, the most severe sufferers are those that were assaulted in environments that they considered safe, such as on campus or at home (Goodman et al., 1993). The most persistent psychological consequences related to sexual abuse include intrusive thoughts, nightmares, disruption in close relationships, fear, depression, guilt, shame, and sexual dysfunction (Cohen & Roth, 1987).

Several additional psychological and behavioral disturbances have been identified in connection with sexual assault. For example, the incidence of obsessive compulsive disorder and alcohol dependency is greater among sexual assault victims compared to nonvictims. One study found that victims were three times more likely to abuse marijuana, six times more likely to abuse cocaine, and 10 times more likely to abuse prescription drugs than nonvictims. Victims that are genetically susceptible to the development of bipolar disorder and schizophrenia, prior to the sexual assault, may be more likely to express such disorders if victimization occurs (Resick, 1993). Victims also tend to smoke, overeat, drink excessively, and ignore basic health needs to a greater degree than nonvictims. Self-destructive behaviors such as self-mutilation, self-neglect, unprotected sex with multiple partners, and reckless driving are commonly reported (Bohn & Holz, 1996). According to Koss et al. (1994), victims of sexual assault are more likely to engage in behaviors that are associated with illness and premature death (e.g., failing to wear a seat belt) than other individuals.

Sexual assault, particularly rape, also often results in physical conditions that negatively impact the health of the individual. On the whole, victims perceive their health less favorably and report more health problems in all body systems, except for the skin and eyes, when compared to nonvictims (Goodman et al., 1993; Koss & Kilpatrick, 2001). Common complaints such as soreness, bruising, genitourinary problems (i.e., vaginal itching, burning, or discharge), disorganized sleep patterns, stomach pain, and nausea are reported. The majority of these symptoms improve within 24–48 hours after the attack. However, in some instances, when sexual assault is more severe, genital soreness may persist for several days or weeks. Many victims develop a sore throat if forced to participate in oral sex (Lenox & Gannon, 1983). The most prevalent medical condition observed immediately after victimization is physical injury. Approximately 39% of rape victims sustain physical injuries including abrasions of the head, neck, face, arms, legs, and trunk (Goodman et al., 1993). Severe injuries such as multiple traumas, major fractures, and major lacerations are reported in some victims. Often, victims may experience posttrauma skeletal muscle tension which can be expressed in the form of fatigue, tension headaches, and sleep disturbances. Acute health conditions should be treated directly following the attack. However, research suggests that only 54% of those sustaining physical injury seek medical treatment. Without professional care, physical injuries may take longer to heal or become infected leading to more serious problems for the victim (Goodman et al., 1993; Koss et al., 1994).

Victimization can also induce long-term chronic health conditions. Sexual assault victims utilize health care at higher rates than nonvictims, approximately 10 more visits per year (Crane, 2003). Also, victims are more likely to be hospitalized and undergo surgical procedures. Victimized women undergo laparoscopy for chronic pelvic pain and experience complications following hysterectomy at higher rates than nonvictimized women (Frampton, 1998). Sexual victimization is associated with a variety of chronic pain disorders including headache, back pain, facial pain, abdominal pain, temporal mandibular joint discomfort (TMJD), chronic pelvic pain, and bruxism (Koss et al., 1994). Chronic conditions such as gastrointestinal disorders (i.e., irritable bowel syndrome), psychogenic epileptic seizures, premenstrual syndrome, dysmenorrhea, painful intercourse, and dyspareunia are diagnosed frequently among victims of sexual assault (Frampton, 1998; Chrisler & Ferguson, 2006; Koss & Kilpatrick, 2001; Koss et al., 1994). Migraines, infections, and hypertension also have been reported (Chrisler & Ferguson, 2006). Furthermore, elevated levels of stress, due to sexual assault, may lead to chronic health conditions. Stress illness theory suggests that stressful life events disrupt the immune system by suppressing its resistance to illness. When the immune system is weakened, overall health can decline. Additionally, victims often engage in destructive behaviors such as alcohol consumption, smoking, and poor dietary habits in order to cope with stress, which can lead to further decreases in immune system functioning (Koss et al., 1994). Common stress-related health conditions consist of sleep disorders, vomiting, diarrhea, constipation, spastic colon, muscle tensions, heart palpitations, hyperventilation, and choking sensations (Bohn & Holz, 1996). However, disclosing a secret trauma is associated with an increase in immune response and may result in positive health outcomes (Koss et al., 1994).

At times, victims report health conditions that have no physiological cause, which are known as somatic complaints. Bohn and Holz (1996) described such complaints as "thick-chart syndrome" because victims frequently visit health care providers with vague symptoms that lack a clear diagnosis. Somatic complaints are more prevalent among victims of sexual assault than other victims of abuse and typically include vomiting, diarrhea, food intolerance, pain during urination, double vision, seizures, convulsions, paralysis, urinary retention, burning in genital regions, and excessive menstrual bleeding (Koss & Kilpatrick, 2001). The exact cause of somatic complaints is unknown. However, researchers agree that symptoms might be the result of stress-induced changes in immune functioning or an intensified focus on physical sensations that produce heightened concerns about bodily health (Chrisler & Ferguson, 2006; Koss et al., 1994). Also, somatic complaints have been associated with residual physical injuries sustained during the violence (Chrisler & Ferguson, 2006). For instance, victims commonly experience pain at the site of old injuries from the assault (Bohn & Holz, 1996).

SEXUAL HARASSMENT VIOLENCE

Sexual harassment is defined as inappropriate sexual behavior associated with employment or student performance that leads to unwanted touching or sex-related comments (Carr, 2007). Approximately 50% of female students experience some form of sexual harassment while in college, and harassment has been associated with elevated levels of fear regarding personal safety in undergraduate students. Both graduate and undergraduate victims reported that they would not attend college if they had the decision to make again. Students encountering an act of sexual harassment often have negative perceptions of the overall campus community. For instance, harassed women tend to feel less respected, accepted, and believe they are treated less fairly than other women on campus (Cortina et al., 1998). Although harassment is widespread, only 2.5% of victims use formal complaint channels to alert others about the attack. Research suggests that students who disclose the harassment experience more negative outcomes than those who do not report the incident. Indeed, psychological and physical health complications increase among victims if they file a formal complaint or seek legal help (Koss, 1990).

When a professor abuses power by committing an act of sexual harassment, the negative effects become entangled in the student's educational experience, which can threaten the pursuit of academic goals (Cortina et al., 1998). At Harvard University, 15% of graduate and 12% of undergraduate victims changed their academic major as a result of sexual harassment (Koss, 1990). In addition, graduate women's evaluations of their academic proficiency and self-efficacy can be negatively affected by such abuse (Cortina et al., 1998). The impact of sexual harassment can cause a student to give up work, research, and educational opportunities (Koss, 1990). According to Paludi and colleagues (2006), 29% of sexual harassment victims report a decrease in academic and professional opportunities and 13% report a decline in grades as well as financial support due to the victimization. Additional consequences such as impaired concentration, decreased educational satisfaction, interference in supervision, scholastic decline, decreased morale, changes in study habits, and unfavorable performance evaluations have been reported by victims (Cortina et al., 1998; Paludi, Nydegger, DeSouza, Nydegger, & Dicker, 2006; Woody & Perry, 1993).

Persistent sexual harassment can elicit avoidant behavior among college students. Typically, avoidance is expressed by absenteeism, dropping classes, changing advisors, or withdrawing from school (Cortina et al., 1998). Since professors typically withhold opportunities from students who resist their advances, the most logical alternative is to withdraw rather than to experience more abuse and disappointment (Koss, 1990). Over 20% of college women who reported harassment also reported an increase in absenteeism; 7% of victims avoided a particular location on campus or dropped out of school completely (Roosmalen & McDaniel, 1998). An example of avoidance is clearly demonstrated in the story of Deborah, "'Looking back, I don't know what I was afraid of,' mused Deborah, some years after her experience as a student worker fondled by a professor, 'but I was terrified each time this man came toward me.' At the end of the semester, Deborah wrote a short note about the professor's advances, gave it to her dorm advisor, and left school. She gave up her ambitions to become a scientist, and didn't return to college for many years" (Quina, 1990, p. 97).

Sexual harassment can function as a stressor that leads to a decline in mental health and well-being. Indeed, 21–85% of victims reported that their psychological and physical health worsened as a result of the harassment (Koss, 1990). Even if the harassment did not involve physical violence, victims reported extreme fear, loss of control, and disruption of normal routines (Quina, 1990). As sexual harassment becomes more severe, negative effects on psychological health become more pronounced (Woody & Perry, 1993). Typically, victims experience a period of generalized distress characterized by shock, emotional numbing, constriction of affect, and intrusive nightmares directly after the victimization. Unfortunately, this distress can induce psychological symptoms that persist for an extended time. Symptoms such as fear, depression, anxiety, irritability, decreased self-esteem, hopelessness, and vulnerability are reported among victims (Koss, 1990). Roosmalen and McDaniel (1998) reported that 9% of harassment victims are diagnosed with some degree of sexual dysfunction. Additional reactions such as nervousness, decreases in energy, guilt, self-consciousness, and disconnection from reality may occur (Esacove, 1998). Victims frequently report increases in emotionality including elevated levels of frustration, powerlessness, insecurity, embarrassment, confusion, helplessness, and isolation (Paludi et al., 2006; Woody & Perry, 1993). In one sample, a majority of victims described feelings of anger, distress, fear, and alienation as a result of the harassment (Koss, 1990). Negative social and interpersonal reactions such as a fear of new people, a lack of trust in others, an inability to focus on specific activities, a preoccupation with self, a change in social networking, a negative attitude toward sexual relationships, and a change in physical appearance are observed among victims (Woody & Perry, 1993). Almost 44% of women victims reported a decrease in their ability to trust men as a result of sexual harassment (Roosmalen & McDaniel, 1998).

Long-term psychological impacts have been documented among harassment victims. Adverse effects such as grief, anger, fear, lowered self-esteem, helplessness, guilt, shame, distortion of body image, sexual dysfunction, and problems in close relationships typically continue for several years after harassment has ended (Quina, 1990). As mentioned, a majority of sexual assault victims are diagnosed with posttraumatic stress disorder. Often, if the act of sexual harassment resembles the trauma of sexual assault, the victim may experience persistent symptoms of PTSD (Rabinowitz, 1990). For instance, flashbacks are frequently reported in harassment victims (Woody & Perry, 1993).

Additionally, chronic health problems often develop in victims of sexual harassment (Roosmalen & McDaniel, 1998). Because harassment is repetitive in nature, health conditions can become more serious as the victimization continues (Paludi et al., 2006). The most recurrent physical symptoms associated with sexual harassment include headaches, sleep disturbances, eating disorders (i.e., binge eating), gastrointestinal disorders (i.e., nausea), jaw tightness, teeth grinding (bruxism), loss of appetite, and crying spells (Koss, 1990; Paludi et al., 2006). Additional disruptions such as chest pain, heart palpitations, sweating, shaking, lethargy, dermatological reactions, genitourinary distress, and respiratory problems have been reported (Esacove, 1998). Rabinowitz (1990) has reported that victims of sexual harassment are at a greater risk for alcohol and drug dependency than nonvictims.

STALKING VIOLENCE

Stalking involves the "willful, malicious, and repeated following or harassing of another person that threatens his or her safety" (Amar, 2006, p. 108). The occurrence of stalking violence is increasing among the general population. In the United States, approximately 1 million women and 400,000 men are stalked annually. The prevalence of stalking is also increasing on campuses (Amar, 2006). Indeed, 20–35% of students are stalked while in college, and many report extreme concern regarding personal safety as a result of the abuse (Amar, 2006; Davis, Coker, & Sanderson, 2002). For women, the likelihood of being stalked is three times higher than the likelihood of being raped (Amar, 2006). One study found that 75% of victims felt that stalking could result in physical harm or life-threatening consequences (Amar & Alexy, 2005). Davis, Coker, and Sanderson (2002, p. 430) speculated that "in the majority of cases, it is the fear of violence and the enduring and unpredictable nature of the intrusions into the person's privacy that seem critical to its impact on victims."

The immediate impact of stalking can lead to changes in schedules and frequent routines (Amar, 2006). For instance, approximately 82% of stalking victims report an adjustment to their daily lifestyles after the abuse begins (Abrams & Robinson, 2002). Victims often lose time from work (26%), avoid social activities (9%), or miss class (4%) due to persistent stalking (Amar, 2006). Victims may change their phone numbers, jobs, and residences to avoid their perpetrator (Amar & Alexy, 2005). Indeed, avoiding the perpetrator, taking extra precautions, and seeking help are the most common behavioral changes observed among victims (Amar, 2006). Changes that result in disruption of normal functioning usually persist for at least one month after the victimization has ended (Amar & Alexy, 2005). Although lifestyle changes are relatively short-lived, some changes may cause unwanted habits.

Victims frequently initiate, or increase the frequency of cigarette smoking and alcohol consumption. Also, some victims tend to carry weapons in order to protect themselves from their stalker. According to Davis et al. (2002), 17% of victims acquire a gun after being stalked.

The most widespread reaction to stalking is psychological degradation (Carr, 2007). Stalking is often described as "emotional rape" or "psychological terrorism" because of its severe impact on mental health (Davis et al., 2002, p. 430). One victim, who experienced both rape and stalking, reported that being stalked was more emotionally harmful than being raped because the stalking "just kept going on and on and on" (Draucker, 1999, p. 478). In the National College Women Sexual Victimization Survey, 30% of women sustained psychological injury from stalking victimization (Amar & Gennaro, 2005). Moreover, negative changes in mental health often lead to a loss of employment and subsequent declines in financial stability among a majority of victims (Abrams & Robinson, 2002).

Stalking can induce anxiety, depression, hostility, and general psychological distress (Amar, 2006). For instance, Pathe and Mullen conducted a study to determine the psychological consequences associated with stalking violence. Among those surveyed, 83% reported heightened anxiety, including panic attacks and hypervigilance, 74% reported sleep disturbances, 55% reported flashbacks, and 24% reported suicidal thoughts. Somatic complaints and lowered levels of functioning also were documented in conjunction with such abuse (Abrams & Robinson, 2002). Among college students, the most frequently reported psychological disturbance is anxiety. Indeed, 85% of victims report elevated levels of anxiety immediately after an incident of stalking (Ravensberg & Miller, 2003). Fears concerning physical safety and premature death commonly are associated with victimization (Amar, 2006). Anxiety disorders, including PTSD and obsessive compulsive disorder (OCD) have been diagnosed at higher rates among victims (Ravensberg & Miller, 2003).

Typically, individuals who have been stalked report significantly more PTSD symptoms than nonvictims (Amar, 2006). For example, victims often experience intrusive recollections and flashbacks following victimization (Draucker, 1999). In one study, nearly 40% of victims met the diagnostic criteria for PTSD and 18% exhibited clinical features of the disorder (Abrams & Robinson, 2002). Stalking also can cause symptoms associated with clinical depression. Symptoms such as hopelessness, powerlessness, suicidal ideation, chronic sleep disturbances, and heightened interpersonal sensitivity are common (Ravensberg & Miller, 2003). The development of depression occurs because the victim has no control over the stalking experience, and the repetitive nature of the victimization leads to even more reductions in perceived control, which exacerbates depressive symptomatology (Amar, 2006). Additional symptoms such as memory impairment, fatigue, poor concentration, and disorganized thoughts may persist for approximately two years after the victimization has ended (Abrams & Robinson, 2002). Several of the psychological symptoms mentioned above, such as hopelessness, heightened interpersonal sensitivity, and anxiety may prevent victims from seeking intimate relationships in the future (Ravensberg & Miller, 2003).

The emotional trauma associated with stalking can also produce negative health consequences among victims (Amar, 2006). Both men and women report a decline in physical health as a result of stalking (Davis et al., 2002). As with sexual assault, physical injury is the predominant health complaint following victimization. Approximately 13% of victims reported being physically injured by their stalker. Common physical injuries include swelling, cuts, scratches, bruises, broken teeth, and knife or gunshot wounds. Additional injuries such as sore muscles, sprains, pulls, welts, black eyes, and cut lips are reported frequently by victims (Amar, 2006). Additionally, men and women who have been stalked report a greater incidence of chronic health conditions than nonvictimized individuals (Davis et al., 2002). As mentioned previously, Pathe and Mullen conducted a study to determine the psychological disturbances associated with stalking. Among victims, several chronic health conditions also were identified. For example, 23–30% developed digestive disease disorders, 47% developed chronic headaches or migraines, and 45–48% developed eating disorders and weight fluctuations (Davis et al., 2002). Moreover, women typically experience more severe symptoms as a result of increased levels of fear and autonomic nervous system activity, which can lead to more severe health outcomes. It is not uncommon for victims to experience cued physiological reactions to stimuli associated with stalking, such as a ringing phone or a knock at the door (Ravensberg & Miller, 2003).

DATING VIOLENCE

Dating violence consists of physical, sexual, or psychological harm toward a current or former dating partner (Carr, 2007). At times, the term "dating violence" is used interchangeably with "intimate partner violence" (IPV). Essentially each term represents the same type of violence; however, to distinguish between the two, researchers often use "dating violence" in reference to college students. Indeed, dating violence is simply intimate partner violence perpetrated at the college level (Amar & Gennaro, 2005). Approximately 8–14% of women, in all age ranges, are assaulted by a husband, boyfriend, or ex-partner every year (Campbell, 2002). The incidence of dating violence among college students remains high as 15–40% experience such abuse (Amar & Alexy, 2005). While dating should be a "carefree period of romantic experimentation," for many, dating can represent the beginning of a wide variety of negative emotional and physical consequences that result from victimization (Amar & Gennaro, 2005, p. 235). Before discussing these consequences, research concerning the impact of dating violence among college women will be reviewed.

Amar and Alexy (2005) conducted a study in which 210 victims of dating violence were required to write a narrative describing the impact of the experience on their daily lives. "The overarching theme of the narrative notes was, 'dissed' by dating violence" (p. 165). According to the authors, to "dis" someone is to treat them without respect or dignity. Among victims, feelings of rejection and psychological turmoil were the result of being "dissed." When the narratives were analyzed, a wide range of emotional and behavioral disturbances were identified among the victims (i.e., emotional distress, distrust, using extra precautions, feeling disconnected and distant in relationships, self-discontentment, denial of the experience, feeling disenfranchised, having one's life disrupted, and moving from disempowerment to empowerment).

The majority of individuals described experiences consistent with emotional distress, including: emotional suffering, mental anguish, and feelings of vulnerability after their encounter with dating violence. Emotions such as anger, guilt, self-blame, fear, depression, and betrayal were frequently recounted. Many described clinical symptoms consistent with PTSD. For instance, one victim wrote, "I often have flashbacks and find myself crying" (p. 166). One victim who experienced date rape wrote, "I felt like people didn't believe me. My father said things that hurt me and made me cry. The policeman said it was my fault. He said if I were your boyfriend, I'd beat you up for being at some guy's apartment" (p. 167). Negative reactions from individuals can result in an individual's reluctance to disclose the trauma.

Several victims reported disruptions to their daily lives similar to those experienced by stalking victims. One victim stated, "I do not answer phone calls that have no caller ID" (p. 168). Changes in daily routines were common. A number of participants mentioned that they "try to take and know different routes to places" since the abuse occurred (p. 168). For some, dating violence led to personal growth. They were able to find meaning in their experience and use it to promote self-knowledge. One victim reported, "I believe that my experience has helped me learn that there is no reason for anyone to harm me. It has made me a stronger person in that I no longer let males take advantage of me" (p. 169).

Victims of dating violence exhibit more mental health symptoms, as suggested by Amar and Alexy (2005), than nonvictims. According to Campbell (2002), depression and PTSD are the most prevalent sequelae associated with dating violence. Episodes of depression are often intensified by stress related to the abuse. Additionally, specific factors associated with dating violence can act as precursors to the development of

PTSD. Factors involving the severity of victimization, one's previous trauma history, and the level of partner violence affect the onset of PTSD in victims (Campbell, 2002). Moreover, individuals often report intense feelings of betrayal, stigmatization, self-blame, fear, powerlessness, and lowered self-worth (Coffey, Leitenberg, Henning, Bennett, & Jankowski, 1996). Such feelings can promote suicidal ideation in some victims (Amar & Gennaro, 2005; Campbell, 2002). Other psychological consequences such as insomnia, sexual dysfunction, social problems, and substance abuse are often reported by those who have experienced dating violence. Typically, women may begin to abuse various substances as a result of their relationship with the abusive partner. Drugs can be a mechanism for coping with the abuse, and they can alleviate the symptoms of PTSD (Campbell, 2002).

Chronic health consequences of dating violence typically result in physical injury and chronic pain, frequently in the head and back, as well as gastrointestinal, gynecological, and central nervous system disorders involving fainting and seizures (Campbell, 2002). Additionally, in one national survey, 66–73% of victims reported minor physical injuries such as scratches, bruises, and welts. Approximately 2–17% of victims in the same survey reported more severe injuries including lacerations, broken bones, dislocated joints, head and spinal cord injuries, chipped teeth, and internal injuries (Amar & Gennaro, 2005). Studies suggest that victims of dating violence are injured in the head, face, neck, thorax, breasts, and abdomen to a greater degree than other victimized individuals. Further, gynecological disorders involving STDs, vaginal bleeding, fibroids, genital irritation, pain from intercourse, chronic pelvic pain, and urinary tract infections are diagnosed among victims of dating violence. Additionally, cardiovascular complications such as hypertension and chest pain also are documented sequelae of dating violence. Typically, immunosuppression due to stress can cause increased rates of colds and influenza in victims as compared to nonvictims (Campbell, 2002). Unfortunately, college students who experience dating violence rarely seek professional help. Also, among victims of dating violence, less than 50% of those that sustain physical injuries seek medical treatment. Amar and Gennaro (2005) suggest that minor physical injuries such as scratches and bruises might signal the presence of dating violence among patients who are unwilling to disclose the abuse. They encourage mental health and medical professionals to screen for dating violence if such injuries are present.

HOMICIDE

Homicide is the "willful (non-negligent) killing of one human being by another" (Asaro, 2001, p. 95). According to the U.S. Department of Education, approximately 23 homicides were committed on college campuses in 2002 (Carr, 2007). Current information regarding the impact of campus homicide is minimal. However, several informative case studies have documented campus-wide reactions to homicide as the event occurred and are applicable to the present discussion. Two such studies will be reviewed in this section.

One case study, conducted by Shelton and Sanders (1973), took place at Oregon State University in February of 1972. The homicide was discovered by police; a female freshman had been killed by a knife wound to her chest. The body was found by students who lived in the same dormitory as the victim. Initial reactions of student survivors, particularly those living closest to where the homicide occurred, included fear, generalized anxiety, grief, depression, vulnerability, and confusion. Sleep disturbances, nausea, vomiting, headaches, and diarrhea were frequently reported. Such reactions became worse as students began to fear a subsequent attack. Apparently, students became preoccupied with explaining the behavior of the perpetrator and engaged in continuous speculation about his motivation for committing the act. As more speculation and discussion occurred among those on campus, more distress was observed. Approximately two days after the homicide, the most severe levels of suffering were reported. Students became fatigued and depressed, which produced feelings of anger and frustration. Those directly affected by the homicide experienced severe deficits in concentration and academic performance during this time. For instance, staff who worked in the dormitory where the homicide occurred showed a decrease in decision-making ability, as well as a reduced capacity to cope with the day-to-day demands of their position. More students began to feel unsafe on campus. One week after the homicide, nearly 70% of students had temporarily left the university. Parents also exhibited similar reactions of fear and panic, and required their children to either return home or stay in their dormitories. According to the authors, some students did withdraw from the university as a result of the homicide. Students that required the longest period of recovery were those that lived in closest proximity to the homicide.

Biernat and Herkov (1994) also observed reactions to campus homicide when five college students were murdered at the University of Florida in Gainesville in August of 1990. Extreme terror among students, faculty, and even the surrounding community was reported. Such overwhelming fear led approximately 700 students to withdraw from the university. Several noticeable behavioral changes occurred among students that remained on campus. These involved increases in the amount of time students communicated with friends and family, in the number of calls made to law enforcement officials, and in the amount of weapons, such as knives, mace, and guns carried by survivors. Additionally, students were more prone to check door and window locks as well as to leave the lights on at night. Nighttime travel and traveling to places alone were avoided. More students utilized mental health services during this time than before the homicides occurred. Common psychological symptoms including distressing thoughts, loss of interest in normal activities, recurrent nightmares, disconnection from others, changes in personality, sleep disturbances, irritability, anger, concentration problems, and an overall increase in a variety of illnesses were reported.

Like all other victims discussed in this chapter, the majority of homicide survivors also develop symptoms of PTSD. Intrusive thoughts related to the homicide, avoidance of homicide-related stimuli, and physiological hyperarousal have been documented among victims. In one study, approximately 23% of homicide survivors developed all the symptoms of PTSD and 50% reported at least one symptom associated with the disorder. The study also found that the development of PTSD is not dependent on whether the individual witnessed the crime. However, living with the victim at the time of the homicide and having a close relationship to the victim are associated with a higher incidence of PTSD symptomatology. Since PTSD is linked with negative health outcomes, it is not surprising that many survivors report a greater number of medical problems. Often survivors report cardiac distress, IBS, chronic pain, and sexual dysfunction. Many report an overall decline in health status subsequent to the homicide (Hertz, Prothrow-Stith, & Chery, 2005).

CONCLUSIONS

The impact of campus violence may alter the lives of students and lead to disorders that impact functionality. As we have seen, sequelae associated with victimization can negatively affect psychological, physical, academic, social, and behavioral outcomes. Although the manifestation, duration, and severity of psychological and physical consequences can vary across the different types of campus violence mentioned in this chapter, many of the disorders are the same for victims who experience different acts of abuse. For instance, mental health symptoms associated with PTSD and depression are commonly reported by victims of sexual assault, sexual harassment, stalking, dating violence, and homicide. However, among these victims, those who experience sexual assault are more likely to meet all the criteria for PTSD and clinical depression as compared to victims who encountered the other types of violence (Amar, 2006; Campbell, 2002; Hertz et al., 2005; Koss et al., 1994; Koss, 1990; Shelton & Sanders, 1973; Woody & Perry, 1993).

Additionally, certain psychological sequelae are not consistently reported for each type of violence discussed; however, they are very similar for several of those listed. For example, victims of sexual assault, sexual harassment, dating violence, and homicide typically experience some degree of sexual dysfunction (Campbell, 2002; Hertz et al., 2005; Koss et al., 1994; Resick, 1993; Roosmalen & McDaniel, 1998). Moreover, suicidal ideation is commonly reported among victims of sexual assault, stalking, and dating violence, but not among those who encounter sexual harassment or homicide (Amar & Gennaro, 2005; Campbell, 2002; Koss et al., 1994; Ravensberg & Miller, 2003). A similar pattern is evident in those who develop low self-esteem following the victimization. Typically, decreases of this nature are associated with sexual assault, sexual harassment, and dating violence (Amar & Alexy, 2005; Koss, 1990; Resick, 1993). Further, substance dependency, involving alcohol, drugs, and nicotine, is reported more often among individuals who have experienced sexual assault, sexual harassment, stalking, and dating violence as compared to homicide survivors (Campbell, 2002; Davis et al., 2002; Rabinowitz, 1990; Resick, 1993).

Similarly, a number of physical/medical conditions are reported across the various types of campus violence. The most common physical disturbances seen in the majority of victims include gastrointestinal and cardiovascular disorders. For example, nausea, stomach pain, irritable bowel syndrome, diarrhea, and vomiting are generally associated with each type of violence discussed in this chapter (Campbell, 2002; Davis et al., 2002; Hertz et al., 2005; Koss, 1990; Koss & Kilpatrick, 2001; Paludi et al., 2006; Shelton & Sanders, 1973). Moreover, cardiovascular complications such as hypertension, chest pain, and heart palpitations have been documented among victims of sexual assault, sexual harassment, dating violence, and those exposed to a campus homicide (Campbell, 2002; Chrisler & Ferguson, 2006; Esacove, 1998; Hertz, 2005).

Although gastrointestinal and cardiovascular disorders are the most prevalent among victims, those who experience sexual assault, stalking, or dating violence typically sustain minor to severe physical injuries (Amar, 2006; Campbell, 2002; Goodman et al., 1993). For instance, abrasions to the head, neck, face, arms, legs, thorax, breasts, and abdomen are commonly reported among victims of sexual assault and dating violence (Campbell, 2002; Goodman et al., 1993). Additionally, chronic pain disorders including headaches, back pain, chronic pelvic pain, and bruxism have been exhibited in those who have encountered sexual assault, sexual harassment, dating violence, and exposure to homicide (Campbell, 2002; Hertz et al., 2005; Koss, 1990; Koss et al., 1994; Paludi et al., 2006). In those victims who experience the most severe sexual abuse (i.e., sexual assault, sexual harassment, and dating violence), gynecological disorders are not infrequent. Indeed, the majority of these individuals report genitourinary problems such as vaginal itching, burning, discharge, STDs, vaginal bleeding, fibroids, and pain during intercourse (Campbell, 2002; Esacove, 1998; Lenox & Gannon, 1983). Finally, chronic sleep disturbances are consistently reported among the majority of victims of campus violence (Biernan & Herkov, 1994; Bohn & Holz, 1996; Campbell, 2002; Koss, 1990; Paludi et al., 2006; Ravensberg & Miller, 2003).

In order for the psychological and physical sequelae associated with campus violence to cease, violence itself must be prevented. To accomplish this task, Carr (2007) suggests the employment of several important strategies. For instance, campuses must realize that violence exists on a continuum and will persist unless addressed at all levels. Additionally, peaceful reconciliation of differences can be promoted by the reduction of anonymity and the strengthening of relationships among the entire campus community. A "zero tolerance" policy for campus violence should be implemented by the university including expulsion or suspension for any serious act of violence committed against another individual (p. 312). Also, students should be warned about criminal activity via campus newspapers, orientations, and Internet communication devices. In order to promote bystander intervention, brochures that explain when and where to report suspicious activity should be distributed to all students on campus.

The majority of campuses nationwide have utilized such strategies to create prevention programs targeted at protecting students, faculty, and staff. Programs typically involve training in social skills, assertiveness, sexual decision making, anger and stress management, conflict resolution, and self-defense (Pezza & Bellotti, 1995). Furthermore, education about campus violence, via theater productions, poster contests, and activities within the community, has been incorporated in prevention programs (Carr, 2007). Several programs aimed at improving campus lighting, escort services, and security personnel and protocol have been effective (Pezza & Bellotti, 1995). Although many prevention programs have been successful at reducing the frequency of campus violence, Carr (2007) suggests that sexual violence programs remain limited. For instance, rape prevention programs are typically designed to address attitudes that contribute to the perpetration of sexual assault. However, few of these programs have documented changes in attitude or student behavior as a result of participation (Carr, 2007).

It seems that a crucial aspect of recovery and prevention involves empathy and understanding on behalf of the victim. If faculty, staff, and health care professionals are aware of the long-term repercussions of campus violence, students may be able to receive the immediate care that they need to maintain productive and happy lives. However, if students do not receive support from those around them, as often is the case, they may suffer from psychological and physical health conditions for a considerable amount of time. Therefore, more research should be conducted to understand the suffering of this population and treatments should be implemented based on the type of violence committed against the student. With this in mind, hopefully the impact of campus violence can be minimized, and students may be able to enjoy their college experience.

REFERENCES

Abrams, K. M., & Robinson, G. E. (2002). Occupational effects of stalking. *Canadian Journal of Psychiatry*, *47*, 468–472.

Amar, A. F. (2006). College women's experience of stalking: Mental health symptoms and changes in routines. *Archives of Psychiatric Nursing*, *20*, 108–116.

Amar, A. F., & Alexy, E. M. (2005). "Dissed" by dating violence. *Perspectives in Psychiatric Care*, *41*, 162–171.

Amar, A. F., & Gennaro, S. (2005). Dating violence in college women: Associated physical injury, healthcare usage, and mental health symptoms. *Nursing Research*, *54*, 235–242.

Asaro, M. R. (2001). Working with adult homicide survivors, part I: Impact and sequelae of murder. *Perspectives in Psychiatric Care*, *37*, 95–101.

Biernat, M., & Herkov, M. J. (1994). Reactions to violence: A campus copes with serial murder. *Journal of Social and Clinical Psychology*, *13*, 309–334.

Bohn, D. K., & Holz, K. A. (1996). Sequelae of abuse: Health effects of childhood sexual abuse, domestic battering, and rape. *Journal of Nurse-Midwifery*, *41*, 442–456.

Campbell, J. C. (2002). Health consequences of intimate partner violence. *Lancet*, *359*, 1331–1336.

Carr, J. L. (2007). Campus violence white paper. *Journal of American College Health*, *55*, 304–319.

Chrisler, J. C., & Ferguson, S. (2006). Violence against women as a public health issue. *Annals of the New York Academy of Sciences*, *1087*, 235–249.

Coffey, P., Leitenberg, H., Henning, K., Bennett, R. T., & Jankowski, M. K. (1996). Dating violence: The association between methods of coping and women's psychological adjustment. *Violence and Victims*, *11*, 227–238.

Cohen, L. J., & Roth, S. (1987). The psychological aftermath of rape: Long-term effects and individual differences in recovery. *Journal of Social and Clinical Psychology*, *5*, 525–534.

Cortina, L. M., Swan, S., Fitzgerald, L. F., & Waldo, C. (1998). Sexual harassment and assault: Chilling the climate for women in academia. *Psychology of Women Quarterly*, *22*, 419–441.

Crane, P. (2003). Psychosocial forensic nursing: The health effects of rape. *On the Edge*, *9*, 4–7.

Davis, K. E., Coker, A. L., & Sanderson, M. (2002). Physical and mental health effects of being stalked for men and women. *Violence and Victims*, *17*, 429–443.

Draucker, C. B. (1999). "Living in hell": The experience of being stalked. *Issues in Mental Health Nursing*, *20*, 473–484.

Esacove, A. W. (1998). A diminishing of self: Women's experiences of unwanted sexual attention. *Health Care for Women International*, *19*, 181–192.

Frampton, D. B. (1998). Sexual assault: The role of the advanced practice nurse in identifying and treating victims. *Clinical Nurse Specialist*, *12*, 177–182.

Goodman, L. A., Koss, M. P., & Russo, N. F. (1993). Violence against women: Physical and mental health effects. Part I: Research findings. *Applied & Preventive Psychology, 2*, 79–89.

Hertz, M. F., Prothrow-Stith, D., & Chery, C. (2005). Homicide survivors: Research and practice implications. *American Journal of Preventive Medicine, 29*, 288–295.

Kaltman, S., Krupnick, J., Stockton, P., Hooper, L., & Green, B. L. (2005). Psychological impact of types of sexual trauma among college women. *Journal of Traumatic Stress, 18*, 547–555.

Kilpatrick, D. G., Resick, P. A., & Veronen, L. J. (1981). Effects of a rape experience: A longitudinal study. *Journal of Social Issues, 37*, 105–122.

Koss, M. P. (1990). Changed lives: The psychological impact of sexual harassment. In M. Paludi (Ed.), *Ivory power: Sexual harassment on campus* (pp. 73–92). Albany, NY: State University of New York Press.

Koss, M. P., Goodman, L. A., Browne, A., Fitzgerald, L. F., Keita, G. P., & Russo, N. F. (1994). The physical and psychological aftermath of rape. In M. P. Koss et al. (Eds), *No safe haven: Male violence against women at home, at work, and in the community* (pp. 177–199). Washington, DC: American Psychological Association.

Koss, M. P., & Kilpatrick, D. G. (2001). Rape and sexual assault. In E. Gerrity, T. M. Keane, & F. Tuma (Eds.), *The mental health consequences of torture* (pp. 177–193). New York: Kluwer Academic Publishers.

Lenox, M. C., & Gannon, L. R. (1983). Psychological consequences of rape and variables influencing recovery: A review. *Women & Therapy, 2*, 37–49.

Norment, L. (2002). Rape and recovery: Survivors speak out. *Ebony, 57*, 152.

Paludi, M., Nydegger, R., DeSouza, E., Nydegger, L., & Dicker, K. A. (2006). International perspectives on sexual harassment of college students. *Annals of the New York Academy, 1087*, 103–120.

Pezza, P. E., & Bellotti, A. (1995). College campus violence: Origins, impacts, and responses. *Educational Psychology Review, 7*, 105–123.

Quina, K. (1990). The victimization of women. In M. Paludi (Ed.), *Ivory power: Sexual harassment on campus* (pp. 93–102). Albany, NY: State University of New York Press.

Rabinowitz, V. C. (1990). Coping with sexual harassment. In M. Paludi (Ed.), *Ivory power: Sexual harassment on campus* (pp. 103–118). Albany, NY: State University of New York Press.

Ravensberg, V., & Miller, C. (2003). Stalking among young adults: A review of the preliminary research. *Aggression and Violent Behavior, 8*, 455–469.

Resick, P. A. (1993). The psychological impact of rape. *Journal of Interpersonal Violence, 8*, 223–255.

Roosmalen, E. V., & McDaniel, S. A. (1998). Sexual harassment in academia: A hazard to women's health. *Women & Health, 28*, 33–54.

Shelton, J. L., & Sanders, R. S. (1973). Mental health intervention in a campus homicide. *Journal of the American College Health Association, 21*, 346–350.

Woody, R. H., & Perry, N. W. (1993). Sexual harassment victims: Psycholegal and family therapy considerations. *The American Journal of Family Therapy, 21*, 136–144.

PART II

From the Research Laboratory to the Classroom: Pedagogical Techniques for Teaching Students About Campus Violence

Chapter 5

Anti-Violence Pedagogy: Strategies and Resources

Jennifer L. Martin

In 2004, there were an estimated 1,367,009 violent crimes nationwide. Of these crimes, 62.5% were aggravated assaults, 29.4% were robberies, 6.9% were forcible rapes, and 1.2% were murders (FBI, 2004). It is not surprising that the violence in our culture has trickled down to college campuses and even to K–12 educational systems. As Bennett-Johnson (2004) states, "American crime and violence have overflowed onto the college/university campus, and are now affecting senior high, junior high and elementary schools" (p. 199). As educators, we have a responsibility to try and combat violence on our campuses; unfortunately, there is not a panacea for this. However, educators can devise a variety of simulations and strategies that can get to the root of many forms of violence; this root, many would argue, is prejudice.

One educator, Jane Elliot, sought to do just this, to combat prejudice in her classroom before it turned to violence. Jane Elliot's now famous "blue eyes/brown eyes" experiment was first conducted in the 1960s. Elliot, then a small-town elementary teacher in Riceville, Iowa, felt compelled to teach her all white class about the effects of racism after the assassination of Dr. Martin Luther King Jr. in 1968. Elliot was pained by the traditional curriculum of "heroes and holidays" that barely scratched the surface of diversity and did not even touch issues of racism or of white privilege. In countering the inadequacies of the curriculum, she divided her class up by eye color and granted privileges only to those with the arbitrarily privileged color. The next day, she reversed the experiment. Her students acted accordingly; those who were given privileges often abused them and the students who were deprived of privileges. Friends were separated and conflict ensued. After the experiment, Elliot discussed with her students the reasons for her choices. The students were forever changed by this experience. Elliot went on to repeat her experiment year after year. Her pedagogical trail blazing has been featured in several books, on the PBS show *Frontline*, and in several teaching videos. (See Web Resources and Video Resources sections of this chapter for further information on Jane Elliot.) Elliot is now a lecturer and a diversity trainer. In short, simulations can be very effective tools to teach students about diversity, racism, and privilege. Diffusing stereotypes is one way to combat the growing problem of violence in schools today.

Multicultural course requirements, ethnic student organizations, and diversity awareness programs are common on America's college campuses. Yet students of color, LGBTIQQ students (Lesbian, Gay, Bisexual, Transgendered, Intersexed, Queer, and Questioning individuals), women, and other minority students still often face difficulty accessing and succeeding in American higher education and face higher degrees of violence on campus. Because of this, courses in multicultural education must include information and awareness of LGBTIQQ issues as a part of the standard curriculum, anti-violence pedagogy, and a commitment to breaking down stereotypes and empowering students to join in the fight to end violence on campus and achieve equity for all.

EMPLOYING SIMULATIONS AND OTHER EXERCISES

"Crossing the Line" is an activity used on many college campuses, particularly by student activities directors and during freshman orientation to expose students to diversity and to indicate to them that similarities between people who may appear different are more common than they may have thought. The simulation involves students standing in the middle of a room, and then "crossing the line," or moving to the other side of the room to indicate a positive response to a question. The questions the facilitator asks of the participants vary from fairly benign questions, such as "you wish you had more money," to more controversial questions such as, "you have had a sexual experience that you regretted." After the simulation the facilitator discusses and debriefs with the group.

Another simulation that can be conducted in a classroom is the "Multicultural Education Simulation" (see Exhibit 5-1 at the end of this chapter). In this simulation, students are exposed to the different pedagogical approaches to the teaching of diversity, and of the inadequacies of approaches throughout history. This simulation can be tailored to students at all levels and can be geared to a variety of topics, and provides a nice introduction to multicultural education and a vehicle for fruitful student discussion.

A more formal way in which to expose students to diversity involves personal reflection in written form. Such an assignment involves asking students to step outside of their comfort zones and expose themselves to a new experience dealing with diversity. Students then write about their feelings having experienced an aspect of culture with which they were unfamiliar and then writing about this experience.

Consciousness-raising groups are another pedagogical tool that can be used on campuses to prevent violence. Violence is often caused through ignorance and the inability of individuals to empathize with those they feel are different from them. These differences are often based upon stereotypes. Individuals often targeted for violence on campuses are members of the following groups: women, LGBTIQQ individuals, racial/ethnic minorities, religious minorities, etc. Consciousness-raising groups can target stereotypes and find commonalities between people. All faculty members can become involved in this, from professors to student activities directors.

Personality assessments/tests, although not scientifically valid, can be used to indicate individual differences and similarities between individuals caused by accidents of birth. These can be used as an introduction to diversity training.

Professors of teacher education can use social justice pedagogy to instill the values of equity and empowerment for all in the next generation of teachers. These teachers will hopefully spread the word in younger students so that they are exposed to egalitarian ideas and anti-violence programs before they reach college age.

INSTITUTING POLICIES

Policies can be a useful pedagogical tool to inform students about the importance of accepting difference. If students are included in the analysis and creation of policies at all educational levels, they will have a more vested interest in the policy and thus more buy-in. (See Exhibit 5-2 for sample policy and Exhibit 5-3 for sample incident reporting form. Both appear at the end of the chapter.)

Teaching students about the change process is a necessary and integral part of their acceptance of change. Changing an organization can be a complicated process but when it comes to issues of reducing harassment/intimidation it is often a necessary process. In terms of gender/sexual harassment and harassment based on sexual orientation, traditional notions of gender often play a part. When traditional notions of gender are perpetuated within an organization, sexual harassment is more likely to exist (Cleveland & Kerst, 1993). As Cleveland and Kerst state:

> Some men (e.g., those who embrace very traditional masculine gender roles) may be more inclined to engage in sexual harassment in a wide

variety of settings. That is, some men may readily and easily demonstrate and accept such behavior. On the other hand, there is evidence that sexual harassment can be inhibited in settings by creating a climate or culture that identifies such behavior and clearly indicates that it is negative and unacceptable. (p. 63)

Organizational cultures that tolerate sexual harassment show an *increase* in incidents of sexual harassment (Welsh, 1999). In a study conducted by Timmerman and Bajema (2000), it was found that unwanted sexual conduct is less of a problem in organizational cultures that are perceived as providing equal opportunities for both females and males. When an organization's norms and values are detrimental to the female population (and perhaps portions of the male population as well), then changes must be made.

Changing an organization's norms and values with regard to gender, racial, and other stereotypes can be beneficial in terms of reducing the occurrence of harassment. However, changing an organization's structure, in terms of instituting policy, may be easier than changing its norms and values; nevertheless, in order to make the policy most effective, the norms and values of the organization that underlie it must change as well. As Schlechty states, "to change an organization's structure ... one must attend not only to rules, roles, and relationships, but to systems of belief, values, and knowledge as well. Structural change requires cultural change" (Schlechty as cited in McAdams, 1997, p. 140). Thus, reform efforts must focus on the culture prior to focusing on restructuring. Timmerman and Bajema also argue that when referring to organizational culture, two aspects become especially relevant to the problem of harassment: the social climate of the organization and the level of rules and procedures. Timmerman and Bajema state:

> ... local norms are not only set by management, but may also evolve out of peer interactions in the workplace. In either case, acceptance or condoning appears to have a disinhibiting effect on men who are likely to harass.... Sexual harassment is fundamentally social behavior, governed by local norms, specifically, management's norms. (p. 189)

In essence, teachers and administrators truly set the tone for the culture of the school. When teachers and administrators hear degrading references and do not intervene, the assumption is that such behaviors are acceptable. This may further contribute to a hostile school culture; it also has devastating effects on the students being harassed. As Wessler (2000) states, "when a teacher does not respond to degrading language, students believe that the silence means that the teacher condones those words.... The students who are most devastated by degrading language are those who believe a teacher heard but did not intervene" (p. 31).

ASSESSING THE CULTURE

Before an organization seeks change in any concrete manner in order to combat situations such as sexual and other forms of harassment, the organization's culture must be assessed. It would be helpful to determine the attitudes of organization members (students, teachers, and administrators) about the existence of prejudice and the amount of harassment that occurs within the culture. It may also be helpful to determine if there are differences between the responses of males and females within the organization, and, if so, how these responses differ. As Hotelling and Zuber (1997) state, "Gender has been demonstrated to be the most influential factor in determining whether incidents are defined as sexual harassment, with women universally more likely to view certain behaviors as sexual harassment" (p. 104). Differences between males and females as to what constitutes sexual harassment can be a major problem within organizations. Once these potential differences are demonstrated, educational programs can be instituted that provide a variety of diverse perspectives on the issue.

CREATING A PLAN

After assessing the attitudes of organization members, it is important for the organization to create a plan. This plan must take into account the best interest of all parties involved. In the case of a school as an organization, the needs and safety of the students should come first, but schools must also take into consideration the needs of teachers, administrators, district and central office staff, and parents. A school's plan may identify the processes of developing a comprehensive anti-harassment policy for faculty, staff, and students; how to involve the students in the process; how to educate all employees and students on all forms of harassment; etc. It may be necessary to provide diversity and/or sensitivity training to students and staff. Because change is systemic it must pervade all aspects of an organization. As Fullan and Miles (1992) state:

> ... reform must focus on the development and interrelationships of all the main components of the system simultaneously—curriculum, teaching and teacher development, community, student support systems, and so on ... [Also] reform must focus not just on structure, policy, and regulations but on deeper issues of the culture of the system. (p. 751)

Because of the nature of harassment, which involves issues of power and/or notions of gender, ideology, etc., it is important that concerned parties are educated on the issue so that all members of the organization will support the change effort and the plan to set this change into motion. As Schwartz (2000) argues, "A serious effort to keep a school free of sexual harassment [and, I would argue, other forms of harassment as well] involves the commitment of the whole school (and district), community and requires a systemic, multidimensional approach and long-term educational strategies" (p. 3). One manner in which to persuade people to change, after they have been educated and made aware of the relevant factors involved in the change and the consequences involved should the organization to continue as it has, is through empowerment. As Hoyle states, "people who must implement the decision must make the decision" (Hoyle, 1992, as cited in Squires & Kranyik, 1995, p. 29).

In order to make effective reform efforts within a school regarding anti-harassment, the strategies for change must target hegemonic and traditional ideologies that perpetuate biases based on racial, gender, socioeconomic, and other differences. Cuban defines the difference between first-order and second-order changes within the school reform process:

> First-order changes try to make what already exists more efficient and more effective, without disturbing the basic organizational features, without substantially altering the ways in which adults and children perform their roles.
> .... Second-order changes seek to alter the fundamental ways in which organizations are put together ... [and] introduce new goals, structures and roles that transform familiar ways of doing things into new ways of solving persistent problems. (Cuban as cited in Goodman, 1995, p. 1)

In order to make second-order changes, the underlying causes of the problem must not only be sought, but also the "old ways" must be replaced with something new. Education is a good start when attempting to bring about a new paradigm within a school. As Glover, Cartwright, and Johnson (1998) state, "Policies cannot exist in isolation and 'are lived through in all aspects of teaching and learning'" (p. 97). Once people are educated on the nature and the effects of the problem, they can then help to formulate solutions, new ways in which to deal with the problem. In essence, the help of all concerned parties should be elicited in bringing about new discursive processes. The development of such processes might then inspire people to take ownership not only of the problem but also of the solutions; people then may become highly invested in the process of change.

According to Glover, Cartwright, and Johnson (1998), the rationale for developing a policy is threefold, "A policy makes clear to everyone in the school community what the school is doing in a particular area of activity and why; it communicates the practice expected within the school and it can be used to monitor progress" (p. 92).

Good policies, however, may not be sufficient in creating positive change within a school. Members of the organization must cope well with the process of change. As Fullan and Miles (1992) have found, successful change requires good coping skills among members of the organization, "The enemies of good coping are passivity, denial, avoidance, conventionality, and fear of being 'too radical.' Good coping is active, assertive, inventive. It goes to the root of the problem when that is needed" (p. 750). It is important that administrators and/or policy implementers educate members of the organization not only about the problem at hand but also about the process of change, how changes will not occur overnight, etc. Fullan (1991) and McAdams (1997) find that even moderately complex changes may take between three to five years.

SUPPORTING THE CHANGES

Administrators and/or policy implementers must also provide a system of support within the organization in order to help individuals understand and accept the changes being made. Wagner (2001) has found that in order to implement successful school change the following elements must first be in place: a shared vision of the goals of learning; an understanding of the urgent need for change; relationships based on mutual respect and trust; and engagement strategies that create commitment rather than mere compliance. Finally, in order to create a successful reform effort within a school, it must be stressed that such a process must be both all-encompassing and ongoing. As Midgley and Wood (1993) argue:

> Those who are calling for pervasive changes in the culture of schools stress that reform is an ongoing process—"steady work" grounded in the day-to-day experiences of students—rather than a series of sporadic attempts to respond to the latest educational innovation. Unfortunately, school reform has continued to stress one change at a time, without considering the specifics of context and culture. (p. 246)

Change is a learning process and thus will always involve a certain degree of uncertainty. It is important to remember when considering change or reform efforts within an organization that the process of change should be considered a journey as opposed to a formulaic process—similar ideas will not be implemented in the same manner in different organizations. Also, change can be a frightening process: individuals and by extension organizations are often resistant to it. As McAdams (1997) states, "Just as the character of a person is deep-seated and resistant to change, so the culture of an organization is difficult to influence. Indeed, many proposed changes are viewed as threats to the existing culture and may be resisted for that reason alone" (p. 140).

REFERENCES

AAUW Educational Foundation (2001/1993). *Hostile hallways: Bullying, teasing, and sexual harassment in school.* Washington, DC: The American Association of University Women Educational Foundation.

ACLU of Michigan (2000). *What schools need to know: Gay, lesbian, bisexual and transgender students and the law.* Detroit, MI: The Gilmour Fund.

Adams, K. L., & Ware, N. C. (1989). Sexism and the English language: The linguistic implications of being a woman. In J. Freeman (Ed.), *Women: A feminist perspective* (4th ed; pp. 470–484). Mountain View, CA: Mayfield Publishing Company.

Adams, M., Blumenfeld, C. R., Hackman, H. W., Peters, M. L., & Zuniga, X. (Eds.), *Readings for diversity and social justice: An anthology on racism, anti-semitism, sexism, heterosexism, ableism, and classism.* New York: Routledge.

Allport, G. W. (1954). *The nature of prejudice.* Reading, MA: Addison-Wesley.

Anderson, J. A. (1988). Cognitive styles and multicultural populations. *Journal of Teacher Education, 39*(1), 2–9.

Anti-Defamation League (1999). Responding to hate-motivated behavior in school. Retrieved January 31, 2003, from http://www.adl.org/tools_teachers/Responding 1.asp

Aruri, N. H. (1969). *The Arab-Americans: Studies in assimilation.* Wilmette, IL: Medina University Press.

Asanti, M. (1988). *Afrocentricity: The theory of social change.* Trenton, NJ: African World Press.

Baker, G. C. (1988). Recognition of our culturally pluralistic society and multicultural education in our schools. *Education and Society, 1*(1), 23–28.

Banks, J. (1988). *Multicultural education: Theory and practice.* Boston: Allyn and Bacon.

Barth, R. S. (1990). *Improving schools from within: Teachers, parents, and principals can make the difference.* San Francisco: Jossey-Bass.

Battle, C. Y., & Doswell, C. M. (Eds.). (2004). *Building bridges for women of color in higher education: A practical guide to success.* Lanham, MD: University Press of America.

Beck, E. (1995). From "kike to JAP": How misogyny, anti-semitism, and racism construct the "Jewish American princess." In M. Anderson & P. Collins (Eds.), *Race, class, and gender: An anthology* (2nd ed; pp. 87–95). New York: Wadsworth Publishing Company.

Bennett-Johnson, E. (2004). The root of school violence: Causes and recommendations for a plan of action. *College Students Journal, 38*(2), 199–202.

Biklen, R. (1985). *The complete school: Integrating special and regular education.* New York: Columbia University Press.

Bogdan, R. (1986). *Special education: Research and trends.* Elmsford, NY: Pergamon.

Boyden, J. E. (2002, December). Zero tolerance: Racial harassment in school worsens for scapegoated students. Retrieved January 30, 2003, from http://www.arc.org/wiret3xt5/021219j_boyden.html

Bullivant, B. (1989). *Multicultural education: Issues and perspectives.* Boston, MA: Allyn and Bacon.

Bush, M. E. L. (2004). *Breaking the code of good intentions: Everyday forms of whiteness.* Lanham, MD: Rowman & Littlefield Publishers, Inc.

Callahan, C. J. (2001). Protecting and counseling gay and lesbian students. *Journal of Humanistic Counseling, Education and Development, 40*(1), 5–10.

Cleveland, J. N., & Kerst, M. E. (1993). Sexual harassment and perceptions of power: An under-articulated relationship. *Journal of Vocational Behavior, 42,* 49–67.

Clinchy, E., & Kolb, F. (1989). *Planning for schools of choice: Achieving equity and excellence.* Andover, MA: Network, Inc.

Collins, D. E. (2004). *Fear of a "black" America: Multiculturalism and the twentieth-century African American experience.* Lincoln, NE: iUniverse, Inc.

Collins, P. H. (2000). *Black feminist thought: Knowledge, consciousness, and the politics of empowerment.* New York: Routledge.

Conley, D. T. (1991). What is restructuring? Educators adapt to a changing world. *Equity and Choice, 6*(3), 45–51.

Cortes, C. (2000). *The children are watching: How the media teach about diversity.* New York: Teachers College Press.

Council on International Books for Children (1987). *Stereotypes, distortions and omissions in U.S. history textbooks.* Council on International Books.

Counts, G. (1932). *Dare the school build a new social order?* Carbondale: Southern Illinois University Press.

Daniels, H. A. (1990). *Not only English: Affirming America's multilingual heritage.* Urbana, IL: National Council of Teachers of English.

Delpit, L. (1995). *Other people's children: Cultural conflict in the classroom.* New York: The New Press.

Dewey, J. (1916). *Democracy and education.* New York: Macmillan.

Federal Bureau of Investigation (2004). *Violent crime in the United States.* Retrieved November 14, 2007, from http://www.fbi.gov/ucr/cius_04/offenses_reported/violent_crime/index.html

Fine, M. (1991). *Framing dropouts: Notes on the politics of an urban high school.* Albany, NY: State University of New York Press.

Fine, M., & Asch, A. (Eds.). (1988). *Women with disabilities: Essays in psychology, culture, and politics.* Philadelphia, PA: Temple University.

Fine, M., & Weis, L. (2003). *Silenced voices and extraordinary conversations: Re-imagining schools.* New York: Teachers College Press.

Fineran, S., & Bennett, L. (1998). Teenage peer sexual harassment: Implications for social work practice in education. *Social Work, 43*(1), 55–64.

Fraschl, M., & Sprung, B. (1986). *Building community: A manual exploring issues of women and disabilities.* Women and Disabilities Awareness Project, Equity Concepts, Inc.

Freire, P. (1974). *Pedagogy of the oppressed.* New York: Seabury Press.

Fullan, M. G., & Miles, M. B. (1992). Getting reform right: What works and what doesn't. *Phi Delta Kappan, 73*(10), 744–752.

Gay, G. (1989). Designing relevant curricula for diverse learners. *Education and Urban Society, 20*(4), 327–340.

Gilroy, P. (2002). *Against race: Imagining political culture beyond the color line.* Cambridge, MA: Belknap Press.

Ginsberg, R. W. (1999). In the triangle/out of the circle: Gay and lesbian students facing the heterosexual paradigm. *The Educational Forum, 64*(1), 46–56.

Giroux, H. A. (1983). *Theory and resistance in education.* London: Heinemann Educational.

Giroux, H. A., & McLaren, P. (1989). *Critical pedagogy, the state, and cultural struggles.* Albany: The State University of New York.

Glide (1998). Glide statistics. Retrieved January 31, 2003, from http://www.social-glide.org/statistics.html

Glover, D., Cartwright, N. G., & Johnson, M. (1998). The introduction of anti-bullying policies: Do policies help in the management of change? *School Leadership & Management, 18*(1), 89–105.

Good, T. L., & Brophy, J. E. (1987). *Looking in classrooms* (4th ed.). New York: Harper and Row.

Goodman, J. (1995). Change without difference: School restructuring in historical perspective. *Harvard Educational Review, 65*(1), 1–29.

Gordon, A. (1979). *The nature of prejudice.* Cambridge, MA: Addison-Wesley.

Grady, S. (2000). *Drama and diversity: A pluralistic perspective for educational drama.* Westport, CT: Heinemann.

Grayson, D. (1986). *The equity principal: An inclusive approach to excellence.* Los Angeles County Office of Education.

Grayson, D. A. (1985). *Infusing an equity agenda into schools districts.* Downey, CA: Los Angeles County Office of Education.

Grossman, H. (1984). *Educating Hispanic children: Cultural implications for classroom instruction, classroom management, counseling, and assessment.* Springfield, IL: C.C. Thomas.

Harvey, G. (1986). Finding reality among myths: Why what you thought about sex equity in education isn't so. *Phi Delta Kappan, 67*(7), 509–512.

Hilliard, A. (1989). Conceptual confusion and the persistence of group oppression through education. *Equity & Excellence, 24,* 36–43.

hooks, b. (1984). *Feminist theory: From margin to center.* Cambridge, MA: South End Press.

hooks, b. (1995). *Killing rage: Ending racism.* New York: Henry Holt and Company.

hooks, b. (2000). *Feminism is for everybody: Passionate politics.* Cambridge, MA: South End Press.

hooks, b. (2000). *Where we stand: Class matters.* New York: Routledge.

Hotelling, K., & Zuber, B. A. (1997). Feminist issues in sexual harassment. In W. O'Donohue (Ed.), *Sexual harassment: Theory, research, and treatment.* Boston: Allyn and Bacon.

Hsu, F. (1985). The self in cross cultural perspective. In A. Marsella, G. deVos, & F. Hsu (Eds.), *Culture and self: Asian and Western perspectives.* New York: Tavistock.

Irvine, J. J. (2003). *Educating teachers for diversity: Seeing with a cultural eye.* New York: Teachers College Press.

Kingston, M. A. (1993). "Ante up": The essential ingredient for social change. *Urban Education, 27*(4), 413–429.

Kirmani, M. H., & Laster, B. P. (1999, April). Responding to religious diversity in classrooms. *Educational Leadership, 56*(7), 61–63.

Klein, S., Dwyer, C. A., Fox, L., Grayson, D., Kramarae, C., Pollard, D., & Richardson, B. (Eds.). (2007). *Handbook for achieving gender equity through education.* NJ: Erlbaum.

Kopels, S., & Dupper, D. R. (1999). School-based peer sexual harassment. *Child Welfare, 78*(4), 435–460.

Levine, D. U. (1990). Creating effective schools: Findings and implications from research and practice. *Phi Delta Kappan, 72*(5), 389–393.

Lightfoot, S. L., & Carew, J. (1979). *Beyond bias: Perspectives on classrooms.* Cambridge, MA: Harvard University Press.

Lomotey, K. (1989). Cultural diversity in the school: Implications for principals. *NASSP Bulletin, 73*(521), 81–88.

Massachusetts Governor's Commission on Gay and Lesbian Youth (1993, July). *Making colleges and universities safe for gay and lesbian students: Report and recommendations of the governor's commission of gay and lesbian youth*. Boston, MA: Massachusetts Governor's Commission on Gay and Lesbian Youth.

McAdams, R. P. (1997). A systems approach to school reform. *Phi Delta Kappan, 79*(2), 138–142.

McCarthy, M. M., & Webb, L. D. (2000). Balancing duties and rights. *Principal Leadership, 1*(1), 16–21.

Menkart, D., Murray, A. D., & View, J. (2004). *Putting the movement back into Civil Rights teaching: A resource guide for K-12 classrooms*. Washington, DC: Teaching for Change and the Poverty & Race Research Action Council.

Midgley, C., & Wood, S. (1993). Beyond site-based management: Empowering teachers to reform schools. *Phi Delta Kappan, 75*(3), 245–252.

Moody, J. (2004). *Faculty diversity: Problems and solutions*. New York: Routledge Press.

Morrison, A. M. (1993). *The new leaders: Guidelines on leadership diversity in America*. San Francisco: Jossey-Bass.

Morrow, R. A., & Torres, C. A. (2002). *Reading Freire and Habermas: Critical pedagogy and transformative social change*. New York: Teachers College Press.

National Gay and Lesbian Task Force (1984). National anti-gay/lesbian victimization report. New York.

Nieto, S. (2004). *Affirming diversity* (4th ed.). New York: Longman.

Oaks, J. (1985). *Keeping track: How schools structure inequality*. New Haven: Yale University Press.

Obiakor, F. E., & Algorzine, B. (2001). *It even happens in 'good' schools: Responding to cultural diversity in today's classrooms*. Thousand Oaks, CA: Corwin Press.

Oliver, O., Hoover, J. H., & Hazler, R. (1994). The perceived roles of bullying in small-town Midwestern schools. *Journal of Counseling and Development: JCD, 72*(4), 416–420.

Ortiz, F. (1988). *Hispanic-American children's experiences in classrooms: A comparison between Hispanic and non-Hispanic children. Race, class, and gender in American education*. Albany: State University of New York Press.

Perlstein, D. (2000). Failing at kindness: Why fear of violence endangers children. *Educational Leadership, 57*(6), 76–79.

Peters, W. (1987). *A class divided: Then and now*. New Haven, CT: Yale University Press.

Pignatelli, F., & Pflaum, S. (1993). *Celebrating diverse voices: Progressive education and equity*. Newbury, CA: Corwin.

Razack, S. H. (2001). *Looking white people in the eye: Gender, race, and culture in courtrooms and classrooms*. Toronto: University of Toronto Press.

Rendon, L. I., Barcia, M., & Person, D. (Eds.). (2004). *Transforming the first year of college for students of color*. Columbia, SC: National Resource Center for the First-Year Experience and Students in Transition.

Reyhner, J. (1986). *Teaching the Indian child: A bilingual/multicultural approach*. Billings: Eastern Montana College.

Rhoads, R. A. (1998). *Freedom's web: Student activism in an age of cultural diversity*. Baltimore, MD: Johns Hopkins.

Riddel, F. S. (1974). *Appalacia: Its people, heritage, and problems*. Dubuque, IA: Kendall/Hunt Publishing.

Rogers, E. M., & Shoemaker, F. F. (1971). *Communication of innovation: A cross-cultural approach*. New York: Free Press.

Sadker, M., & Sadker, D. (1990). *Sex equity handbook for schools*. New York: Longman.

Schwartz, W. (2000). *Preventing student sexual harassment* (Report No. EDO-UD-00-9). Washington, DC: Office of Educational Research and Improvement. (ERIC Document Reproduction Service No. ED448248)

Seller, M. S. (1988). *To seek America: A history of ethnic life in the United States*. Englewood, NJ: Jerome S. Ozer.

Smith, W. A., Altbach, P. G., & Lomotey, K. (2002). *The racial crisis in American higher education: Continuing challenges for the twenty-first century* (Frontiers in Education). New York: SUNY Press.

Spring, J. (1985). *American education*. White Plains, NY: Longman.

Spring, J. (1989). *The sorting machine*. White Plains, NY: Longman.

Spring, J. (2004). *Deculturalization and the struggle for equality*. Boston, MA: McGraw Hill.

Squires, D. A., & Kranyik, R. D. (1995). The Comer Program: Changing school culture. *Educational Leadership, 53*, 29–32.

Stein, N. (1995). Sexual harassment in school: The public performance of gendered violence. *Harvard Educational Review, 65*(2), 145–162.

Stein, N. (1996). From the margins to the mainstream: Sexual harassment in k-12 schools. *Initiatives, 57(3)*, 19–26.

Steineger, M. (1997). *Preventing and countering school-based harassment: A resource guide for k-12 educators*. (Report No. ED420113). Northwest Regional Educational Lab. Washington, DC: Department of Education. (ERIC Document Reproduction Service No. EA029089)

Tanaka, G. (2003). *The intercultural campus: Transcending culture and power in American higher education*. New York: Peter Lang Publishing.

Thompson, C. (1985). *As boys become men: Learning new male roles*. Cambridge, MA: Resources for Change.

Wagner, T. (2001). Leadership for learning: An action theory of school change. *Phi Delta Kappan, 82*(5), 378–383.

Ward, J., & Anthony, P. (1992). *Who pays for student diversity? Population changes and educational policy*. Newbury Park, CA: Corwin.

Webb, L. D. (1997). What schools can do to combat student-to-student sexual harassment. *NASSP, 81*(585), 72–79.

Weinberg, M. (1986). *Because they were Jews: A history of anti-semitism*. Westport, CT: Greenwood Press.

Wells, A. S. (1989). *Hispanic education in America: Separate and unequal*. New York. ERIC Clearinghouse on Urban Education 59, Teachers College, Columbia University.

Wessler, S. L. (2000, December/2001, January). Sticks and stones. *Educational Leadership, 58*(4), 28–33.

Wiggens, G. (1991). Standards not standardization: Evoking quality student work. *Educational Leadership, 48*(5), 18–20.

Videos

Elliot, J. (1996). *Blue eyed* [Video recording]. (Available from Employee University, 702 S. Ewing St., Lancaster, OH 43130)

Hadleigh-West, M. (1998). *War zone: A film about sex, power, and what happens when men threaten a woman's right to walk undisturbed on the street* [Video recording]. (Available from The Media Education Foundation, 26 Center Street, Northampton, MA 01060)

Jhally, S. (1995). *Dream Worlds II: Desire, sex and power in music video* [Video recording]. (Available from The Media Education Foundation, 26 Center Street, Northampton, MA 01060)

Katz, J. (1999). *Tough Guise: Violence, Media & the Crisis in Masculinity* [Video recording]. (Available from The Media Education Foundation, 26 Center Street, Northampton, MA 01060)

Kilbourne, J., Vitagliano, J., & Stallone, P. (Producers). (1979). *Killing us softly: Advertising's image of women* [Video recording]. (Available from Cambridge Documentary Films, P. O. Box 390385, Cambridge, MA 02139-0004)

Web Resources

Jane Elliot

Jane Elliot's "Blue Eyes/Brown Eyes" experiment on PBS's *Frontline*: http:// www.pbs.org/wgbh/pages/frontline/shows/divided/etc/view.html

Multicultural Education and Teaching for Social Justice

American Civil Liberties Union: http://www.aclu.org/

Anti-Defamation League: http://www.adl.org/

Bureau of Justice Statistics: http://www.ojp.usdoj.gov/bjs/

Center for Multicultural Education: http://depts.washington.edu/centerme/ home.htm

Civil Rights Organization: http://www.civilrights.org

Diversity Web: An Interactive Resource Hub for Higher Education: http:// www.diversityweb.org/diversity_postings/resources/publications.cfm

EdChange (dedicated to diversity, equity, and justice in schools and society): http://www.edchange.org/

Educators for Social Responsibility: http://www.esrnational.org/

Evaluation Tools for Racial Equity: http://www.evaluationtoolsforracialequity. org/evaluation/01/1bResource.htm

Facing History and Ourselves: http://www.facinghistory.org/

Hate Crime: http://hate-crime.net

Hate Crimes: http://www.partnersagainsthate.org/

Multicultural Education: http://www.ncrel.org/sdrs/areas/issues/educatrs/ presrvce/pe3lk1.htm

Multicultural Education and Ethnic Groups: Selected Internet Sources: http:// wwwlibrary.csustan.edu/lboyer/multicultural/main.htm

Multicultural Pavilion: http://www.edchange.org/multicultural/

Multicultural Web sites Directory: http://www.public.iastate.edu/~savega/ multicul.htm

National Association for Multicultural Education: http://www.nameorg.org/

National Multicultural Institute: http://www.nmci.org/

Prejudice Institute: http://www.prejudiceinstitute.org

The Universal Declaration of Human Rights: http://www.un.org/Overview/ rights.html

U.S. Department of Education, Office for Civil Rights: http://www.ed.gov/ offices/OCR/

Ethnicity

American-Arab Anti-Discrimination Committee: http://www.adc.org/
American Jewish Committee: http://www.ajc.org/
Center for the Study of White American Culture: http://www.euroamerican.
    org/
Mexican American Legal Defense and Educational Fund: http://www.maldef.
    org
National Asian Pacific American Legal Consortium: http://www.napalc.org/
National Association for the Advancement of Colored People: http://
    www.naacp.org/
National Congress of American Indians: http://www.ncai.org
National Council of La Raza: http://www.ncir.org/
Organization of Chinese Americans: http://www.ocanatl.org/
Puerto Rican Legal Defense and Educational Fund (PRLDEF): http://
    www.prldef.org

Gender

Al-Raida: Institute for Women's Studies in the Arab World: http://www.lau.
    edu.lb/centers-institutes/iwsaw/raida.html
American Association of University Women: http://www.aauw.org/
The Convention on the Elimination of all Forms of Discrimination Against
    Women: www.cedaw.org
Feminism: www.feminist.org/education
Gender Equity: www.sadker.org
National Coalition for Women and Girls in Education: www.ncwge.org
National Council for Research on Women: www.NCRW.org
National Organization for Women: http://www.now.org/index.html
National Women's Law Center: http://www.nwlc.org/
2000 U. N. Millennium Development Goals Relating to Gender and Education:
    www.un.org/millenniumgoals
U.S. Women Connect: http://www.uswc.org

Language

Bilingual Education Links: http://jan.ucc.nau.edu/~jar/BME.html
National Association for Bilingual Education (NABE): http://www.nabe.org
National Clearinghouse on English Language Acquisition and Language
    Instruction Education Programs (NCELA): http://www.ncela.gwu.edu
School Effectiveness for Language Minority Students: http://www.ncela.gwu.
    edu/ncbepubs/resource/effectiveness/
Teachers of English to Speakers of Other Languages (TESOL): http://www.
    tesol.org

Poverty

Institute for Research on Poverty: http://www.irp.wisc.edu/
Southern Poverty Law Center: http://www.splcenter.org/
U. S. Census Bureau: http://www.census.gov/hhes/www/poverty.html

Religion

Multi-faith and Religion Site List: http://www.conjure.com/religion.html
Promoting Religious Tolerance: http://www.religioustolerance.org/

Sexual Orientation

Anti-Violence Project: http://www.avp.org/homepage.htm
Gaynet: http://www.qrd.org/qrd/electronic/email/gaynet
Gay-Straight Alliance Network: http://www.gsanetwork.org/
GLBT Anti-Violence Project: http://www.lambda.org
Matthew Shepard Foundation: http://matthewsplace.com/foundtext.html
National Gay and Lesbian Task Force: http://www.thetaskforce.org/
Statistics About Homophobia: http://www.now.org/issues/lgbi/stats.html
University of Maryland Diversity Database: http://www.inform.umd.edu/
    EdRes/Topic/Diversity/Specific/Sexual_Orientation/

Transgender Information

Gay, Lesbian, Bisexual, Transgender Student Services: http://www.glbtss.
    colostate.edu/transgender/
Gender Talk: Transgender Resources: http://www.gendertalk.com/info/
    resource/index.shtml
http://www.annelawrence.com/tgresources.pdf
http://www.usc.edu/student-affairs/glbss/PDFS/TransgenderInformation.pdf
Transgender Information: http://www.debradavis.org/gecpage/gectransinfo.
    html

Exhibit 5-1

Multicultural Education Simulation

    James Banks, "the father of multicultural education," argues that there are three basic approaches to curriculum, in reference to multiculturalism:

1. The mainstream-centric approach allows for the traditional canonized authors and does not allow for room for multiple perspectives. It is presented as a closed hermeneutic or interpretive system. It takes the dominant culture as its core, its center, and teaches that, leaving everything else out.

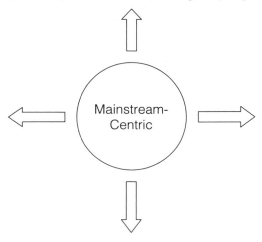

2. The ethnic additive approach still takes the mainstream as its center, but adds on bits and pieces such as Black History Month, Women's History Month, and/or "snippets" of information about "others." There is no integration of these "additions" with the core curriculum. Thus, the curriculum does not change in any meaningful way.

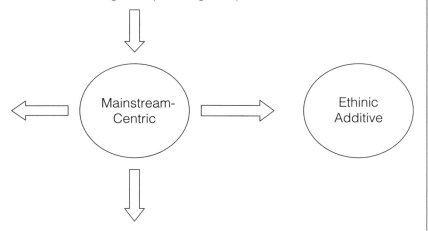

3. The national and global approach shifts the center of curriculum. Issues are explored from multiple perspectives.

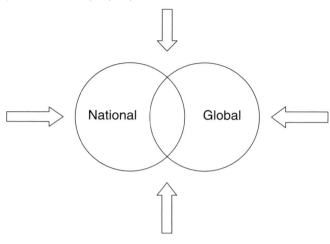

Simulation Directions
   One can easily create three pictorial representations of these three perspectives that would be meaningful to teach in a university classroom. An interesting approach to this would be to create three puzzles that students would have to put together that represent each curricular perspective. Materials needed: three stand-ard-sized sheets of poster board, crayons, markers, or colored pencils.

Mainstream-centric puzzle:
   Divide the poster board into eight shapes. Keep all of these pieces white and think of eight representative people of traditional culture/curriculum. Here are some suggestions:

1. Thomas Jefferson
2. George Washington
3. Christopher Columbus
4. Mark Twain
5. William Shakespeare
6. Abraham Lincoln
7. Edgar Allan Poe
8. Ralph Waldo Emerson

You may want to laminate your puzzle first, and then cut it into its puzzle pieces.

Ethnic additive puzzle:
   Create the same puzzle as the one you created for the mainstream-centric repre-sentation with one important difference. This puzzle will have *four additional pieces*. These four pieces will represent various ethnic additions of your choosing.

Continued

Exhibit 5-1 Continued

The four pieces should be drawn in each of the four corners of the poster board. Each of these four pieces should be shaded a different color but the eight pieces (similar to the mainstream-centric puzzle) will remain white. Some suggestions for your ethnic additives:

1. Betsy Ross
2. Poncho Villa
3. Geronimo
4. Martin Luther King Jr.

National global puzzle:

Divide your poster board into 20 different shapes. Write 20 names representing various national, cultural, ethnic perspectives from a variety of disciplines (and these points of view do not necessarily have to be names). For example:

1. Toni Morrison
2. Caesar Chavez
3. Gandhi
4. The Grimke sisters
5. Amy Tan
6. Allen Ginsburg
7. James Baldwin
8. Kate Chopin
9. Sojourner Truth
10. Jane Pittman
11. Amiri Baraka
12. Louise Erdrich
13. Maya Angelou
14. Sandra Cisneros
15. John Lennon
16. Trail of Tears
17. Eleanor Roosevelt
18. Malcolm X
19. Sappho

Shade each of these pieces a different color but *leave one space in the puzzle white and blank* (this will represent the eventual inclusion of new perspectives).

Facilitation Directions

1. Please inform your participants that there is to be no talking during the construction. Instead, have participants and observers take notes on what they see happening.

2. Pass out the first puzzle to two people in the class to put together. The two people you select should be members of the mainstream culture (if possible), e.g., white males.

3. Upon completion of the first puzzle, pass the second puzzle out to the same people but give the colored pieces to a person who is not a white male. You may want pass the ethnic additive pieces to more than one non-white male or female.

4. Upon completion of the second puzzle, divide the third puzzle among the members of the entire class. Encourage all students to take part in the construction.

5. Ask students to determine what they think the three puzzles represent. Ask them why only certain students participated in certain constructions. Ask them to discuss the significance of these factors. Ask students what the implications of these three approaches are for our lives in a diverse world. Etc.

Exhibit 5-2

Policy to Promote Social Justice

Everyone is entitled to a safe school environment that is free from bullying, harassment, and intimidation in any manner.

Students are prohibited from engaging in conduct, whether written, verbal, or physical, that unreasonably interferes in another's (students and staff) participation in or enjoyment of school or school-related activities. Students are prohibited from intimidating or attempting to intimidate or harass others based on (but not limited to) the following: sexual orientation, physical or mental disability, race, ethnicity, socioeconomic status, gender, religion, appearance, or any other personal or behavioral characteristic. The intent of the harasser is irrelevant. It is the impact of the action that determines whether or not harassment has occurred.

Intimidation includes but is not limited to:

Language

- Students will not use language to taunt and degrade other individuals. For example, "You are gay," "Do you know Sue? I heard she is a dyke," or "Lose some weight."
- Students will not use language in a generic manner to degrade others. For example, "Those pants are gay" (ugly), "You got jewed" (ripped-off), or "You throw like a girl" (weak).

Bullying

Students will not intimidate or attempt to intimidate others by any means or methods, including: taunts, name-calling, put-downs, discriminatory harassment, extortion, exclusion, violence or threat of violence.

- For example, purposely bumping into another student in the hallway, because s/he is new, not liked, looks different, etc.

Continued

Exhibit 5-2 Continued

Hazing
   Students will not initiate another student into any grade, school or school-related activity by any means or method that may cause physical or emotional pain, embarrassment, or discomfort.

- For example, coercing a new student into the bathroom in order to initiate him/her into the school by violence or threat of violence.

Harassment
   Harassment is conduct, including verbal conduct, that interferes with a student's educational benefits, opportunities, performance, or general well-being.
   Students will not engage in unwelcome sexual advances, requests for sexual favors, or other verbal or physical conduct relating to a person's sex, sexual orientation, race, color, national origin, religion, height, weight, marital status, disability, etc.
   Quid Pro Quo sexual harassment: Requesting sexual favors from another individual in exchange for a benefit or avoidance of negative consequences.

- For example, "if you perform _____ sexual act, I won't tell Mr. Smith you cheated on the exam."

Hostile Environment sexual harassment: Engaging in behaviors of a sexual nature, overtly or covertly, that create a coercive, embarrassing, unsafe and/or intimidating environment for individuals or groups.

- For example, questioning, describing, or discussing a person's sexuality whether or not s/he is present, graffiti of a sexual nature on the bathroom wall, grabbing, touching, sexual innuendo, etc.

Consequences
   Consequences for violation of this policy will vary from suspension to expulsion depending upon the frequency and severity of the behavior. Students should be aware that all claims of harassment/intimidation will be investigated promptly and thoroughly. Confidentiality will be protected and retaliation against individuals reporting behaviors that violate this policy will result in possible expulsion from school.
   The following steps are general disciplinary guidelines to be used at the administration's discretion. Steps may be skipped/omitted, depending on the severity of the offense. In addition to the consequences listed below, students will be involved in a variety of programs intended to promote positive behavior and peer interaction including: conflict mediation/resolution, counseling, etc.
   First Offense: Administrative intervention (warning that behavior will not be tolerated and more severe consequences are to follow). Student will write a statement that describes the incident from her/his point of view and offers possible constructive ways to deal with the conflict.
   Second Offense: 30 minute detention (during lunch or after school). Student will work on assignments with topics related to their offenses. If student does not have anything to work on, an assignment will be provided.

Third Offense: One day of in-school suspension (ISS) and mandatory after-school sensitivity class.

Fourth Offense: Three days of out-of-school suspension.

Fifth Offense: Five to 10 days of out-of-school suspension.

Sixth Offense: Administrative review of student's history. Possible expulsion hearing.

Reporting

There are a variety of ways in which one may report incidents/behaviors that are in violation of the tolerance policy.

1. All teachers are aware of this policy and of what to do in the case of observed and reported incidents. A student may report violations to a teacher. This teacher will then report the incident to the administration where it will be dealt with promptly.

2. Violations of the tolerance policy may be reported directly to the administration.

3. Violations of the tolerance policy may be reported to the school counselor or social worker.

4. Violations of the tolerance policy may be reported by filling out the enclosed *Harassment Incident Report Form*. You may find this form in the counseling office and in the main office. There are various places that this form may be submitted for investigation. There are boxes outside the offices of the counselor and the social worker for this purpose. There is also one in the main office and one in each classroom. Students may also turn forms into their teachers if they so choose.

Exhibit 5-3

Harassment Incident
Report Form

All forms of harassment and intimidation are strictly prohibited in this school. All members of the study body, faculty, staff, and administration are to be treated with dignity and respect. If you believe you are or have been a victim of harassment, please complete this form. If you require assistance in filling out this form, please consult a staff member or counselor. Your complaint will then be investigated by the proper school authorities.

Please fill out as much of this form as possible that you feel comfortable with.

Student: _____

Address: _____

Parent's Name: _____

Telephone: _____

Continued

Exhibit 5-3 Continued

Parent Work Telephone: _____

Date(s) of Alleged Incident(s): _____

Name(s) of Person(s) You Believe Harassed You:

_____

Witnesses Present:

_____

_____

Where Did the Incident(s) Occur:

_____

Describe the Incident(s) in as much detail as possible. Attach additional pages if needed.

_____

_____

_____

_____

_____

_____

_____

_____

_____

_____

_____

I pledge that the information I have provided on this form is true, and complete to the best of my knowledge.

Student Signature: _____

Date: _____

Received by: _____

Date: _____

Chapter 6

"A" Is for Activism: Classroom-Based Approaches to Preventing Campus Violence

Joan C. Chrisler
Mab Segrest

Learning by doing has long been a desirable technique for any level of instruction. A goal of many Women's Studies faculty, whether stated explicitly on the syllabus or not, is to move students toward activism and a deep engagement with their realities. When formerly passive students work on issues of importance to them, they learn lessons that expand beyond the course material (e.g., what it means to be a citizen), they develop skills they will use throughout their lives (e.g., public speaking), and their self-concepts are altered in ways they did not expect (e.g., increased self-respect, empowerment). The life-changing effects of Women's Studies courses have been well documented in the behavioral science literature (e.g., Hoffmann & Stake, 1998; Malkin & Stake, 2004; Stake & Rose, 1994).

In the first author's Psychology of Women course, the activism assignment is worded as follows on the syllabus:

> For the term paper you are to perform a consciousness-raising activity in which you teach others about an important issue that was covered in this course. Think of an action that you would not (or could not) have done prior to taking this course. Think about the topics covered in the texts and how the experiences of different people were presented. Then perform a liberating act that is positive, consciousness-raising (both for you and others), and representative of one of the course themes. Your action

must be nonviolent (i.e., no harm may come to you or others, either mentally or physically), must be legal, and may not also be submitted for credit in another course or program. For example, you might choose to create and display/enact an affirmative work of art/street theater; construct a Web site, blog, or zine about women's issues; volunteer at the Southeastern Connecticut Women's Center; or work on a project with the campus Women's Center or the local chapter of the Feminist Majority or the National Organization for Women. In your paper:

(1) describe the action you took and why you took it;

(2) explain why and how the action served to raise your consciousness and/or that of others and estimate how successful you were in doing so;

(3) analyze your thoughts and feelings about the action and the issues involved. How much did you know and how did you feel about the issues before taking this course? How much do you know and how do you feel about the issues now? Do you think you might do more consciousness raising and/or political activism in the future?

Psychology students often find this assignment daunting at first, but then rise to the challenge. Project topics are quite varied (e.g., images of women athletes, risk factors for eating disorders, positive aging), but violence against women is a popular choice. Students have produced powerful zines (self-published booklets) by collecting accounts from survivors of rape, child abuse, or domestic violence. One student made a series of colorful posters that she put up across campus; the posters contained abusive comments about women from contemporary music under the heading "Think about it." Another student distributed plastic bracelets stamped with the text "End Violence Against Women"; the bracelets were accompanied by statistics about the incidence of various forms of violence on campuses and in the general population. Two projects had a longer impact on campus. In one case the student designed a brochure about coping with street harassment, which was later distributed by the Study Away Office to students planning to attend universities in countries known for this behavior. In the other case a student developed a psychoeducational workshop on verbal abuse, which she delivered for several years (including post-graduation) to incoming students during their orientation week.

Like other Women's Studies and Psychology faculty, we find that students often seek us out to share their personal struggles. Over the years, we have heard stories of acquaintance rape, attempted rape, sexual and gender harassment, verbal abuse, and stalking, and some of these events have taken place on our campus, often in connection with alcohol abuse. Indeed, the second author has become increasingly alarmed by stories students in her Transnational Feminism course tell about binge drinking on campus. She regularly spends a special class meeting (students come to her home in small groups for apple pie and discussion) on campus violence, which begins by having the students read aloud the sexual misconduct policy from the students' handbook, after which upperclass students give first-year students advice about how to stay safe. Class discussions typically reveal the mistaken belief that the college does not want cases of sexual misconduct brought forward (in order to protect its reputation), confusion over drinking and sexual activity, power imbalances in heterosexual relationships (and casual hook-ups) on a campus where women outnumber men by 50%, women's lowered self-esteem following incidents of misconduct, dorms that function as "domestic spheres" with attendant silences (like residence hall advisors who keep quiet), and young women's quite reasonable hesitation about the repercussions of bringing a charge of misconduct on such a small campus or through the city's criminal justice system.

These discussions inspired the development of a one-credit field placement course for the Department of Gender & Women's Studies. In the first two years the course was offered, the focus on "countering campus violence" was the most popular option. Students began their work by taking an intensive 24-hour training course on sexual assault that was conducted by the Southeastern Connecticut Women's Center, which runs a rape crisis hotline and a domestic violence shelter. The students then participated in a Think Tank on Sexual Assault, which consisted of themselves, the second author, the college's affirmative action officer, and several members of the student life staff. The Think Tank assessed the problem (both nationally and on our campus), reviewed the college's policies and procedures, and recommended changes, and considered other aspects of campus life and the college budget that could be improved (e.g., increased funding for counseling services, better training for peer counselors and students who work in the residence halls, more supervision of alcohol use on campus, changes to the college Web site and student handbook to highlight sexual misconduct policies). The knowledge gained from outside the campus permitted students to take a more assertive stance toward campus policies and practices. The second author is currently making plans to follow up on the work of the Think Tank with a semester-long focus on the application of a human rights framework to campus sexual assault. Plans include a conference, during which outside experts will give formal talks and also meet less formally with the campus community to work with us to establish best practices and benchmarks to help create a safe climate for women on campus.

Activist course assignments such as these benefit not only the students and faculty in the particular classes, but also friends with whom they discuss the assignments; members of the campus community who see their posters, zines, or other materials; and future students who will be affected for the better by changes in policy and procedures or by encountering the educational materials developed by these young feminist activists. In carrying out these assignments students learn how to identify problems, how to teach others about important issues, and how to work for change within and outside the system, beginning always with where they are. In the course of the assignments they become empowered, and, we hope, they develop the courage and skills they will need later in life to continue to confront social problems whenever and wherever they find them.

REFERENCES

Hoffmann, F. L., & Stake, J. E. (1998). Feminist pedagogy in theory and practice: An empirical investigation. *NWSA Journal, 10*, 71–97.

Malkin, C., & Stake, J. E. (2004). Changes in attitudes and self-confidence in the women's and gender studies classroom: The role of teacher alliance and student cohesion. *Sex Roles, 50*, 455–468.

Stake, J. E., & Rose, S. (1994). The long-term impact of women's studies on students' personal lives and political activism. *Psychology of Women Quarterly, 18*, 403–418.

Chapter 7

Stalking as a Form of Campus Violence: Case Studies

Janet Sigal

Aggression is a major topic area in my social psychology course. Aggression is defined as "behavior intended to harm another person who is motivated to avoid the harm" (Baumeister & Bushman, 2008, p. 292). The harm can either be physical or psychological. One of the areas that I describe in my lectures on aggression is stalking.

Stalking is often described as persistent pursuit that causes the average person to experience fear or distress. Stalking behavior can take many forms and affects many types of victims. There are many causes of stalking including psychopathological behavior (e.g., when a person stalks someone, believing it is a way to get a date with that person), but the most common causes of stalking include the breakup of a relationship or marriage, and when someone is rejected by a potential date or romantic partner. The stalking can take the form of numerous phone calls, letters, or e-mails, more in-your-face approaches such as waiting for someone outside their workplace or university, and finally in a more extreme form, following the victim on foot or in a car. Further escalation into violence may also occur. There are few effective methods of responding to stalking. Most experts advise the person to indicate very clearly that she or he is not interested in a relationship and then cease communication entirely. If the victim adopts this "detach and watch" approach, the stalker may pursue the person for a period of time and then give up, or it may make the stalker angry and the stalking may escalate into direct violence. The advice generally is to "detach and watch" rather than "engage and enrage." Although earlier examples primarily focused on direct approaches, more recently, cyber-stalking through the Internet also has become a focus of study.

A number of studies have investigated stalking of college students. For example, Bjerregaard (2000) questioned a large number of college students and found that over 20% of college women, and approximately 10% of college men in their sample reported having been stalked. In general, college students report that the stalkers were known to them.

In the course of my lecture on stalking, I present my class with several cases of students or faculty members who have been stalked. Most recently, I taught an undergraduate student who approached me, showing extreme distress. She had been followed while driving back to the dormitory, and a few nights later she began receiving threatening phone calls in the middle of the night. One night when she was out, her roommate picked up the phone and recorded the stalker's threat that he would put out her eyes. The student recognized the stalker as her uncle who was engaged in a violent family dispute with her mother and the uncle was arrested. This example illustrates both the very negative effects on stalking victims (she was unable to concentrate, was fearful all the time, and was in constant distress) as well as the difficulty in dealing with the stalker. In order to allow the police to arrest the stalker, it seemed to be necessary to provide audiotaped evidence of his violent intentions.

Other students have been stalked by individuals with whom they have been romantically involved. One of my graduate students (another case that I present in class) was married to an extremely controlling individual. While we were away at a conference, he called her every hour to determine where she was. At times he would demand to talk with me to provide corroborating evidence that she was not having an affair with someone at the conference. Although she finally divorced her husband, he continued to phone her and she had to move away and have an unlisted phone number.

Another case example that I use in my lecture involved a graduate student who was at the clinic seeing patients. Her therapy relationship with one of the patients was terminated and he was transferred to another therapist. However, every time she held a group session in a room with a door that was glass on top, he would be staring at her through the window. He also would follow her out to her car. In a study also investigating this type of stalking, Purcell, Powell, and Mullen (2005) reported results from a survey of psychologists in Australia. Approximately 20% of the therapists indicated that they had been stalked for a period of time, generally either because of a romantic attachment on the part of a client or because the client was angry (e.g., in cases of child custody). Many of the therapists reported that they changed their practice in some way (e.g., to increase security) and some therapists actually were thinking of changing professions.

Another example of a stalking victim was a graduate student who received many phone calls in the middle of the night without the speaker identifying himself. Fortunately, the telephone company was able to trace the number even though it was blocked, and it was another student who had asked her out at a party and whom she rejected. In a similar situation, one of our undergraduates refused to date someone. He became angry and stalked her on her campus. The student actually transferred to our university to avoid the stalker and he followed her and enrolled in our university as well.

Finally, I described an experience that I had with a student who stalked me. She indicated interest in joining our research team, but when she was told that our meetings were during the day, she informed me that she worked and wondered why the team couldn't meet at night. Following that e-mail interaction, she sent me a lengthy e-mail detailing her objections to not being included on the team. For about a year, I received an e-mail from her almost every day. Even after that year she sometimes sent me e-cards. The experience was so distressing that I forwarded copies of her e-mails to the chair of the department to save as a record.

Students find this topic and my case examples quite interesting and relevant both to the field of aggression and to behavior of college students. I encourage colleagues to integrate case studies in their teaching, with the intent both to illuminate the nature of stalking as well as to offer, perhaps, solutions and relief.

REFERENCES

Baumeister, R. F., & Bushman, B. J. (2008). *Social psychology: Human nature.* Belmont, CA: Thomson Wadsworth.

Bjerregaard, B. (2000). An empirical study of stalking victimization. *Violence and Victims*, 15, 389–406.

Purcell, R., Powell, M. B., & Mullen, P. E. (2005). Clients who stalk psychologists: Prevalence, methods, and motivation. *Professional Psychology: Research and Practice, 36,* 537–543.

Chapter 8

The Psychology of Women Course as a "Catalyst for Change" for Campus Violence

Michele A. Paludi
Florence L. Denmark
Darlene C. DeFour

Several authors have noted a "developmental process" that is observable in students during their participation in a psychology of women course (e.g., Paludi et al., 2007; see Chrisler & Segrest, this volume). This process, first identified by Downing and Rousch (1985), includes the following stages: passive acceptance; revelation; embeddedness/emanation; synthesis; and active commitment.

Students who can be characterized as being in the passive acceptance stage of this model frequently state that discrimination is no longer present in politics, economics, education, or the family. However, the topics that are usually covered in the psychology of women courses (e.g., communication differences between women and men, sexual harassment, reproductive rights, rape, bias in counseling women) begin students' questioning of these long-held assumptions.

By discussing topics in the psychology of women course, a common transition occurs from the passive acceptance stage to revelation (Paludi, 2002). For example, students begin to remember how they in fact have been discriminated against because of their sex, race, sexual orientation, or religion. They notice magazine advertisements, music videos, and television programs that objectify women. They also recall being referred to by derogatory names because they wore glasses, were overweight, had acne, wore braces, and other reasons that are rooted in claims linked to a lack of femininity or female attractiveness. It is during this stage of the developmental process that students may become angry with themselves about why they allowed these comments to be made and why they didn't speak up about them when they occurred (Paludi, 2002).

When students in the course share their anger about these issues, they frequently want to spend time connecting with others, sharing their experiences and asking others how they have handled discrimination in their lives. This stage is referred to as the embeddedness/emanation stage. This stage is replaced by the synthesis stage, in which statements are made acknowledging the discriminatory practices against women, especially ethnic women, aged women, lesbians, and physically challenged women. Frequently, students will make statements reflecting their transcendence of gender-role stereotypes. They describe women and men as individuals, not as members of their respective sex categories.

Students who are in the active commitment stage report wanting to take more courses on women and gender, conduct research in the psychology of women, and/or volunteer at a rape crisis center or Planned Parenthood.

Walsh (1985) suggested the psychology of women course can serve as a "catalyst for change" at the individual, organizational, and societal levels. We have found the psychology of women course to help change students' perceptions and attributions about campus violence. Examples of change at the individual level include working for equality in interpersonal relationships and leaving a relationship that is characterized by intimate partner violence. Examples of change at the organizational level include ensuring campus policies are in place and enforced that prohibit hazing, sexual harassment, stalking, hate crimes, and sexual assault. Finally, societal level changes include lobbying legislators for stricter penalties for rapists.

The psychology of women course provides students with ways to work for change at each of these three levels, especially through the pedagogical techniques instructors implement in the course that encompasses adult learning principles. Research in educational psychology and the psychology of women (see Lord, 1982; Paludi, 1996) has identified that women prefer learning situations that:

- Are practical and problem-centered
- Promote their positive self-esteem
- Integrate new ideas with existing knowledge
- Show respect for the individual learner
- Capitalize on their experience
- Allow choice and self-direction

Thus, the psychology of women course can help promote change in individuals in the following ways:

- Provide overviews, summaries, case studies, and behavioral rehearsals to link research and theory to practice;
- Use collaborative, authentic problem-solving activities;
- Assist individuals in becoming more effective and confident through guided practice and establishing routines;
- Ask individuals what they would like to know about the topic;
- Provide a quality, well-organized, differentiated experience that uses time effectively and efficiently;
- Validate and respect participants' existing knowledge;
- Create activities that use individuals' experience and knowledge.

Types of pedagogical techniques that are commonly used in the psychology of women course include: small group discussion, case studies and scenarios, and behavioral rehearsal. Several pedagogical techniques are presented in this chapter that we have used in the psychology of women course. The goal of these techniques is to help students move from passive acceptance to active commitment in their individual relationships as well as toward organizational and societal change with respect to violence and victimization. Similar work has been reported by Fischer (1986) in a human sexuality course that addressed date rape. Students were more rejecting of date rape, more sure that the behavior was rape, and slightly more liberal in their attitudes toward women at the end of the course than at the beginning.

SAMPLE PEDAGOGICAL TECHNIQUES

Lobbying Legislators

Have students call or write state assembly members or state senators about bills that have been introduced in the legislature that deal with campus violence (see Paludi, 2002). Questions to consider asking the legislators include:

- How long have the bills been under consideration?
- Do the bills take into account students who are especially vulnerable to sexual victimization?
- Do the bills provide for curriculum development to teach students about violence?

Have the students consider what they can do to assist legislators regarding the passage of these bills.

Sexual Harassment of Students

Provide students with scenarios that illustrate sexual harassment. Paludi (1996, pp. 29–30) has identified the following:

> In your biology class your professor smiles and comments on your appearance as a greeting each morning. Before this professor's lecture on female anatomy, the professor tells the class that you will be the class's visual aid today since you are well-built and a fine specimen of female anatomy.
>
> You are taking a math course that includes a unit on statistics. You know that this course is important to your career and a good grade in math can increase your chances of getting into graduate school. You have been having some difficulty in understanding probability theory. You decide to talk with your TA about this topic. You tell your TA about your concern about the material and your wish to get a good grade because you want to go to graduate school. Your TA makes it clear that all you have to do is to comply with your TA's sexual requests.

Ask students how they would handle each situation if they were the student in each scenario.

Ask students to discuss the benefits and costs of each method of responding to the situations of sexual harassment that was generated by the class.

Have your campus's sexual harassment educator/Title IX coordinator discuss the campus's sexual harassment policy and investigatory procedures. Distribute copies of the policies to students.

Discuss issues of retaliation, confidentiality, due process, and therapeutic support available for individuals seeking resolution of their complaint of sexual harassment.

Portfolio

Ask students to prepare a portfolio to be submitted at the end of the course. The portfolio must include work in one of the following areas:

- Sexual assault
- Hazing
- Intimate partner violence
- Sexual harassment
- Hate crimes

Students should select one area from the above list that reflects a program or practice in their current or previous campus. For example, students may select a campus policy on hate crimes to review. Work in the selected area should include the following:

- Write a narrative describing the background, major issues, practices, and problems/challenges based on personal knowledge/experiences, observations, and/or interviews. The narrative or "problem statement" should be in essay form and be no more than two single-spaced pages.

- Provide a copy of any materials in reference to the program or practice, for example, a policy statement or investigatory procedures. Note: The professor will keep materials confidential and will not share the materials with others.
- Locate at least five published (peer reviewed) articles (in addition to those assigned in class) related to the selected topic area. Students should look for material that provides strategic direction concerning how to address the problem or challenge they have identified above. These resources must be listed in the portfolio. (The instructor will provide students with a list of journals on sexual victimization that students may use for this section of their portfolio.)
- Provide an evaluation of the program or practice in light of knowledge of the topic gained in the course, readings, and in the selected articles. Based on this evaluation, provide recommendations for the improvement of the effectiveness of the program or practice (no more than 10–12 single-spaced pages).

Attitudes Toward Victim Blame and Victim Responsibility

Provide students with statements similar to those offered by Paludi (1996, p. 18):

- A sexually victimized woman is a desirable woman.
- The extent of the woman's resistance to sexual violence should be the major factor in determining if violence has occurred.
- Any woman may be sexually victimized.
- A sexually victimized woman is usually an innocent victim.
- A woman should blame herself for sexual victimization.
- Virtually all women who have reported sexual victimization are able to rebuild their lives and believe in their own competence.

Ask students to get into small groups of 5–10. Each group can appoint a recorder/moderator who will report back to the entire group.

Ask students to indicate whether they agree or disagree with each statement or if they are uncertain.

Have the moderator/recorder indicate the reasons for students' agreements and disagreements with the statements.

Ask each moderator/recorder to summarize for the entire class the discussion that occurred in their small group.

Facilitate a lecture and discussion about perceptions and attributions of violence against women.

Ask students to identify ways they can help dispel myths related to violence against women.

Bullying and Hazing Exercises for Students

Interview 10 college students. Ask them whether they have been bullied or have experienced hazing while at college. Ask them to describe the situation and how they reacted.

Ask students if hazing is ever acceptable. If they answer yes, ask students to indicate what forms would be acceptable, questionable, or unacceptable initiation activities. Finally, ask students how they make their decision.

Find out whether hazing is occurring on your campus.

- Interview members of athletic teams, sororities, and fraternities to find out.
- Do males and females differ in their use of hazing?

Men Working to Reduce Violence Against Women

Purpose:
During the semester we discussed the importance of men as allies in dealing with gender issues. This exercise is designed to increase your awareness of men's groups that focus on reducing violence against women or gender discrimination. The violence can be rape, sexual harassment, intimate partner violence, bullying, or hazing.

Instructions:

- Research one men's organization that has as one of its goals the reduction of violence against women.
- Give the name and describe the organization you researched. When and where did it originate? Is it a local, national, or international group? Indicate where the organization is located.
- What are the main objectives of the organization?
- How does the group attempt to obtain its objectives? (Lobbying local, state, or national officials, education via workshops for men on campus, etc.)
- Supply a copy of any resources that the organization uses to put forth its program.
- List the organization's Web site.
- What is the mechanism for becoming a part of this organization?

This exercise is adapted from Richabaugh (1998).

Empowerment via Historical Analysis

One gender stereotype is "real women" are weak and compliant. Women are viewed as physically weak and incapable of physically warding off attacks. Women are frequently socialized to be nice and not make waves. This is clearly a misrepresentation of women. Historically women have fought back against injustice both overtly and covertly. Fighting back gives women a sense of power. Even on the individual level women who fight back reduce their chances of being raped. Fighting back also seems to speed psychological recovery after an assault (Rozee, 2005). So being able to take care of oneself (e.g., by taking a self-defense class, working to create change on campuses by creating policies, speaking up in relationships) is not antithetical to being a "real woman." The purpose of the exercise is to get students to see that "fighting back" is part of women's history.

Ask students to research a woman or a historical movement that illustrates women's "fighting spirit." Either ask students to pick a woman or a social movement from history or provide a list like the two below. If names are given, an effort should be made to have women and social movements from diverse backgrounds (i.e., women in Africa, Asia, Europe, etc.) and periods of history.

Movement or Event
The Aba Revolution of 1929 (aka The War of The Women)
The Black Women's Club Movement
1933 Puerto Rican Needleworkers Strike
Women's Internal League for Peace and Freedom
1982 New York Chinatown Garment Strike
First Jewish Women's Movement

Women

Yaa Asantewaa	Queen Tomyris
Queen Artemisia	Queen Boudica
Trung Sisters	Nefertiti
Cleopatra VII	Kaitchknoa Winema
Dahteste Mescalero	Wang Cong'er
Lozen	Nanye-hi
Mary Owens	Frances Clayton
Tomeo Gozen	Hanguaku Gozen
Bushi Women	Mary Church Terrell
Fanny Lou Hammer	Victoria Clafin Woodhull

- Provide the name of the person or social movement that you selected. Give the dates that the person lived or the dates of the event or movement.

- Write a one to two page, single-spaced description of the person or social movement. Be sure to include the major issues for the movement, major contributions for the person, and how the person or social movement demonstrates a "fighting spirit."

- Did you identify issues other than gender that played a role in the movement (e.g., race, ethnicity, social class, sexual orientation)?

- Discuss how the social movement or what the person accomplished is related to current feminist principles.

Interviewing a Researcher or Advocate in Campus Violence

Provide students with a list of individuals who have agreed to participate in this interview. The purpose of this interview is to determine the perspective of their role in social change with respect to campus violence. This interview should give students an idea of the issues facing individuals in campus violence research and advocacy today and of the rewards of these professions.

Ask students to provide a written summary of the interview.

Also ask students to give an oral presentation to the entire class.

Sample questions for students to ask the professionals include:

- What made you select this area of study/advocacy?
- What educational background do you have that prepared you for this career?
- Who were your role models and/or mentors in helping you get into this career?
- Did you have any gatekeepers who wanted you not to pursue this field?
- How has your worked changed individuals with respect to campus violence?
- What do you want to accomplish next to help prevent campus violence?

Content Analysis of Hate Crimes Depicted in Films and Music

Ask students to watch a movie about a topic related to violence and hate crimes (e.g., *North Country, Philadelphia,* or *Crash*) in order to apply the course concepts through an analysis of the film. As an alternative, ask students to listen to the lyrics of popular music (e.g., Melissa Etheridge's "Scarecrow," that was inspired by the hate crime toward Matthew Shepard because he was gay).

Ask students to content analyze the film or lyrics by answering the following question: Describe a scene in the movie (lyrics in the song) that depicts a hate crime. Describe how the scene/lyrics portray a myth about hate crimes. Counter this portrayal with the reality about hate crimes, based on the research cited in the course.

Also ask students to explore their own feelings and thoughts about hate crimes. Distribute your campus's policy on hate crimes so students know their rights and responsibilities with respect to hate crimes.

REFERENCES

Downing, N., & Rousch, K. (1985). From passive acceptance to active commitment. *The Counseling Psychologist, 13,* 695–709.

Fischer, G. (1986). College student attitudes toward forcible date rape: Changes after taking a human sexuality course. *Journal of Sex Education and Therapy, 12*, 42–46.

Lord, S. (1982). Research on teaching the psychology of women. *Psychology of Women Quarterly, 7*, 96–104.

Paludi, M. (1996). *Exploring/teaching the psychology of women: A manual of resources* (2nd ed.) Albany, NY: State University of New York Press.

Paludi, M. (2002). *The psychology of women*. Upper Saddle River, NJ: Prentice Hall.

Paludi, M., Dillon, L., Stern, T., Martin, J., DeFour, D., & White, C. (2007). Courses in the psychology of women: Catalysts for change. In F. L. Denmark and M. A. Paludi (Eds.), *The psychology of women: A handbook of issues and theories*. Westport, CT: Greenwood.

Richabaugh, C.A. (1998). *Sex and gender. Student projects and exercises*. New York: McGraw Hill Publishers.

Rozee (2005). Rape resistance: Successes and challenges. In A. Barnes (Ed.), *The handbook of women psychology and the law* (pp. 265–270). San Francisco: Jossey-Bass.

Walsh, M. R. (1985). The psychology of women course: A continuing catalyst for change. *Teaching of Psychology, 12*, 198–203.

PART III

Dealing with and Preventing Campus Violence: Laws, Policies, Procedures, and Training Programs for Students and Employees

Chapter 9

Laws Affecting Postsecondary Institutions' Efforts to Prevent, Respond to, and Recover from Acts of Violence on Campus

Linda Gordon Howard

While [Seung Hui] Cho was a student at Virginia Tech, his professors, fellow students, campus police, the Office of Judicial Affairs, the Care Team [established to intervene with troubled students], and the Cook Counseling Center all had dealings with him that raised questions about his mental stability. There is no evidence that Cho's parents were ever told of these contacts, and they say they were unaware of his problems at school. Most significantly, there is no evidence that Cho's parents, his suitemates, and their parents were ever informed that he had been temporarily detained, put through a commitment hearing for involuntary admission, and found to be a danger to himself. Efforts to share this information was impeded by laws about privacy of information, according to several university officials and the campus police.
Report of the Review Panel Presented to Governor Kaine, Commonwealth of Virginia, August 2007

Since 1999, mass shootings on high school and university campuses have shocked and disturbed the nation. The tragic deaths of 32 students and faculty and the injuries of 17 others at Virginia Tech University on April 16, 2007, brought new attention to educational insitutions' efforts to prevent campus violence. Virginia Governor Timothy Kaine and President George W. Bush commissioned reports to determine what happened, to conclude what lessons could be learned from the murders, and to make recommendations as to how future tragedies might be prevented and addressed. One key finding emerged from both reports. There is widespread confusion and misunderstanding among educators, mental health providers, and others about what information they can share about students. The confusion stems from misinterpretations and misapplications of the privacy laws that govern when student information may be shared and when it may not be shared.

The reports concluded that Virginia Tech officials misinterpreted federal privacy laws and believed that they were prohibited from sharing information about the troubled student who did the shootings, in circumstances where they could have shared information. As a result, no single official at Virginia Tech had the full picture that could have emerged from this student's interactions with his fellow students, his suitemates, his teachers, the university counseling center, the university police department, an outpatient psychiatric center, and the judge who conducted a commitment proceeding.

There is a question as to whether sharing the information that was not shared would have made any real difference. There is doubt among mental health practitioners as to whether it is possible to predict violent behavior. In addition, it is not possible to know whether officials and health care providers would have acted if they had the information or whether they would have acted promptly or effectively if they had acted. In any event, university officials require access to critical information if they are to prevent, respond to, and restore the community environment in the aftermath of disruptive, violent incidents on campus. Discharging that responsibility requires concerted action on the part of many individuals and the sharing of information where it is appropriate and allowed by law.

Typically, when institutions seek to comply with the law, they are concerned with the actions the law requires them to take or prohibits them from taking. Institutions are left uncertain when certain privacy laws allow them to disclose information and records about a student under certain circumstances and to certain people, but do not require them to disclose the information. For the most part, the provisions addressed in this chapter also *allow* the disclosure of information under certain circumstances. Whether to disclose or not to disclose is left to the discretion of the institution.

Sharing of student information by educational institutions will tend to be the subject of institutional policy or individual decisions by individual officials. Being aware of the law is only the start. Training is required for officials to understand the possible scope of institutional policies, the range of their individual discretion, and the possible actions that individual officials can take. Institutions must establish policies that direct how they will exercise the discretion the law grants them. Individuals must consider whether they will act where the law permits them to act.

Information sharing also affects the institution's recovery from a violent campus event. Recovery includes identifying victims and their families, informing the campus community about what happened and why it happened, and communicating efforts to prevent it from happening again. Having access to the facts and being fully aware of the institution's ability to disclose them to those immediately affected, officials, investigating authorities, review panels, the public, and the media, supports the institution's ability to recover with grace, compassion, and speed.

Information sharing is not the only legal arena that institutions must consider as they create and implement policies regarding potential and actual violent incidents on campus. They must also address whether guns, explosives, and other dangerous materials will be allowed on campus, whether they can deny admission to, suspend, or expel students who pose a potential or actual risk. Finally, there are many laws, including laws that prohibit hazing, violent crimes, sexual offenses, and other activities, of which institutions need to be aware.

This is not intended to be, nor can it be, an exhaustive treatment of all such laws. Because of the lack of understanding about the effect of privacy laws at educational institutions around the country, and because of the central role that information sharing plays in the institution's ability to recognize and respond to risks, this chapter focuses heavily on laws that regulate the disclosure of student records and information.

Institutions are advised to get specific guidance from the Office of Civil Rights of the United States Department of Education, their state's attorney general, and their institutional counsel about this and other laws mentioned in this chapter.

This chapter addresses three categories of laws:

- Privacy laws and other laws affecting the disclosure of information about students.
- Laws that affect an institution's ability to prohibit certain kinds of activities on campus, including the institution's ability to ban guns on campus.
- Laws that affect the admission, suspension, expulsion, and discipline of troubled students.

PRIVACY LAWS AFFECTING THE DISCLOSURE AND SHARING OF INFORMATION ABOUT POSTSECONDARY STUDENTS

Federal Laws Governing the Disclosure of Student Records

The Family Education Rights and Privacy Act of 1974 (FERPA). The Family Education Rights and Privacy Act of 1974 (commonly known as ''FERPA'') and regulations issued by the Secretary of Education are the major authorities governing the privacy of student information held by educational institutions. FERPA requires postsecondary institutions to ask a student for written consent before disclosing a student's personally identifiable information contained in educational records. For students in elementary and secondary school who are under the age of 18, the written consent must come from the student's parents. Postsecondary institutions must also withhold personally identifiable information from even the student's parents, unless the student gives written consent to the disclosure.

There are a number of circumstances under which FERPA allows colleges and universities to disclose information about a student *without* the student's written consent. Each of these exceptions and exemptions can assist institutional officials to share information and to act when campus safety requires action.

- Observations may be disclosed. FERPA restricts the institution's disclosure of educational *records*. FERPA does not apply to information that is not contained in educational records, such as observations of teachers, students, officials, or anyone else. For example, if a teacher observes a student acting in a disruptive or disturbing way in the classroom or anywhere else, nothing prohibits the teacher from calling the student's parents and informing them of the behavior. Likewise, if a student expresses concern to a university official about another student's unusual behavior, the university official may call the student's parents or the security office and share the observation.

- Educational records may be disclosed to parents under certain circumstances. An exception to FERPA allows educational institutions to share information with parents if:

  a. The student is a dependent for income tax purposes.

  b. A health or safety emergency involves their son or daughter.

  c. The student is under age 21 and has violated any law or school policy concerning the use or possession of alcohol or a controlled substance.

- Educational records may be disclosed to certain officials in a health or safety emergency. An exception to FERPA allows the institution to share educational records with appropriate officials in a health or safety emergency, while the emergency exists.

- Educational records may be shared with officials who have a legitimate educational interest. This exception to FERPA requires the institution to determine what officials, such as counselors, college or university police, have a legitimate educational interest and to designate them as such officially, allowing education records to be shared with them.

- Disciplinary records may be disclosed under certain circumstances. An exception to FERPA allows the institution to disclose the final results of a disciplinary proceeding against the alleged perpetrator to the victim of violent crime or nonviolent sex offense. In addition, the institution can

disclose to anyone—not only to the victim—the final results of a disciplinary proceeding when it determines that student is an alleged perpetrator
of a violent crime or non-forcible sex offense, and with respect to the allegation, the student has committed a violation of the school's rules or policies.

• An exception to FERPA says educational records may be disclosed to
  another institution to which a student transfers or seeks to transfer. Institutions that are considering admitting a student can obtain all records
  maintained by the student's current institution.

• Law enforcement records may be disclosed. FERPA does not cover
  records maintained by the "law enforcement unit" of the institution.
  Records of requests for assistance, responses, investigations, and deten-
  tions may be disclosed. The institution would have to declare the appropriate office or department to be a "law enforcement unit" and maintain
  law enforcement unit records separate from educational records.

Health Insurance Portability and Accountability Act of 1996 (HIPAA). HIPAA
is a federal privacy law that was passed in response to a concern for
electronically shared health information. HIPAA requires that all health
providers maintain the confidentiality of patient health information
and limits when and to whom information can be shared. HIPAA does
not apply to records that are covered by FERPA. Health records maintained by educational institutions that also provide health care to students are deemed to be educational records and may be disclosed in
the same manner as educational records covered by FERPA. Health
records are also subject to the same exceptions and exemptions
described above that allow educational records to be disclosed.

There are some instances in which FERPA is not clear when health
treatment records may be disclosed. For example, it is unclear whether
an educational institution's health provider can disclose a student's
treatment records to an outside health provider who is treating the
same student. The Virginia Tech Review Panel recommended that the
Department of Education issue guidance clearing up these questions.

Student and Exchange Visitor Information System. FERPA allows educational institutions to cooperate with the Department of Homeland Security by providing requested information about international exchange
students.

Clery Act. The Clery Act (The Jeanne Clery Disclosure of Campus Security Policy and Campus Crime Statistics Act) requires postsecondary
institutions to provide timely warnings of crimes that represent a threat
to the safety of students or employees. It also requires institutions to
make public their security policies and to collect, report, and dissemi-
nate campus crime statistics to the campus community and the Department of Education on an annual basis.

Campus Sexual Assault Victims' Bill of Rights. This bill of rights (2002) requires that colleges and universities that participate in federal student aid programs afford sexual assault victims certain rights. In addition to other rights, survivors must be informed of their options to notify law enforcement.

Campus Sex Crimes Prevention Act. This act (2000) provides for the collection of and disclosure of information about convicted, registered sex offenders either enrolled in or employed at postsecondary institutions.

State and Local Laws Governing Disclosure of Student Records and Information

Once the institution has determined that federal law allows certain information or records to be disclosed, it must look to see whether state law prohibits, or even requires, the disclosure. For example, Virginia's Freedom of Information law requires campus police departments to keep basic information about crimes open to the public (Va. Code 23–232.2 2(B)). Virginia law also requires health providers to disclose certain information, such as evidence of child abuse or neglect.

The nature and complexity of federal and state laws governing privacy of student information and records requires colleges and universities to look beyond compliance and to develop policies and action plans that allow the responsible officials to exercise the discretion the law allows. Every institution should examine its current policies to determine whether they are based on erroneous interpretations of privacy laws and make needed changes. The lives of their students and employees depend on institutions using all their available resources and authority.

LAWS THAT AFFECT THE INSTITUTION'S ABILITY OR OBLIGATION TO PROHIBIT CERTAIN KINDS OF ACTIVITIES ON CAMPUS

Campus Gun Bans

State law generally grants to the governing boards of colleges and universities the power to impose whatever rules or regulations they deem to be necessary to fulfill their responsibilities, unless the rules and regulations violate a specific provision of state law. Where that power is not specifically granted by state law, courts have generally accepted that colleges and universities have broad authority to regulate activities on their campuses. This authority has been generally accepted to include the power to ban concealed weapons on campus, unless state law includes specific limitations on that power.

A 2003 survey showed that 80% of the postsecondary institutions surveyed imposed some form of ban of firearms on campus. Most institutions banned guns on campus altogether. Others made specific exceptions. The exceptions fall into five categories: guns that are stored in a campus storage facility, guns that are authorized for specific purposes (such as ROTC, rifle team, or a specific educational activity), guns that are registered with the institutions, or guns for which students have received prior authorization.

Many states have enacted laws that allow most people to carry a concealed firearm on their person. Most of these laws include an exception for college and university campuses, but some do not. Recently, campus gun bans have been challenged as violating state law. In 2006, the Utah Supreme Court ruled that the University of Utah's 30-year-old prohibition against guns on campus violated a 2004 amendment to the state's constitution that allows people to carry concealed weapons. In 2003, a student at a Virginia college who had a permit to carry a concealed weapon disputed the college's campus gun ban, arguing that the ban violated state law. After the Virginia attorney general intervened, a college official granted the student permission to carry his gun on campus.

Campus gun bans are the subject of intense controversy in many communities. Opponents argue that campus gun bans not only violate state law, but that they also disarm students and employees who could otherwise defend themselves. Proponents argue that guns on campus increase the likelihood of violence. Some institutions persist in enforcing their gun bans, despite state law. At the time of the Virginia Tech massacre, Virginia Tech had declared its campus to be a "gun-free zone."

Institutions should consult state law to determine their authority to regulate firearms on campus and any specific restrictions on that authority.

Criminal Laws

Stalking. Federal law and the laws of all 50 states and the District of Columbia prohibit stalking in some form. Educational institutions have the authority to call the police when students violate these laws, to establish campus stalking policies, and to discipline students who violate campus stalking policies.

Hazing. Forty-three of 50 states have enacted laws that address hazing, most of which impose criminal penalties and/or heavy fines. Hazing can sometimes be violent and lead to injury and death. Universities typically have the authority to prohibit hazing.

LAWS THAT AFFECT THE ADMISSION, SUSPENSION, EXPULSION, AND DISCIPLINE OF TROUBLED STUDENTS

Among the preventive measures colleges and universities can take to avoid and respond to campus violence are to deny admission to certain students and suspend or terminate students for violating laws or campus policies. A number of laws apply to these actions. Key among these is Section 504 of the Rehabilitation Act of 1973, which prohibits discrimination on the basis of disability in educational programs and institutions that receive federal funding. In addition, the Americans with Disabilities Act contains provisions similar to those of Section 504 and applies to public colleges and universities regardless of whether they receive federal funding.

Admissions

Institutions may not deny admission to an applicant based on the student's disability, which includes a diagnosis or history of mental disorder or disability. If the student is qualified to participate in the educational program and can perform with the support of a reasonable accommodation, the institution must provide the reasonable accommodation.

Section 504 requires institutions to make assessments and to draw distinctions that most institutions are typically not equipped to make. Assessing a physically disabled student's ability to perform in an educational program is relatively straightforward. It is either necessary to see, to hear, to walk, or to use one's hands to perform adequately in the essential aspects of an academic program, or it is not. The student can either perform the required tasks or the student cannot.

Most institutions no longer rely on initial and outdated impressions of physically disabled applicants. Institutions now routinely conduct disciplined analyses of what is required to participate in educational programs, consider students' abilities as indicated by medical professionals, and make fair assessments of students' abilities to perform in their programs, and design a workable reasonable accommodation. We have moved far from the days when college officials believed (and some argued), for example, that performing in law school required a student to be able to stand and reach books on a high library shelf.

What is a reasonable accommodation is sometimes a much more difficult question. The expense of the accommodation, the degree to which it would alter essential aspects of the educational program, and the availability of the needed equipment or personnel all have to be taken into account. Even so, physical disabilities are relatively simple to assess.

Assessing a mentally disabled person's qualification is a fundamentally different matter. Educational institutions treat mental disabilities very differently, whether because of a lack of understanding them, lack of experience, lack of training, fear of being associated with the mentally disabled, or the social stigma and negative assumptions that attach to mental disability.

Section 504 is of limited usefulness as part of a program to prevent campus violence.

First, Section 504 requires an assessment of the student's ability to perform in a program. This law was designed to assure access to programs and activities for qualified disabled applicants. It was neither designed to be, nor intended to be, a means of protecting the community from possible violent acts.

Second, Section 504 contemplates that the student will disclose the disability to the institution and request an accommodation that will allow him to perform with the disability. Relying upon the troubled student to seek assistance that will allow him to function in the campus environment has obvious drawbacks. Students may not seek assistance for a variety of reasons, including the belief (whether actual or imagined) that they can function well without assistance, the fear of being stigmatized or ridiculed, or poor judgment.

Third, decisions made on the basis of mental disability, unlike decisions made on the basis of physical disability, are predictive in nature. That is, it is necessary to ask, given the nature of the disability, "How will this person function in the future?" (If the person is displaying symptoms in the moment, the decision becomes easier.) In cases where the institution proposes to act to prevent some future violent behavior, some argue that it is not possible to predict the future actions of mentally disturbed persons. There is a real debate as to whether concerns and fears about the possibility of violence from mentally disturbed persons are based in fact or myth. Despite the tragic events at Virginia Tech, many people with mental disabilities function quite well in society with the appropriate support, and that many acts of campus violence have been committed by mentally healthy, though misguided individuals.

Fourth, even if it is possible to predict the future actions of mentally disturbed persons (or mentally healthy persons, for that matter), there are legitimate questions as to whether college admissions officials should be in the business of making that prediction and whether they are competent to do so.

Fifth, even if we determine that college admissions officers can and should assess the likelihood that an applicant may erupt into a violent episode, those officers are hampered by a lack of the information they would need to make sound decisions. College admissions officers have only the file in front of them to deal with. They can ask questions of students either pre- or post-admission, but they must rely on information provided by the student or the student's family that may be inaccurate, incomplete, or simply not provided at all. Observations from the applicant's teachers and counselors are usually not offered, medical records are protected by information privacy laws, and criminal records of minors have typically been sealed or expunged. At best, institutions must base these critical decisions on woefully inadequate information.

Governor Kaine said, in a statement issued upon the release of the Virginia Tech Review Panel Report, "There was an intense awareness within Cho's family, counselors, and the Fairfax County [Va.] school system that he was troubled, had contemplated violence, and needed some fairly intense services to be able to function. The system surrounded him with those services, and he succeeded. However, despite serious concerns about whether he would be able to continue to succeed at Virginia Tech, the university never received any information about his challenges and the strategies that had enabled him to succeed up to that point in his life."

Discipline

While Section 504 prohibits discrimination on the basis of a disability, it does not prohibit decisions made on the basis of behavior. Applicants who have engaged in dangerous, criminal, or disruptive behavior before admission can be denied admission on the theory that past behavior is a fairly reliable indicator of future behavior. Current students who engage in such behavior may be disciplined, suspended, or expelled. Applicants and students who engage in suspicious or troubling behavior that may not be dangerous, criminal, or disruptive can be offered supportive services. For example, two students complained that Cho, the Virginia Tech gunman, had engaged in stalking behavior. Stalking is a crime.

Without making any reference to a student's mental condition or disability, the institution may remove a student from the campus who is found to have engaged in threatening or criminal behavior. However, in instances where students have taken the overt action of attempting suicide and institutions have placed them on immediate mandatory leave, the Office of Civil Rights of the U.S. Department of Education (OCR) has found the institutions to be in violation of Section 504. Students have sued institutions and won substantial settlements after being suspended and barred from their dormitory rooms following suicide attempts. On the other hand, courts in two cases in West Virginia and Massachusetts held college administrators and an institution liable because they failed to intervene to prevent the deaths of students who had previously attempted suicide. The courts said that the officials owed a duty to protect the students who were known suicide risks.

These legal developments have left college officials concerned that they will be held legally responsible for a student's death no matter what they do. Some institutions avoid collecting personally identifiable records on student suicide attempts to escape any claim that they knew the students were in danger.

In any event, if students cannot function within the campus society or perform academically because of mental instability, institutions must find effective ways to provide the needed support or to remove these students from the campus.

Institutions tend toward blanket policies. In the case of troubled students, neither a blanket "do nothing" policy, nor a blanket mandatory leave policy will satisfy the law. The better course of action is to make individual decisions based on the individual circumstances and the best medical and academic interests of the student. Students are entitled to due process and an opportunity to be heard before they are suspended or expelled.

Managing this responsibility at a large university with tens of thousands of students is an enormous challenge. I sit on the board of trustees of a small college with about 1,100 students, and it is still a challenge to know what is going on with all the students and to respond appropriately and effectively when a student's ability to function mentally or emotionally has been compromised. We have found that what works is encouraging students and faculty to share information with the responsible administrators, having early warning systems in place, and responding swiftly and persistently to individuals' different needs.

Whatever program of preparedness, intervention, and response an institution designs, the critical elements of the program will be well-functioning relationships among all college offices and officials, recognition of warning signals, a protocol of coordinated effective action, and individual responses to different circumstances. All of these elements depend on the broadest possible lawful sharing of available information.

The applicable laws do not offer a road map to institutions for an effective program of campus safety or security. Indeed, many laws appear to operate as roadblocks to an institution's ability to prevent campus violence.

The laws discussed here and their associated regulations can be described as an uncoordinated patchwork of dictates that were never designed to support institutions to respond to the risk of campus violence. Nearly all of the laws discussed here need review and change. Until the needed changes are made, institutions will still have to make decisions every day that affect the lives of the people on their campuses. While doing so, they must balance individual rights of privacy and personal freedom against the new threats to the community of incomprehensible, sometimes unpredictable and terrible violence.

REFERENCES AND RESOURCES

Cases

Schieszler v. Ferrum College, 233 F.Supp. 2d 796 (W.D.Va. 2002)
Shin v. Massachusetts Institute of Technology, et al., No. 02–0403 (Superior Ct. Mass, June 27, 2005)

Reports

Report of the Review Panel—Mass Shootings at Virginia Tech, April 16, 2007, Report of the Review Panel Presented to Governor Kaine, Commonwealth of Virginia, Chapter V. Information Privacy Laws Report, August 2007. http://www.governor.virginia.gov/TempContent/tech PanelReport

Report to the President on Issues Raised by the Virginia Tech Tragedy, submitted by Secretary of Michael O. Leavitt, Department of Health and Human Services, Secretary Margaret Spelling, Department of Education, Attorney General Alberto Gonzales, Department of Justice (June 13, 2007) www.hhs.gov/vtreport.html

Virginia Tech Internal Review

- Security Infrastructure Working Group Report, Presidential Working Paper, August 17, 2007
- Information and Communications Working Group Report, Presidential Working Paper August 17, 2007
- Interface Working Group Report, Presidential Working Paper, August 17, 2007

Laws

Family Educational Rights and Privacy Act 20 U.S.C. § 1232g (2000)
Outline available: http://www.ed.gov/policy/gen/guid/fpco/ferpa/index.html
Health Insurance Portability and Accountability Act. 42 U.S.C. § 1320(d) (2000)
    Statute & Fact Sheets Available: http://www.hhs.gov/ocr/hipaa/
Jeanne Clery Disclosure of Campus Security Policy & Campus Crime Statistics Act (1990). Part of Campus Security Act, Pub. L. No. 101–452, 1990 (Codified as amended at 18 U.S.C. § 1092(f)). Handbook available: http://www.ed.gov/admins/lead/safety/campus.html
Americans with Disabilities Act. Pub. L. No. 101–336, 1990 (Codified as 42 U.S.C. 2101)
Section 504 of the Rehabilitation Act of 1973, Pub. L. No. 93–112, 1973 (Codified as 29 U.S.C. §794)
Violent Crime Control and Law Enforcement Act of 1994 (Federal stalking law), Public Law 103–322, Title IV, Subtitle B, Chapter 110A, 2261–2266 and National Defense Authorization Act for Fiscal Year 1997, Public Law 104–201, § 1069, (codified as 18 U.S.C. 2261, 2261A, and 2262)
Virginia Health Records Privacy Act (VHRPA)
Virginia Freedom of Information Act (VFOIA) Chapter 37 Va. Code Title 2.2

Studies

National Survey of College Campus Gun Possession Policies (The Alliance for Justice) Spring 2003

Government Agencies and Government Resources

Resources on School Violence including articles and studies may be found at the Federal Bureau of Investigation's Web site, www.fbi.gov.

Additional information and guidance on FERPA may be found at the Family Policy Compliance Office's Web site at: www.ed.gov/policy/gen/guid/fpco/index.html

Additional information about HIPAA requirements may be found at www.hhs.gov

Organizations

Association of Governing Boards www.agb.org

International Association of Campus Law Enforcement Administrators (ICLEA)

National Association of Attorneys General www.naag.org

National Association of College and University Attorneys www.nacua.org

National Center for Victims of Crime, Legislative Database

Chapter 10

Sexual Harassment Education

Amy J. Ramson

While people tend to think of sexual harassment as a problem unique to the business environment, this illegal behavior is also frequently found on our country's college and university campuses. Most research has found that 20–40% of female college students, employees, and professors report some type of sexual harassment (Kelley & Parsons, 2000). According to a recent study conducted in spring 2005 commissioned by the American Association of University Women Educational Foundation, nearly two-thirds of college students experience sexual harassment at some point during their college experience (Hill & Silva, 2006). The study examined a survey that was nationally representative of both male and female college students.

Harassment can have a disastrous impact on the finances, personal lives, and physical and emotional health of staff, faculty, and students. In addition, studies have found that professional consequences vary from lowered morale to decreased job satisfaction to job loss (Dziech & Weiner, 1990; Fitzgerald et al., 1988; Welsh, 1999). Educational institutions had been protected from legal responsibility for sexual harassment until recently, when two landmark Supreme Court decisions rendered in the late 1990s instituted a new standard of liability for educational institutions where students are harassed. This change in law, in addition to the evidence by recent legal imperatives that training is an important prevention tool, has prompted educational institutions to focus more strongly on this issue and to improve their anti-harassment training.

This chapter will explore the educational program designed by Hostos Community College, a program that uses a multimedia approach paired with discussion to educate its academic community about sexual harassment. This blended technique has been successful in both meeting the prevention requirements under current law and the needs associated with the complex environment of a metropolitan college.

Part of the City University of New York (CUNY) system, Hostos Community College (Hostos) is a two-year college. CUNY, the largest urban university campus in the country, serves more than 400,000 students per year and is composed of 19 colleges, including senior, community, and technical colleges, a graduate center, a law school, and a medical program. A majority of the student population and a large percentage of the staff and faculty at CUNY are minorities, primarily African American and Latino. Of all the CUNY colleges, Hostos's student population, distinctively, has the highest number of minorities and women.

SETTING THE STAGE

The United States' most significant federal civil rights legislation, the Civil Rights Act of 1964, provides the details of sexual harassment law. The Civil Rights Act's Title VII outlaws sex discrimination by employers. A 1986 Supreme Court case, *Meritor Savings Bank FSB v. Vinson,* found that sex discrimination also takes the form of sexual harassment. Title IX of the Education Amendments of 1972 extends these same rights to students and other educational community members at public and private academic institutions and training programs that receive federal funding. Academic institutions must follow both employment and academic laws regarding sexual harassment because their communities are comprised of both employees and students.

The United States Equal Employment Opportunity Commission (EEOC) enforces Title VII of the Civil Rights Act of 1964, by issuing regulations, handling workplace sexual harassment cases, and providing legal advice. The EEOC published regulations in 1980 that were amended in 1990, putting into action Title VII of the Civil Rights Act, entitled *Guidelines on Discrimination Because of Sex.* The workplace rules in this act (29 C.F.R. section 1604.11) specify two types of conduct that amount to sexual harassment. Each type includes an abuse of power in which physical, verbal, or non-verbal behavior relating to sex is unwanted by the victim.

The first type of sexual harassment is *quid pro quo,* which is a Latin term meaning "this for that." Quid pro quo harassment generally comes about when a person with more authority wields power over a subordinate or person of less power by making sexual advances, requesting sexual favors, or engaging in other behavior of a sexual nature. With quid pro quo sexual harassment, submission to or rejection of the conduct is made a condition of employment or academic evaluation. Quid pro quo harassment might occur when a professor persistently asks a student out to dinner even after the student has said no.

The second, and more common, type of sexual harassment is hostile environment sexual harassment. This occurs between people with equal power. The conduct excessively compromises the victim's work or academic performance or creates a threatening, antagonistic, or offensive work or academic environment. This behavior could happen when a group of faculty members regularly jokes about women's anatomy during meetings, making a female professor refrain from attending those meetings even though they are mandatory.

Until recently, educational institutions were protected from sexual harassment lawsuits. In 1998 and 1999, the Supreme Court handed down two landmark decisions that raised the possibility for schools to be monetarily liable in private actions where a student is sexually harassed by a teacher or another student: *Gebser v. Lago Vista Independent School District* (1998) and *Davis v. Monroe County Board of Education* (1999). Both cases require that a number of narrow conditions be met in order for legal responsibility to be assigned, most importantly that the school knew of the conduct and showed a deliberate indifference to it. Although these conditions make for a formidable burden of proof, making it difficult for most plaintiffs to win, the possibility now exists for future sexual harassment suits against schools.

MEETING A LEGAL RESPONSIBILITY

Since identifying sexual harassment as a legal action distinct from sex discrimination in *Meritor* (1986), legal sources have supported prevention as the best tool for eliminating sexual harassment. In the beginning, seminal Supreme Court decisions and federal agency regulations interpreting the Civil Rights Act of 1964 and The Education Amendments of 1972 promoted the creation of internal policies and complaint mechanisms as prevention tools. More recently, both the EEOC and the U.S. Department of Education's Office for Civil Rights (OCR) have issued guidelines that push academic institutions to add the training of personnel and students to their prevention plans.

The EEOC's 1980 *Guidelines on Discrimination Because of Sex*, which were amended in 1990, stated the best method for eradicating sexual harassment is prevention. In addition, the rules required that this prevention includes informing employees of their right to raise the issue as well as creating methods to sensitize employees.

In 1998, the Supreme Court handed down two landmark decisions that made employers indirectly liable for sexual harassment committed by a supervisor where an actual action has been taken against the victim: *Faragher v. City of Boca Raton* (1998) and *Burlington Industries Inc. v. Ellerth* (1998). The decisions gave a specific incentive to employers to prevent sexual harassment. The decisions said that where harassment has happened but no actual action has been taken, an employer could present an affirmative defense to legal responsibility if it has demonstrated reasonable care to prevent and stop the sexually harassing conduct.

In 1999, the EEOC issued *Enforcement Guidance: Vicarious Employer Liability for Unlawful Harassment by Supervisors,* which gives employers the specific elements of reasonable care to prevent sexual harassment and emphasizes that employers should be aggressive in their prevention of sexual harassment in order to avoid liability. The guidance states the importance of training employees as a prevention tool in addition to implementing a policy and procedures for complaints. The EEOC indicates that the employer's responsibility to practice reasonable care to prevent sexual harassment includes providing "training to all employees to ensure that they understand their rights and responsibilities" (EEOC, 1999, Policy and Complaint Procedures section, para. 2). Responsibility to exercise due care also includes making sure that supervisors recognize their responsibilities under the policy and complaint procedures, an understanding which regular training could achieve.

The guidelines specify the elements of supervisor training: "Such training should explain the types of conduct that violate the employer's anti-harassment policy; the seriousness of the policy; the responsibilities of supervisors and managers when they learn of alleged harassment; and the prohibition against retaliation" (EEOC, 1999, Other Preventive and Corrective Measures section, para. 4). Although the EEOC's guidelines have no power over the courts and do not have the strength of regulations, the courts use them when rendering decisions.

The OCR, which executes Title IX of the Education Amendments of 1972 by publishing regulations, dealing with claims of academic sexual harassment, and offering legal guidance, also has indicated that training is key to the prevention of sexual harassment. According to the OCR's (2001) *Sexual Harassment Guidance: Harassment of Students by School Employees, Other Students, or Third Parties,* institutions should provide training of administrators, teachers, and staff as well as age-appropriate classroom information so that individuals can recognize sexual harassment behaviors and know how to respond to them.

ENACTING AND COMMUNICATING NECESSARY POLICIES

Kelley and Parsons (2000) suggest that sexual harassment continues at educational institutions because training has not kept up with the enactment of policies. Riggs, Murrell, and Cutting (1993) recommend three key steps for institutional leaders to take to prevent sexual harassment at academic institutions. They indicate these steps are derived from a decade of experience at institutions that have focused on this problem. The steps include drafting a policy, developing an accessible grievance procedure, and continuously educating the entire academic community about sexual harassment behaviors and their potential for harm.

Enacting policies that identify the behaviors that are considered to be sexually harassing and implementing procedures that provide the steps for making a complaint are the essential foundation for prevention. However, it appears the policies and procedures must be communicated in such a way that all persons in the academic community comprehend them, as well as recognize their part in the prevention of sexual harassment. In a study at the University of Massachusetts at Amherst, Williams, Lam, and Shively (1992) explained that the decrease in complaints in the years immediately following the enactment of a college policy against sexual harassment was a result of both the existence of a policy and its being effectively conveyed through publication on campus and intense educational efforts. Thus, if policies and procedures are not effectively broadcast to the academic community, they will not have the desired result.

EXAMINING POLICIES AND PROCEDURES AT HOSTOS

In 1995, the CUNY Board of Trustees announced its original *Policy Against Sexual Harassment* (Policy) and *Procedures for Implementation of The City University's Policy Against Sexual Harassment* (Procedures), which are applicable to employees (faculty and staff) and students on all of the CUNY campuses. In January 2005, both of these documents were modified. Because of the intricacies associated with this new legal area, the policy and procedures are necessarily complicated and dense. However, the basic message of the Policy is clearly stated:

> It is a violation of University policy for any member of the University community to engage in sexual harassment or to retaliate against any member of the University community for raising an allegation of sexual harassment, for filing a complaint alleging sexual harassment, or for participating in any proceeding to determine if sexual harassment has occurred. (CUNY, 2005a, Section A, Prohibited Conduct section, para. 1)

The 1995 Procedures demanded that each CUNY college president install a Sexual Harassment Panel to deal with complaints and a Sexual Harassment Education Committee (Education Committee) to constantly educate the whole college community by disseminating printed material, including the Policy and Procedures, and holding workshops. The goal of the campus Education Committee is proactively to prevent the illegal behavior. The Procedures also stipulate that a panel be set up on each campus to deal with the complaints made against college community members: faculty, staff, or student. The panel's job is to try to resolve complaints informally. If no informal solution is possible, a formal investigation begins and the panel coordinator details its discoveries to the college president. The president is responsible for the final resolution, including disciplinary and corrective action.

The Policy and Procedures that were revised in January 2005 eliminated the panel but set up a coordinator and deputy coordinators with the same roles. The Sexual Harassment Awareness and Intake Committee (Awareness and Intake Committee) has replaced the Education Committee and is charged with the additional task of handling complaint intake as well as educating the entire college community. The goal of providing an informal complaint resolution mechanism remains, so no resort to the court system is necessary.

Although the committees recently have been reorganized, the educational component will proceed under the new format.

ADDRESSING THE CHALLENGES AT HOSTOS

The Education Committee at Hostos identified several obstacles to its mission. As mentioned previously, sexual harassment is surprisingly common on university campuses. Women are more likely than men to become targets of sexual harassment on a campus (Fitzgerald et al., 1988). The Hostos community is especially at risk because it is primarily female and minority. As noted earlier, several studies discovered that 20–30% of women students report being sexually harassed (Dziech & Weiner, 1990). Fitzgerald et al. (1998) concluded that as many as 76% of female students encounter sexual harassment by professors. Paludi and Barickman (1998) have reported that women who are economically disadvantaged and of color are more vulnerable to sexual harassment. Dziech and Weiner (1990) theorize that minority women are at higher risk to sexual harassment because of their lack of self-confidence or because men find these women to be mysterious. Because most of Hostos's demographics fall in these categories, they may be at the highest risk for sexual harassment.

Many Hostos community members are first-generation Hispanic Americans and even recent immigrants, so the Education Committee also needed to break down cultural barriers. In the predominant cultures at Hostos, many of the behaviors that are illegal under U.S. sexual harassment laws are normal and acceptable to both men and women. In a survey of undergraduate men and women, Kalof, Eby, Matheson, and Kroska (2001) found that while students report personally experiencing behavior that is defined as sexual harassment, the students' cultural or ethnic background may cause them not to label such behavior as sexual harassment.

Finally, it is important to note that anti-sexual harassment training at CUNY is not required, so any program the Education Committee developed needed to be interesting as well as relevant and informative to entice people to participate. Holzl (1997) suggests that any method that instructors use must engage the students to learn the material and then retain what they have learned.

In addition, in keeping with the limited resources of public educational institutions, the Education Committee was given a limited budget, which has to cover faculty and staff effort, any materials needed for workshops, and the distribution of written materials.

LEADING BY EXAMPLE

While the Education Committee is required to educate the entire Hostos community, it decided to focus initially on training faculty and top administration leaders, with a secondary emphasis on administration employees. With a minimal budget and time constraints, the Education Committee felt that a college's leaders should set the standards for the whole community. It is hoped that training will, at the very least, dissuade these leaders from committing harassment themselves as well as demonstrate to the community that the college's leadership supports the effort to eliminate harassment. More ambitiously, the Education Committee hopes that college leaders will put a stop to harassment in their classrooms and offices and teach their coworkers and students about the limits of acceptable behavior. As a result, the program was first tailored to this group, along with those of administration employees.

In regards to college policy and laws, the president, vice president, and academic deans are the supervisors of both the faculty and administrative employees. In the academic world, the administration (top tier of staff) is responsible and accountable for implementing governmental laws, policies, and procedures for the whole campus. As discussed, the Sexual Harassment Panel (and now the Awareness and Intake Committee) is responsible for dealing with complaints, and the college president is in charge of the final resolution of complaints. So the college's top officials were trained first, along with the members of the Sexual Harassment Panel and those of the Education Committee.

A college's faculty members are also its leaders and role models, setting the tone for appropriate behavior, both in the classroom and beyond. It was hoped that an intervention at the faculty level would have far-reaching results, in terms of both preventing harassment and demonstrating the priority of sexual harassment at Hostos. So the training of this group began promptly after the education of top administration officials.

University faculty members are sexually harassed more frequently than might be expected. In a small study of college faculty by McKinney (1990), 9% of men and 20% of women reported harassment by a colleague; 19% of men and 22% of women reported being harassed by a student. In a study by Dey, Korn, and Sax (1996), 15.1% of faculty women and 3.1% of faculty men reported harassment. A study by Kelley and Parsons (2000) found that 22% of female faculty reported sexual harassment. Fitzgerald et al. (1988) indicate that 50% of women faculty have encountered sexual harassment.

This harassment has a sizeable effect on how female faculty members perceive their colleges or universities. A study by Dey et al. (1996) states that "harassed women are much more likely to hold negative views of institutional norms toward respect for others, fairness toward women, and manner in which the campus administration operates" (p. 166). Welsh (1999) examined many studies of the job consequences of sexual harassment, which found consequences such as lowered morale, absenteeism, decreased job satisfaction, and damaged interpersonal work relationships.

GETTING THE BEST RESULTS WITH A MULTIMEDIA APPROACH

Numerous studies have shown that people learn best when they process material actively (Nunn, 1996). At the least technological level, it appears that students master material better when they articulate that material before a group (Gullette, 1992; Nunn, 1996). In addition, multimedia presentations show particular promise for improving the effectiveness of education and training. At the simplest level, it is evident that students prefer multimedia presentations to more traditional teaching (Nowaczyk et al., 1998).

The program designed by the Hostos Education Committee merges an online course with 90 minutes of material broken into a three-part workshop, which serves as the focal point of the program. The program includes a video, a Microsoft PowerPoint presentation, and a discussion period.

The workshop is intended for a small group of participants, ranging from five to 25 faculty or staff that is grouped by office, department, and unit, or a group that represents a cross-section of faculty. Students usually are grouped by classes, as government or club leaders, by work-study status, or as tutors. A study by McCormick, Adams-Bohley, Peterson, and Gaeddert (1989) suggests using this approach, saying that "small workshops, directed at natural groups of students and faculty, may be a more effective approach for teaching people about sexual harassment and convincing them they can and should do something about it" (p. 22).

The program is very flexible. It can be adjusted to meet the needs of a specific constituency, group size, or setting, or to serve a specific need, such as addressing an incident which involves a faculty member who already has undergone training. Adjustments include removing portions of the workshop, lengthening the discussion period, and offering the online course instead of the workshop for a second round of training.

The program begins with an online course. Individualized online learning is a rising trend in education, especially in community colleges (Ausburn, 2002). It is helpful not only for academic but also for administrative instruction. An individualized approach is a great benefit to teaching a diverse population that varies tremendously in many factors that affect learning, such as age, skills, and reading comprehension (Ausburn, 2002). Computer-based instruction assists individualized learning by providing lessons in a module format that the learner can access in the order, place, and time he or she chooses, as well as at his or her own pace (Ausburn, 2002). This format also gives the learner privacy—a critical element, given the delicate nature of the materials.

The online course, entitled "Preventing Sexual Harassment," is a customized program created by New Media Learning (2005). The course generally is viewed prior to the workshop to introduce the learner to the Policy and Procedures, sexual harassment behaviors, and consequences of these behaviors. It begins with the CUNY policy statement by the CUNY chancellor and CUNY's Policy and Procedures. (This section is customized by New Media Learning to each college or university's policy statement.) The program then displays a drop-down menu of content areas, which includes the crucial portions of the sexual harassment law, the most recent case law in the area, pretest quizzes, and exercises. After reviewing these materials, learners take a test to assess their mastery of the subject. Once the test is passed, the program creates a printable certificate. Both faculty members and administrative-administration employees can request to have this certificate included in their personnel files.

While online teaching has many benefits, it may not be best for learners who lack proper reading comprehension skills (Ausburn, 2002). Although the mastery test can indicate competence, this test can be passed with just a scanning of the material. In disagreement with Wellbrock (1999), who suggests that computer-based training alone is enough to train successfully in the area of sexual harassment, the Education Committee sees the online course as a supplement to the workshop rather than a complete tool in itself. The Education Committee believes that learning should be interactive and that the nuances and intricacies of sexual harassment require both a role-playing and a discussion component in the training.

The workshop also includes a video, which runs about 20 minutes, that depicts various scenarios in which students and faculty interact and cross personal boundaries. These visual examples can dramatize the often subtle manifestations of sexual harassment in ways other mediums cannot clearly show (Waldrop, 1994). Videos may also make the training more interesting to students (Nowaczyk, Santos, & Patton, 1998).

Choosing a suitable video can be difficult. Many of the videos available show actors and situations that are unrealistic and inappropriate. Most videos currently available present exclusively academic or exclusively workplace environments, which does not accurately suit both constituencies of an academic setting. As a result, the Education

Committee uses an academic environment video for faculty, students, and staff members who interact frequently with students but a work-place environment video for staff members who maintain and police the campus and rarely have student interaction.

The scenes portray all three possible parties in a sexual harassment situation—the harasser, the victim, and the third-party victim—as well as both genders as harassers and victims. The videos also demonstrate equal and unequal power situations, such as where the student is the harasser and the faculty member is the victim.

The video is then followed by a PowerPoint presentation. While the online course presents mostly federal law and provides a great amount of detail, the PowerPoint presentation, which lasts between 30 and 40 minutes, reviews the most critical aspects of the CUNY Policy and Procedures as well as federal law in an engaging, to-the-point format. Holzl (1997) suggests that using PowerPoint presentations can accomplish a teacher's dual mission of engaging students' attention and helping the student retain the material. Mayer, Bove, Bryman, Mars, and Tapangco (1996) found that a brief summary of complex material is more effective for retention of material than the lengthy version of the material. In addition, they found that a multimedia summary that marries visuals with limited text is the most effective for retaining the information.

The discussion period following the video and PowerPoint presentation is an essential element of the education program. Discussions usually last between 20 and 30 minutes. Participation is not required, but discussions frequently become quite animated. Workshop presenters explain the material by referring to the video, by giving real-life examples, or by answering the participants' questions, which usually focus on specific situations and unclear areas in university policy or in the law.

Undoubtedly, any discussion of sexual harassment must be handled with sensitivity and respect. Workshop presenters (Education Committee members) are trained for three days using the model of social identity development (Goodman, 1995). Training guarantees that the presenters themselves have a clear and nuanced understanding of the complicated materials so that they can be comfortable and understandable in their presentations. Presenters also are educated about the handling of sensitive topics and the making of thoughtful decisions. As Goodman observes, culturally based misunderstandings often cause problems to grow (Kochman, 1981; Tannen, 1990; Goodman, 1995). To prevent this, the presenters learn to identify and share an awareness of cultural differences in communication. Finally—and most importantly—the presenters are trained to empower workshop members to respond to sexual harassment appropriately and effectively. Participants are also empowered by simply being allowed to talk. As Gullette (1992) discovered, "the event of speaking as an agent prefigures acting as an agent-exerting power in the outside world" (para. 8).

REACHING OUT TO STUDENTS

The last constituency of the academic community to be trained initially was students. It is important to note that the Education Committee's mission is to educate all three constituencies of the academic community on a continuous basis. Students have been consistently the most challenging to reach owing to their quantity and the competing demands for their attention, including course work, employment, and family obligations. During the fall 2007 semester, there were approximately 5,353 students enrolled at Hostos. In the planning stages of the program, the Education Committee determined that various venues should be targeted in order to reach all categories of students, including full-time and part-time and day and night students. The Committee further realized that the format and length of the full workshop should be modified to both appeal to the student population and to meet the time constraints imposed by the various settings, which include class sessions, college-wide presentations, leadership retreats, etc.

Hauck and Leslie (2006) set forth guidelines for training teenagers and college-aged individuals in sexual harassment. They suggest that training be interactive, inclusive of popular culture, and to ensure understanding, be extremely clear. In addition, training must communicate channels for reporting incidents and should engender trust so students feel comfortable reporting incidents.

Contemporaneous with educating staff employees, the Committee began to educate students who were employed on the campus as tutors and work-study students in small groups of three to 10 students. The arrangement of chairs in a circle and the small number of participants lent an air of intimacy to the workshop. After showing a video and giving a short talk on the CUNY Policy and Procedures, the Committee initiated discussion. Where possible, they discussed real-life problems that had occurred in the students' work environment such as the case in which a student had reported to the area director that her tutor was sitting regularly in such close proximity to her that she felt uncomfortable during the sessions.

This abbreviated program has become a model for use with small groups of students, such as student-workers or student leaders. It became evident to the committee that the intimate nature of the model engenders an environment of trust, where students feel secure to reveal or ask questions about potential sexual harassment situations that they are currently or previously experienced in a work, school, or other context, including their community.

For visits to particular classes, where the atmosphere and seating arrangement is more formal, the modified program is more didactic. The program consists of showing the academic video or PowerPoint presentation and initiating discussion. The discussion generally focuses on clarification of the Policy and complaint Procedures and its unfamiliar components, such as the inclusion of same-sex sexual harassment in the definition of sexual harassment.

The Education Committee crafted a distinct program for a large setting, such as a college-wide forum, student assembly, or meeting of several campus clubs. After the introduction of the Education Committee members to the participants, the brochure and other printed information are disseminated and a presentation of short scenarios follows. Hostos students role-play students, faculty, and staff in five or six situations. The scenarios depict ambiguous behavior, such as one student repeatedly asking a fellow student out on a date. The scenes also explore unfamiliar components of the law, such as a third-party claim of sexual harassment against two students being romantic in a lounge/ study area or sexual harassment. A question and answer period about the scenarios proceeds, which leads to a discussion with the audience.

The Education Committee regularly coordinates its presentation with the Department of Public Safety because of their shared responsibility for the safety of the college community. The Department of Public Safety is the first responder in a number of cases of sexual harassment and the three highest ranked director/officers of the Department have been appointed to the Education Committee. The Department of Public Safety presentation following the Education Committee's scenarios and discussion takes the form of a quiz on sexual assault, which the audience is asked to take. The answers are reviewed as a group and a discussion of certain questions results. The Education Committee has found that these programs are successful in helping students properly identify sexual harassment behaviors and emboldening them to make complaints. Students often approach Education Committee members after these programs with concerns and complaints.

In order to infuse popular culture into the training, the Education Committee devised an activity based upon a popular game show. In conjunction with career week, students are invited to participate in a customized version of *Who Wants to Be a Millionaire?* in which student volunteers are asked questions about sexual harassment on campus and at work, and questions about disabilities and affirmative action. The format of the game show is loosely followed and students are given an audience lifeline to aid in answering questions and obtaining prizes for correct answers.

In order to reach out to students and professors through course curriculum, the Education Committee devised a 10-page document containing a myriad of resources with hot links, which was disseminated through the college distribution list, the list of teaching faculty, and the student distribution list (see Exhibit 10-1 at the end of this chapter). The resources include online resources for classroom integration: scenarios/case study descriptions; questionnaires; role-play exercises and "Myths and

Realities of Sexual Harassment"; online journals/articles/documents; college and organization Web sites on sexual harassment; compilations of video lists from other campuses; film titles; and curriculum kits/guides.

In addition, the Education Committee works to encourage both faculty and student knowledge on sexual harassment and its effects. To further this end, the Education Committee developed a sexual harassment subject guide, which is found on the library Web site and provides a list of sexual harassment materials available in the Hostos library, and links to laws, tutorials, and the online course, "Preventing Sexual Harassment,"

> The Education Committee took the show on the road and visited all the academic departments to introduce the resource document and subject guide to the faculty. The mission of the visits was to educate the faculty about the importance of integrating the issue into their curriculum. Since the Education Committee anticipated some resistance, the resource document contains a variety of rationales for said inclusion. These include: everyone in the college community deserves respectful treatment; the prevalence of sexual harassment; Hostos students fall into the groups most vulnerable to sexual harassment; the impact of sexual harassment on students' careers and attitudes towards school; the impact of education; and the legal imperatives.

CONTINUING EDUCATIONAL EFFORTS

In addition to its formal training, the Education Committee distributes the CUNY Policy and Procedures and various supplemental materials through electronic mail and in hard copy several times during each semester. These materials include a summary of the policy and procedures, an overview of relevant legal statutes and cases, and significant and interesting articles in legal and non-legal publications. Plus, the Education Committee has strategically placed campus posters with visuals that reinforce the anti-sexual harassment message and has created brochures for quick reading.

The Policy and Procedures also are printed in the college catalogue and in a Hostos student publication of laws and policies entitled the *Annual Student Right to Know Report*. Students receive these materials plus the brochure at registration, which ensures that every community member has received the Policy and Procedures and knows that sexual harassment is illegal and not condoned on campus.

In addition to distributing the established Policy and Procedures, the Education Committee works to encourage both faculty and student knowledge on sexual harassment and its effects. To further this study, the Education Committee has developed a sexual harassment subject guide and provided a list of sexual harassment materials available in the Hostos library.

DELIVERING EMPOWERMENT AND EDUCATION

Colleges and universities have many obvious incentives for bolstering their educational efforts in the area of sexual harassment: the need to protect vulnerable community members, the ability to provide a risk-free atmosphere where people want to work and study, and the consideration of school finances given the looming potential for monetary liability. Studies and important scholarship indicated that training is a key tool for preventing sexual harassment. Legal imperatives also show that prevention, which includes training of the academic community, may protect against liability.

Hostos's multimedia program appears to meet the objectives of providing legal information and of commanding the attention of its audience in a cost-effective and exciting manner. By combining an online course with a multimedia workshop, the program presents a large amount of sensitive and complicated material in a way that allows a very diverse group of learners to absorb information at their own pace, using their own cognitive styles. The animated discussions that occur during the discussion period show that the education program has begun to engage its participants into rethinking how their behaviors can hurt others.

The mission of this training program is to prevent sexual harassment at Hostos. This is a lofty goal, given the extent of the problem and the ignorance of this issue in society. It also is still too soon to see if the program has achieved its mission. However, it is clear that the program has caused Hostos community members to deal with this complex and problematic issue, and in a way that suits the college's education, budget, and legal parameters. It allows for both privacy and interactive discussion. It is cost-effective, adaptable, and relatively simple to expand. It can be documented, allowing the college to show that it has met its legal responsibility to provide training.

To date, the Education Committee has effectively educated each department on campus. Through its constant efforts, each faculty member is educated at least once during a three-year period. And while protecting the institution from legal recourse, the program also provides that which Hostos is dedicated to delivering: empowerment and education. The community's consciousness has been raised, and faculty members and other campus leaders are mindful of this issue.

REFERENCES

Ausburn, L. J. (2002). The freedom versus focus dilemma in a customized self-directed learning environment: A comparison of the perceptions of adult and younger students. *Community College Journal of Research and Practice, 26*, 225–235.

Burlington Industries Inc. v. Ellerth, 524 U.S. 742 (1998).

City University of New York (1995a). *Policy against sexual harassment*. New York.

City University of New York (1995b). *Procedures for implementation of the City University's policy against sexual harassment*. New York.

City University of New York (2005a). *Policy against sexual harassment* (Rev. ed.). New York.

City University of New York (2005b). *Procedures for implementation of the City University's policy against sexual harassment* (Rev. ed.). New York.

Civil Rights Act of 1964. Pub. L. No. 88–352, section 78 Stat. 241 (1964).

Davis v. Monroe County Board of Education, 526 U.S. 629 (1999).

Deloney, L. A., & Graham, C. J. (2003). Wit: Using drama to teach first-year medical students about empathy and compassion. *Teaching and Learning in Medicine, 15*(4), 247–251.

Dey, E. L., Korn, J. S., & Sax, L. J. (1996). Betrayed by the academy: The sexual harassment of women college faculty. *The Journal of Higher Education, 67*(2), 149–173.

Dziech, B. W., & Weiner, L. (1990). *The lecherous professor*. Urbana: University of Illinois Press.

Equal Employment Opportunity Commission (1999). *Enforcement guidance: Vicarious employer liability for unlawful harassment by supervisors*. Retrieved January 6, 2005, from the LawMemo.com database.

Faragher v. City of Boca Raton, 524 U.S. 775 (1998).

Fitzgerald, L. F., Shulman, S. L., Bailey, N., Richards, M., Swecker, J., & Gold, Y., et al. (1988). The incidence and dimensions of sexual harassment in academia and the workplace. *Journal of Vocational Behavior, 32*, 152–175.

Gebser v. Lago Vista Independent School District, 524 U.S. 274 (1998).

Goodman, D. J. (1995). Difficult dialogues. *College Teaching, 43*(2), 47–53. Retrieved January 20, 2004, from the Academic Search Premier database.

Guidelines on Discrimination Because of Sex for the U.S. Equal Employment Opportunity Commission, 29 C.F.R. section 1604.11 (1980, 1990).

Gullette, M. M. (1992). Leading discussion in a lecture course. *Change, 24*(2), 32–40. Retrieved January 20, 2004, from the Academic Search Premier database.

Hauck, W. E., & Leslie, C. A. (2006). Is your training reaching the most vulnerable? *T+D, 60*(2), 15. Retrieved September 5, 2007, from the Academic Search Premier database.

Hill, C., & Silva, E. (2006). Drawing the line: Sexual harassment on campus. AAUW Educational Foundation. Retrieved October 1, 2007, from www.aauw.org/dtl

Holzl, J. (1997). Twelve tips for effective PowerPoint presentations for the technologically challenged. *Medical Teacher, 19*(3), 175–180. Retrieved January 6, 2005, from the Academic Search Premier database.

Kalof, L., Eby, K. K., Matheson, J. L., & Kroska, R. J. (2001). The influence of race and gender on student self-reports of sexual harassment by college professors. *Gender and Society, 15*(2), 282–302. Retrieved March 4, 2005, from the JSTOR database.

Kelley, M. L., & Parsons, B. (2000). Sexual harassment in the 1990s: A university-wide survey of female faculty, administrators, staff, and students. *The Journal of Higher Education, 71*(5), 548–568.

Kochman, T. (1981). *Black and white styles in conflict.* Chicago: University of Chicago Press.

Mayer, R. E., Bove, W., Bryman, A., Mars, R., & Tapangco, L. (1996). When less is more: Meaningful learning from visual and verbal summaries of science textbook lessons. *Journal of Educational Psychology, 88*(1), 64–73. Retrieved January 13, 2005, from the PsycARTICLES database.

McCormick, N., Adams-Bohley, S., Peterson, S., & Gaeddert, W. (1989). Sexual harassment of students at a small college. *Initiatives, 52*(3), 15–23.

McKinney, K. (1990). Sexual harassment of university faculty by colleagues and students. *Sex Roles, 23*(7, 8), 421–438.

Meritor Savings Bank FSB v. Vinson, 477 U.S. 57 (1986).

New Media Learning (2005). Preventing sexual harassment [online course]. Retrieved February 24, 2006, from http://www.cuny.edu/sexualharassment

Nowaczyk, R. H., Santos, L. T., & Patton, C. (1998). Student perception of multimedia in the undergraduate classroom. *International Journal of Instructional Media, 25*(4), 367–382.

Nunn, C. E. (1996). Discussion in the college classroom. *The Journal of Higher Education, 67*(3), 243–266.

Office for Civil Rights (2001). Sexual harassment guidance: Harassment of students by school employees, other students, or third parties. Retrieved January 13, 2005, from http://www.ed.gov/offices/OCR/archives/shguide/

Paludi, M. A., & Barickman, R. B. (1998). *Sexual harassment, work, and education: A resource manual for prevention* (2nd ed.). Albany, NY: State University of New York Press.

Riggs, R. O., Murrell, P. H., & Cutting J. C. (1993). Sexual harassment in higher education: From conflict to community (ASHE-ERIC Report No. 2). Washington, DC: George Washington University School of Education. (ERIC Reproduction Services No. ED364134)

Tannen, D. (1990). *You just don't understand: Women and men in conversation.* New York: William Morrow.

Waldrop, J. (1994). Sex, laws, and video training. *American Demographics, 16*(4), 14–16. Retrieved July 10, 2002, from the Academic Search Premier database.

Wellbrock, R. D. (1999). Sexual harassment policies and computer-based training. *Community College Review, 26*(4), 61–69. Retrieved January 20, 2004, from the Academic Search Premier database.

Welsh, S. (1999). Gender and sexual harassment. *Annual Review of Sociology, 25*(1), 169–191. Retrieved on October 31, 2007, from the Academic Search Premier database.

Williams, E. A., Lam, J. A., & Shively, M. (1992). The impact of a university policy on the sexual harassment of female students. *The Journal of Higher Education, 63*(1), 50–64. Retrieved March 4, 2005, from the JSTOR database.

Exhibit 10-1

Sexual Harassment Awareness and Intake Committee 2006
Integration of the topic of sexual harassment into the curriculum
Why should you integrate sexual harassment into your curriculum?

1. Everyone in the college community deserves respectful treatment.
2. Prevalence of sexual harassment
   - According to a current AAUW survey of 10 campuses (Jan. 2006), approximately 62% of students reported having been sexually harassed. An article in *The Chronicle of Higher Education* about this survey can be found at the following Web site: http://www.aauw.org/research/upload/DTLFinal.pdf
   - Dziech and Weiner in *The Lecherous Professor: Sexual Harassment on Campus* conclude that certain groups are the most vulnerable to sexual harassment such as women of color, women working full-time or part-time, etc., or at the poverty level. Our students fall into the most vulnerable groups of students.
3. Impact of sexual harassment
   - Sexual harassment interferes with the ability of students to function in the academic environment and impacts their attitude toward the college.
4. Impact of education
   - Education will help students in the workforce.
   - Students will less likely engage in SH behavior themselves and will be better prepared to cope with SH if it occurs. See article entitled "Inappropriate patient behavior tough on nurses: Sexual harassment a widespread problem, health officials say" found at Web site: http://www.msnbc.msn.com/id/10484939/from/RL.2/.
5. Legal imperatives
   - The Civil Rights Act of 1964 (Title VII) and the Education Amendments of 1972 (Title IX) are the federal statutes that govern SH at colleges.
   - The CUNY Policy Against Sexual Harassment and the CUNY Procedures to Implement the Policy. Sexual harassment is not tolerated on CUNY campuses. The Hostos library Web site http://www.hostos.cuny.edu/library/HHCL_New_Web/REF_RES_readyFRAMES.htm is the Reference and Research Guides site. From this site, one needs to click on the link Pathfinders (Subject Guides). Once this site is open, it is possible to find the link entitled Sexual Harassment containing the afore-mentioned information.
   - Two recent Supreme Court decisions have held that schools may be monetarily liable for teacher to student or student to student SH where conditions exist (*Gebser v. Lago Vista Independent School District* (1998) and *Davis v. Monroe County Board of Education*)

Continued

Exhibit 10-1 Continued

Integrate Sexual Harassment Into the Curriculum
Rationale for prevention strategies
    Preventive education strategies such as using training videos, readings, workshops, group discussions, etc. have been documented to effectively help the student identify SH behavior. See article "Educational Strategies on College Student's Identification of Sexual Harassment" by Birdeau, Somers, and Lenihan appearing in *Education*, March 2005 at the following Web site: http://www.findarticles.com/p/articles/mi_qa3673/is_200504/ai_n13633256.
Strategies

1. Role-playing by students
2. Readings
3. Videos
4. Group discussions
5. Online courses/tutorials

Resources
I. Hostos Library Web Site SH Subject Guide (with active links) compiled by Prof. Rhonda Johnson, HCC library. The library's Reference and Research Guides Web site at http://www.hostos.cuny.edu/library/HHCL_New_Web/REF_RES_readyFRAMES.htm provides access to the page with the listings of the subject guides, like the following:

1. Policies, laws, documents: Federal laws, NY State law, NY City law, CUNY Policy Against Sexual Harassment found at above subject guide.
2. Online courses/tutorials: the CUNY online course and the NYS employee online course "Preventing Sexual Harassment"–CUNY online course (1 hour 30 minutes).

    We strongly recommend that all students, faculty, and staff take the CUNY online course. At the conclusion of the course, a test can be administered and a certificate awarded. This certificate can be put in one's personnel file and can be useful for students to put on their curriculum vitae and attach.

3. Book titles in the Hostos library collection on SH. Access as described earlier can be gained by going to the library's Web site "Research and Reference Guides" located at: http://www.hostos.cuny.edu/library/HHCL_New_Web/REF_RES_readyFRAMES.htm

II. List of online resources for classroom integration: SH scenarios/case study descriptions/questionnaires/role-play exercises/"Myths and Realities of SH":

- http://www.de2.psu.edu/harassment/cases/school.html describes cases occurring in academic settings. Copyright protected but useful as starting points to develop your own descriptions.
- http://www.state.mn.us/ebranch/dhr/sex_harass_over.html from Minnesota.
- Dept. of Human Rights provides several case histories of SH in both the academic and workplace setting.

- http://www.meq.gouv.qc.ca/cond-fem/publications/21-0003a.pdf from the Dept. of Education in Quebec, Canada, allows access to their brochure "Sexual Harassment in Schools: Activity Guide for Students." The brochure, which includes exercises such as questionnaires and Myths and Realities of SH, is designed for secondary school students but can be adapted for our older students.
- http://www.sexualharass.com/sexual-harassment/case-studies.htm describes four case studies. It also provides links to an online quiz on SH and several other pages relating to SH.
- https://www.healthforums.com/library/1,1258,article~9704,00.html#calc Button provides an interactive online quiz on SH.
- http://www.campus-adr.org/cmher/ReportResources/Edition1_2/Roleplay1_ 2.html from North Central College in Illinois has a role-play exercise relating to SH. N.B. It is copyright protected but can be used as a starting point to develop your own.
- http://www.mith2.umd.edu/WomensStudies/GenderIssues/SexualHarassment/ UMDManual/prevention from the U. of Maryland has a "manual" on SH prevention. The manual includes questionnaires, section on myths associated with SH, and discussions regarding the roles of supervisors, employees, and student workers at the university setting.
- http://www.mith2.umd.edu/WomensStudies/GenderIssues/SexualHarassment/ provides links to various SH-related resources such as the N.Y. State Task Force report from 1993 and excerpts of the 1991 transcripts of Prof. A. Hill and Judge C. Thomas before the Committee of the Judiciary regarding the nomination of Judge C. Thomas to the Supreme Court.
- http://www.northeastern.edu/csss/mvp/mvphome.html provides information on The Mentors in Violence Prevention (MVP) Playbook and Trainer's Guide and MVP program. The Guide is commercially available for a small fee. The site also links to a sample SH-related scenario.
- http://womenscenter.virginia.edu/sdvs/harassment/myths.htm from the Women's Center at the U. of Virginia offers an interesting discussion regarding "Myths and Realities regarding SH."
- http://www.copsite.com/corbin/lesson072001.html from the company Corbin & Associates, Inc. contains a "Lesson Plan of the Month" for high school students. The lesson plan, which can be adapted for our students, includes a questionnaire and a role-play exercise. N.B. To see its contents, one needs to access via the cached text.
- http://www.sexualharassmentsupport.org/stories.html from the organization Sexual Harassment Support describes SH-related stories and experiences.
- http://www.sexualharassmentsupport.org/stories.html from the organization Sexual Harassment Support also provides links to other sites discussing AAUW reports, etc. and a site on Myths about SH.

Continued

Exhibit 10-1 Continued

III. Online journals/articles/documents on SH:

URL	Name	Description
http://www.sexual harassmentjournal.com/	*The Sexual Harassment Journal*	Contains summaries of actual cases and links to local publications re. the cited cases
http://web31.epnet. com/selectdb.asp? tb=1&_ug=sid+ 8BA4FBDA%2D3360% 2D4F6C%2D85C7% 2DAE86942C9999% 40sessionmgr4+0E01 &ft=1	*The Chronicle of Higher Education*	Obtain SH-related articles in HTML format via EBSCO full-text database (Academic Search Premier)
http://www.aauw.org/ research/dtl.cfm	"Drawing the Line: SH on Campus" (2006) (Amer. Assn. Univ. Women [AAUW])	Discusses the survey and provides links to other AAUW sites on SH issues, e.g., "Harassment-Free Hallways"
http://www.bernices andler.com/	Bernice Sandler: Godmother of Title IX	This site connects to other Sandler sites with links to full-text articles by Ms. Sandler (Senior Scholar in Residence of the Women's Research and Educ. Inst.)
http://www.aaup.org/ issues/womeninHE/ sexhar.htm	Amer. Assn. Univ. Prof. (AAUP) site on Sexual Harassment	Comments on SH and has links to AAUP publications on SH
http://www2.edc.org/ womensequity/resource/ alldigest/index.htm	Women's Educational Equity Act Resource Center at the Education Dept. Center	Includes links to two digests on SH and Title IX (with several articles each)
http://www.now.org/ issues/harass/	National Organization for Women on topic of SH	Has links to several articles on SH and related topics
http://www.washrag. org/	Home page of "The Wash Rag" from The Women Against Sexual Harassment (W.A.S.H.)	The home page links to the W.A.S.H. publication, *The Wash Rag*, which collects information on SH
http://www.ed.gov/ offices/OCR/archives/ Harassment/index.html	Protecting Students from Harassment and Hate Crime: A Guide for Schools	Contains archived U.S. government document and relevant appendices with other resources

URL	Name	Description
http://www.sex harassmentattorneys.com/ Sexual-Harassment-News. htm	Sexual Harassment and Employment Law News	Compilation of links to a number of newspaper articles on SH related issues
http://www.icasa.org/ uploads/updated_nan_ stein_fall_2001_article. pdf	"Gender Violence in Elementary and Secondary Schools" by Nan Stein (2001)	Article focuses on peer to peer SH in lower grades but information can be extrapolated for college level students
http://www.firstamend-mentcenter.org/speech/ pubcollege/topic.aspx? topic=sexual_harassment	"Sexual Harassment" by David L. Hudson, First Amendment Center	This article by research attorney David L. Hudson relates to free speech on public campuses (i.e., academic freedom with respect to SH concerns)
http://www2.gsu.edu/ ~lawppw/lawand. papers/harass.html	"Gender Harassment on the Internet" by V. Bell and D. de la Rue, Georgia State Univ.	This is an 18 page article that also provides links to legal documents, etc.
http://www.nasbe.org/ Educational_issues/ Reports/Sexual%20 Harrass.pdf	"Sexual Harassment in School: What It Is What to Do: A Policy Guide" issued by the National Association of State Boards of Education.	The policy guide written by Kathryn Wells Murdock and David Kysilko explores several issues that are relevant to our population even though it is more geared for secondary schools, etc.
http://www.thesport journal.org/2003Journal/ Vol6-No3/abusive.asp	"Student-Athletes Perception of Abusive Behaviors By Coaches in NCAA Division II Tennis Programs" by Vicki-Lynn Martin, D.S.M.	This article which appeared in *The Sports Journal*, 6(3), 2003 deals with SH in the university setting concerning athletes and their coaches.
Title IX documents: A) http://www.ed.gov/ offices/OCR/archives/ pdf/shguide.pdf B) http://www.usdoj.gov/ crt/cor/coord/titleix.htm	"Revised Sexual Harassment Guidelines: Harassment of Students by School Employees, Other Students or Third Parties" / Title IX (2001) Coordination & Review Section, Civil Rights Division, Dept. of Justice	Archived document issued by the U.S. Dept. of Education Office of Civil Rights. Government site that contains information on Title IX as well as links to various Title IX-related documents

Continued

Exhibit 10-1 Continued

URL	Name	Description
http://www.hamfish.org/pub/nan.pdf	"Incidence & Implications of SH and Sexual Violence in K-12 Schools" by Nan Stein, Ed.D. (1999)	112-page document written by Dr. Stein for the Hamilton Fish National Inst. On School & Community Violence via George Washington Univ. and the U.S. Dept. of Justice
http://www.findarticles.com/p/articles/mi_qa3617/is_199909/ai_n8871539	"Peer Sexual Harassment Outlawed" by Michael D. Simpson (Sept. 1999)	Article published by NEA Today re. the U.S. Supreme Court case *Davis v. Monroe County Board of Education*
http://www.wendymcelroy.com/articles/shi.html	"Understanding Sexual Harassment" by W. McElroy	Article on SH appeared in *Liberty* magazine Dec. 2001
http://www.ncwge.org/TitleIXReport.pdf	"Report Card on Gender Equity" written by NCWGE	The National Coalition for Women and Girls in Education (NCWGE) issued this statement on gender equity issues on the 25th anniversary of the enactment of Title IX. It includes a section on SH.
http://www.sexualharassmentsupport.org/SilTreat.html	"The Silent Treatment" by Naomi Wolf	Article about Ms. Wolf's experiences with SH at Yale Univ.

IV. Organization/college Web sites on the issue of SH:

- http://www1.ncaa.org/membership/ed_outreach/gender_equity/resource_materials/index.html, which is entitled "Gender Equity/Title IX" (from the National Collegiate Athletic Association) has a wide variety of online resources including links to videos on the subject of Title IX and SH as well as articles, case law discussions, etc.
- http://www.wcwonline.org/zerotol/index.html, entitled "Zero Tolerance," relates to a SH prevention project directed by Dr. Nan Stein of The Wellesley Centers for Women. The Web site provides links to other projects funded by this organization such as "SH and Schools."
- http://www.mun.ca/sexualharassment/Classroom.html is assembled by Ms. Yetman, the SH prevention officer of the Memorial Univ. of Newfoundland. Her statements at this site regard "Safe and Inclusive Classrooms," "Gender Awareness," and "Warming the Chilly Climate." This includes a discussion of sex discrimination and sex stereotyping in the classroom. This campus has

a Peer Theatre Group composed of students dedicated to enlightening the community.

- http://www.cpn.org/tools/manuals/Work/harassment.html is a brochure entitled *The Busy Citizen's Discussion Guide: Sexual Harassment* provided by the Civic Practices Network (CPN). It has useful commentary on the topic of SH.
- http://www.edc.org/hec/pubs/factsheets/fact_sheet1.html from the U.S. Dept of Education's Higher Education Center for Alcohol and Other Drug Abuse and Violence Prevention contains relevant sections on SH and stalking. It also provides useful references.

V. Film titles that deal with SH:
Documentaries

> *The 20th Century with Mike Wallace: Sexual Harassment and Pornography* (1996)
> *The Workplace Hustle: A Film About Sexual Harassment of Working Women* (1980) (moderated by Ed Asner)
> *Out of Work* (1997)
> Fiction and dramatized accounts based on fact
> *North Country* (2005)
> *Disclosure* (1994)
> *Brilliant Lies* (1993)
> *Anchorman* (2004)
> *Nine to Five* (1980)
> *I Can Make You Love Me* (TV movie) (1993)
> *Wildrose* (1984) (N.B. related to situation described in movie *North Country*)
> *Business as Usual* (1987)
> *Hostile Advances: The Kerry Ellison Story* (1996)
> *Oleanna* (1994—and if interested see related Web site contains commentary on *Oleanna* by Prof. J.K. Curry re. SH in the Academy presented at Third Annual Conference on Intellectual Freedom, 4/97)
> *Pretty Persuasion* (2005)

VI. Videos — *at present most of the videos mentioned below are not available from college library*

> A. Possessed by the SHAIC committee and available upon request:
> "Sexual Harassment in the Academic Workplace," from Capstone Communication
> B. Compilation of video lists from other college campuses and other assorted listings/ads:
> http://web.uccs.edu/affirm/policy_files/sexual%20harrass/resources.htm contains a list from U. of Colorado Affirmative Action Office.
> http://www.uwplatt.edu/pers/videos.htm contains a list from the U. of Wisconsin-Platteville Affirmative Action Office. N.B. Videos #12 - #19 are on SH; however, a few of them may be locally produced and not commercially available.

Continued

Exhibit 10-1 Continued

> http://www.niu.edu/aadr/videos.htm contains a list from Northern Illinois U. Affirmative Action Film Collection. N.B. Several of the videos relate to SH at the college setting.
>
> http://www.gov.sk.ca/shrc/vid9.htm contains a list from the Saskatchewan Human Rights Commission.
>
> http://www.evergreen.edu/equalop/film/view.asp?id=68 contains a description re. Sexual Harassment: Building Awareness on Campus by Jean Kilbourne, Media Education Fdn.
>
> http://www.sexualharass.com/ contains an ad for the video "Sex, Power and the Workplace."
>
> http://www.coastalhr.com/sexual_harassment.html has a list of videos on SH and other tools from Coastal.
>
> http://newtraditionsmissouri.org/resources/resources/?subj=Gender+Equity&subset=Sex+Discrimination%2C+Stereotyping is from New Traditions: Gender Equity Resources (a Missouri educator resource) and contains a long list of videos as well as book titles.
>
> http://www.pbs.org/ttc/prev_shows.html is a Web site regarding the PBS all-women news analysis series "To The Contrary." From this site, one can search year by year (from 1998–present) for episodes devoted at least in part to the topic of SH. For example, episode No. 826 (1999) is entitled "Student-on-Student Sexual Harassment" and includes an interview with Ms. Verna L. Williams (at that time with the National Women's Law Center).

VII. Curriculum kits/guides that include videos:

> http://www.grantsandfunding.com/libraries/grantmanage/sink/index.html, contains an ad from Thompson Publishing for the "Educator's Guide to Controlling Sexual Harassment." The guide includes sample questionnaires, examples of SH, etc. Purchase of the guide provides access to newsletters on the latest court rulings, etc.
>
> http://www.electrolab.ca/sexual_harassment_programs.htm describes videos and toolkits available through Electrolab. This site includes an ad for the video "Preventing Sexual Harassment: What Educators Need to Know Trainer's Toolkit." Additional information for this video can be found at http://www.coastal.com/coastalACB/showdetl.cfm?&DID=7&Product_ID= 7189

Chapter 11

Sample Policies and Procedures for Preventing and Dealing with Campus Violence

Michele A. Paludi
Carmen Paludi, Jr.
Maritza Santos

The following policies and procedures are intended to provide colleges and universities with suggestions for developing or modifying their resources on campus violence, including workplace violence. These resources are based in case law and scholarly research cited in the first part of this book. Human Resource Management Solutions (and its president, Michele Paludi) has used these policies in its consulting with campuses and workplaces.

We recommend that campus administrators adapt these policies and procedures to meet their unique needs, including a unionized faculty and/or staff. We advise campuses to have all of their policies and procedures reviewed by their legal counsel. Additional policies may be found in Paludi, Nydegger, and Paludi (2006).

Why include policies on discrimination, HIV/AIDS, substance abuse, or religious observance? Differences among individuals are often at the root of hate crimes. A hate crime is a crime which in whole or part is motivated by the offender's bias toward the victim's status. Hate crimes are intended to hurt and intimidate individuals because they are perceived to be different with respect to their race, color, religion, national origin, sexual orientation, sex, or disability. Furthermore, alcohol and other substance use/abuse very often are implicated in sexual assaults.

Some policies were adapted from Michele Paludi, Rudy Nydesser, and Carmen Paludi, *Understanding Workplace Violence: A Guide for Manager and Employees,* Copyright ©2006, Praeger Publishers. Reproduced with permission of Greenwood Publishing Group, Inc., Westport, CT.

SAMPLE POLICY ON HATE CRIMES

[Name of Campus] fosters a civil, open, and interactive community.

At [Name of Campus] we are committed to maintaining an environment free of discrimination and all forms of coercion that diminish the dignity of any member of the campus. It is the policy of [Name of Campus] not to discriminate against any individual on the basis of race, color, religion, national origin, sex, sexual orientation, marital status, age, disability, or veteran status in matters of recruitment or education/employment in accordance with civil rights legislation. [Name of Campus] has issued separate policies on discrimination and sexual harassment.

Definition of Hate Crime

A hate crime can be generally defined as a crime which in whole or part is motivated by the offender's bias toward the victim's status. Hate crimes are intended to hurt and intimidate individuals because they are perceived to be different with respect to their race, color, religion, national origin, sexual orientation, sex, or disability.

Legislation lists specific crimes that are identifiable as a hate crime, including murder, manslaughter, robbery, aggravated assault, burglary, motor vehicle theft, arson, forcible and non-forcible sex offenses, intimidation, destruction, damage or vandalism of property, and other crimes involving injury to any person or property in which the victim is intentionally selected because of their actual or perceived race, sex, religion, sexual orientation, ethnicity, or disability.

Definition of Bias-Motivated Incidents

When the behavior does not fall into one of the listed criminal categories identified above, hate offenses are referred to as bias-motivated incidents. These incidents may include cases of verbal slurs, etc. and be precursors to more serious hate-motivated violence.

Impact of Hate Crimes on Individuals

Research has identified that victims of hate crimes are vulnerable to subsequent attacks and feelings of alienation, helplessness, suspicion, and fear. Hate crimes affect the ability to learn and work at [Name of Campus] and depart from the standard for civility and respect.

Procedure for Dealing with Hate Crimes and Bias-Motivated Incidents

A student or employee of [Name of Campus] who is involved in or witnesses behavior that poses imminent danger should immediately contact the police. In situations that do not involve imminent danger or for advice on the appropriate course of action, the student or employee is to notify _____on campus.

The sanctions imposed for violations of these regulations include, but are not limited to, fines, restitution for damages, probation, suspension, expulsion, and termination from employment.

Visitors, vendors, and the families of students, faculty, administrators, and employees are expected to comply with the provisions of this policy. Noncompliant behavior leads to removal from the premises.

Guidance for identifying potential threatening or violent behavior and for the best ways to deal with incidents may be obtained from your dean or supervisor.

Remember: Hate crimes are against the law. Students and employees found to be involved in hate-crime-related incidents are subject to legal action. Hate crimes are also a violation of [Name of Campus]'s rules and regulations.

* * *

JEANNE CLERY DISCLOSURE OF CAMPUS SECURITY POLICY AND CAMPUS CRIME STATISTICS ACT

The Jeanne Clery Disclosure of Campus Security Policy and Campus Crime Statistics Act is the landmark federal legislation, originally referred to as the Campus Security Act, that requires college/university campuses in the United States to disclose information about crime on and around their campuses. This legislation is enforced by the United States Department of Education. According to this law:

> Schools must publish an annual report disclosing campus security policies and three years' worth of selected crime statistics;
> Schools must make timely warnings to the campus community about crimes that pose an ongoing threat to students and employees;
> Each institution with a police or security department must have a public crime log;
> The United States Department of Education centrally collects and disseminates the crime statistics;
> Campus sexual assault victims are assured of certain basic rights;
> Schools that fail to comply can be fined by the Department of Education.

[Name of Campus]'s Campus Safety Committee will provide upon request all campus crime statistics as reported to the United States

Department of Education, as well as the annual campus security report.

The campus security report includes: (1) the campus crime statistics for the most recent calendar year and the two preceding calendar years; (2) campus policies regarding procedures and facilities to report criminal actions on campus; (3) policies concerning the security of and access to campus facilities; (4) policies on campus law enforcement; (5) a description of campus programs to inform students, administrators, faculty, and employees about campus security procedures and practices and to encourage individuals to be responsible for their own security and the security of others; (6) campus crime prevention programs; (7) policy concerning the monitoring through the police of criminal activity at off-campus locations of student organizations officially recognized by the college; (8) policies on illegal drugs, alcohol, and underage drinking; (9) where information provided by the state on registered sex offenders may be obtained; and (10) policies on campus sexual assault programs aimed at the prevention of sex offenses and procedures to be followed when a sex offense occurs.

The campus crime statistics and the annual campus security report are available at the reference desk of the campus library and the following locations on campus: [insert locations].

This report is also available online at: [insert URL].

In accordance with the federal Campus Sex Crimes Prevention Act, a registered sex offender is now required to register the name and address of any college at which he or she is a student or employee.

* * *

SAMPLE POLICY PROHIBITING HAZING

[Name of Campus] prohibits hazing. From a legal perspective, hazing is a crime. From a student and employee's perspective, hazing damages the self-esteem of the targets of the hazing. From an organizational perspective, hazing degrades the values of the institution. From a work community perspective, hazing creates an environment of disrespect that contradicts the values of our institution. For all of these reasons, [Name of Campus] takes a strong position against any and all forms of hazing.

Definition of Hazing

Hazing means any act committed by a person, whether individually or in concert with others, against a student or employee in connection with being initiated into, affiliating with, holding office in, or maintaining membership in any organization that is affiliated with [Name of Campus]; and that is intended, or should reasonably be expected, to have the effect of humiliating, intimidating, or demeaning a student or employee or endangering the mental or physical health of a student or employee. Hazing also includes soliciting, directing, aiding, or otherwise participating actively or passively in such acts.

Such activities and situations include, but are not limited to: physical brutality; paddling in any form; forced consumption of food, alcohol, or other drugs; creation of excessive fatigue; required calisthenics; "kidnapping"; physical and psychological shock; engaging in public stunts; morally degrading or humiliating games and activities; activities that are not normally performed by the active membership; and any other activities that are not consistent with the policies of [Name of Campus].

Hazing occurs regardless of the consent or willingness of a person to participate in the activity. Hazing may occur on or off the [Name of Campus] property.

This policy is intended to be consistent with state law. The policy will be reviewed periodically and revised in light of legal developments.

Reporting Hazing

Students and employees are strongly encouraged to report hazing incidents.

To maximize safety, all reports of hazing should first be to the police. Administrators at [Name of Campus] who receive reports of hazing will refer such reports immediately to the police.

Since hazing may violate more than one policy of this institution, the same incident may be referred for resolution to [Name of Campus] under more than one category, e.g., discrimination, sexual harassment, or hate crimes. [Name of Campus] has issued policies and procedures on each of these issues.

Investigation of Hazing

Any allegations of hazing reported to [Name of Campus] will be investigated by a trained investigator.

Upon receipt of a written complaint, the investigator will ask the individual if there are any witnesses he or she would like to be interviewed. Individuals will complete a form providing names of witnesses as well as the issues to which the witnesses may address. Complainants will provide the investigator with a signed statement giving permission to contact these witnesses.

The investigator will immediately forward a copy of the complaint, along with a copy of this institution's Hazing Policy Statement and Procedures, to the individual complained against and request a meeting with this individual within three business days.

During the meeting with the respondent, the investigator will ask the individual if there are any witnesses that he or she would like to be interviewed.

Individuals will complete a form providing names of witnesses as well as the issues to which the witnesses may address. Complainants will provide the investigator with a signed statement giving permission to contact these witnesses.

Names or other identifying features of witnesses on behalf of the complainant and respondent will not be made known to the opposing party. This will help ensure participation by witnesses in the investigation.

The investigator will investigate all complaints of hazing expeditiously and professionally. To the maximum extent possible, the investigation will be completed within two weeks from the time the formal investigation is initiated.

The investigator will also maintain the information provided in the complaint and investigation process confidential. Parties to the complaint will be asked to sign a confidentiality form in which they state they will keep the complaint and complaint resolution confidential.

A safe environment will be set up for the complainant, respondent, and witnesses to discuss their perspectives without the fear of being ridiculed or judged.

No conclusions about the veracity of the complaint will be made until the investigation is completed. All documents presented by the parties to the complaint will be reviewed by the investigator. Documents include, but are not limited to: letters, photos, and notes.

Following the completion of an investigation, the investigator will make one of the following determinations:

- Sustain the Complaint: A finding of hazing has been made and recommendations for corrective action will be identified. Recommended corrective action may include an apology, written or oral reprimand, relief from specific duties, expulsion, suspension, or termination.
- Not Sustain the Complaint: A finding of no hazing has been made.
- Insufficient Information: Insufficient information exists on which to make a determination. The investigator will reinvestigate all parties named in the complaint.

Following any determination and recommendations for corrective action, the investigator will issue a written decision with findings to the President. The severity of the penalty for a hazing offense will be determined in proportion to the hazing activity. The President will correspond with the complainant and person complained against of the findings of the investigation and recommendations for corrective action. The President will make appropriate statements of apology to individuals involved in the complaint.

If employees are not satisfied with the attempts to resolve the complaint of hazing, they may seek resolution as described in the Collective Bargaining Agreement.

Any party to a complaint resolution may do so without fear of reprisal. The President can, in extreme cases, take whatever action is appropriate to protect the college community.

Each complaint against the same individual will be handled independently. Similarly, knowledge that the complainant has filed complaints against other individuals in the past will not enter into the investigative process. Such information may be taken in to account in determining sanctions for violation of the hazing policy.

Referrals for therapists and medical personnel for all individuals involved in an investigation will be made available upon request. [Name of Campus] will also support any victims of hazing if they want to speak to the local police about the possibility of pressing criminal charges.

* * *

SAMPLE POLICY ON DOMESTIC VIOLENCE AS A WORKPLACE CONCERN

Employees of [Name of Campus] must be able to work in an atmosphere of mutual respect and trust. As a place of work, [Name of Campus] should be free of violence and all forms of intimidation and exploitation. [Name of Campus] is concerned and committed to our employees' safety and health. The campus refuses to tolerate violence in our community.

[Name of Campus] has issued a policy prohibiting violence in the workplace. We have a zero tolerance for workplace violence.

[Name of Campus] also will make every effort to prevent violent acts in this workplace perpetrated by spouses, mates, or lovers. The campus is committed to dealing with domestic violence as a workplace issue.

Definition of Domestic Violence

Domestic violence—also referred to as battering, spouse abuse, spousal assault, and intimate partner abuse—is a global health problem. This victimization is defined as violence between adults who are intimates, regardless of their marital status, living arrangements, or sexual orientations. Such violence includes throwing, shoving, and slapping as well as beatings, forced sex, threats with a deadly weapon, and homicide.

Domestic Violence: Myths and Realities

Myth: Domestic violence affects a small percentage of employees.

Reality: Approximately 5 million employees are battered each year in the United States. Domestic violence is the leading cause of injury and workplace death to women in the United States.

Myth: People must enjoy the battering since they rarely leave the abusive relationship.

Reality: Very often victims of battering do leave the relationship. Women and men remain in a battering relationship not because they are masochistic, but for several well-founded reasons, such as:

- Threats to their lives and the lives of their children, especially after they have tried to leave the batterer.
- Fear of not getting custody of their children.
- Financial dependence.
- Feeling of responsibility for keeping the relationship together.
- Lack of support from family and friends.
- The batterer is not always violent.
- They still love the batterer.

Myth: Individuals who abuse their partners do so because they are under a great deal of stress, including being unemployed.

Reality: Stress does not cause individuals to batter their partners. Society condones partner abuse. In addition, individuals who batter learn they can achieve their goals through the use of force without facing consequences.

Myth: Children are not affected by watching their parents in a battering relationship.

Reality: Children are often in the middle of domestic violence. They may be abused by the violent parent. Children may also grow up to repeat the same behavior patterns they witnessed in their parents.

Myth: There are no long-term consequences of battering.

Reality: There are significant long-term consequences of battering, including depression, anger, fear, anxiety, irritability, loss of self-esteem, feelings of humiliation and alienation, and a sense of vulnerability.

Myth: Domestic violence only occurs in poor and minority families.

Reality: Domestic violence occurs among all socioeconomic classes and all racial and ethnic groups.

Threat Assessment Team

[Name of Campus] has established a Threat Assessment Team to assist with dealing with workplace violence. Part of the duties of the Threat Assessment Team is to assess the vulnerability of the campus to domestic violence and serve as advocates for victims of workplace violence, including domestic violence that has carried over into the workplace.

Each of these members of the Threat Assessment Team has received specialized training in workplace violence issues, including domestic violence as a workplace concern.

Services Offered for Employees Who Are Victims of Domestic Violence

[Name of Campus] will offer the following services for our employees who are victims of domestic violence:

- Provide receptionists and building security officer with a photograph of the batterer and a description of the batterer.
- Screen employee's calls.
- Screen employee's visitors.
- Accompany the employee to her/his car.
- Permit the employee to park close to the office building.
- When there is a restraining order, the President will send a formal notification to the batterer that indicates that his/her presence on campus premises will result in arrest.
- Referrals for individual counseling.

Threat Assessment Team Members: [Insert names and contact information]

* * *

SAMPLE POLICY STATEMENT ON SEXUAL HARASSMENT

[Name of Campus] has an obligation to create a learning and work environment for all individuals that is fair, humane, and responsible—an environment that supports, nurtures, and rewards career progress on the basis of such relevant factors as academic and work performance.

All students and employees of [Name of Campus] have a responsibility to cooperate in creating a climate at [Name of Campus] where sexual harassment does not occur. We have a zero tolerance for sexual harassment of our students and employees. All students and employees at all levels of [Name of Campus] must not engage in sexual harassment.

The following policy statement is designed to help employees of [Name of Campus] become aware of behavior that is sexual harassment and the procedures [Name of Campus] will use to deal with sexual harassment in a way that protects complainants, witnesses, and respondents.

Definition of Sexual Harassment

Sexual harassment is legally defined as "unwelcome sexual advances, requests for sexual favors, and other verbal or physical conduct of a sexual nature" when any one of the following criteria is met:

- Submission to such conduct is made either explicitly or implicitly a term or condition of the individual's employment or academic standing;

- Submission to or rejection of such conduct by an individual is used as the basis for employment or academic decisions affecting the individual;
- Such conduct has the purpose or effect of unreasonably interfering with an individual's work performance or creating an intimidating, hostile, or offensive learning or work environment.

There are two types of sexual harassment situations that are described by this legal definition: quid pro quo sexual harassment and hostile environment sexual harassment.

Quid pro quo sexual harassment involves an individual with organizational power who either expressly or implicitly ties an employment decision to the response of an employee to unwelcome sexual advances. Thus, a professor may promise a reward to a student for complying with sexual requests (e.g., a better grade, letter of recommendation) or a supervisor may threaten an employee's job for failing to comply with the sexual requests (e.g., threatening to not promote the employee, threatening to give an unsatisfactory performance appraisal).

Hostile environment sexual harassment involves a situation where an atmosphere or climate is created on campus that makes it difficult, if not impossible, for a student or employee to learn or work because the atmosphere is perceived by the individual to be intimidating, offensive, and hostile.

For purposes of this policy, sexual harassment includes, but is not limited to the following:

- Unwelcome sexual advances.
- Sexual innuendos, comments, and sexual remarks.
- Suggestive, obscene, or insulting sounds.
- Implied or expressed threat of reprisal for refusal to comply with a sexual request.
- Patting, pinching, brushing up against another's body.
- Sexually suggestive objects, books, magazines, poster, photographs, cartoons, e-mail, or pictures displayed in the work area.
- Actual denial of a job-related or academic-related benefit for refusal to comply with sexual requests.

Thus, sexual harassment can be physical, verbal, visual, or written. These behaviors constitute sexual harassment if they are committed by individuals who are in supervisory positions or are peers. And, these behaviors constitute sexual harassment if they occur between individuals of the same sex or between individuals of the opposite sex. [Name of Campus] prohibits these and other forms of sexual harassment. Any student or employee who engages in such behavior will be subject to disciplinary procedures.

What Isn't Sexual Harassment?

Sexual harassment does not refer to relationships between responsible, consenting adults. Sexual harassment does not mean flirting. Giving compliments does not mean sexual harassment. Sexual harassment refers to unwanted, unwelcome behavior. Not every joke or touch or comment is sexual harassment. The key is to determine if the behavior is unwanted and unwelcome. Furthermore, sexual harassment interferes with an employee's and student's ability to get work/learning done.

Costs of Sexual Harassment

There are high costs of sexual harassment to individuals. They include depression, feelings of helplessness, headaches, anxiety, sleep disturbances, and disordered eating. The cost of sexual harassment to our campus includes decreased productivity, absenteeism, and decreased morale.

What Should Individuals Do If They Believe They Are Being Sexually Harassed?

Students and employees who have complaints of sexual harassment, including any faculty member, supervisor, student, coworker, vendor, client, or visitor, are urged to report such conduct to [Name of Investigator] so that (s)he may investigate and resolve the problem. Employees are encouraged to bring their concerns to [Name of Investigator] within 60 days of the alleged incident(s).

[Name of Investigator] will investigate all complaints as expeditiously as possible in a professional manner. The confidentiality of the investigative procedures will be maintained. The complaint will be investigated and resolved typically within a two-week period.

Complainants and those against whom complaints have been filed will not be expected to meet together to discuss the resolution of the complaint.

Investigatory procedures have been developed and are fully explained in another memorandum: *[Name of Campus] Sexual Harassment Complaint Procedure.*

Any student or employee who is found to have engaged in sexual harassment will be subject to disciplinary action, as indicated in [Name of Campus] complaint procedure.

Discussions About Sexual Harassment: No Complaints

Students and employees at [Name of Campus] have the right to seek advice and information about sexual harassment from [Name of Investigator], who will maintain such consultation in confidence. Such discussions do not constitute filing a complaint of sexual harassment.

Retaliation

There will be no retaliation against individuals for reporting sexual harassment or assisting [Name of Investigator] in the investigation of a complaint. Any retaliation against such individuals is subject to disciplinary action, including verbal and written reprimands, transfers, demotions, and dismissal.

False Complaints

If after investigating any complaint of sexual harassment it is discovered that the complaint is not bona fide or that an individual has provided false information regarding the complaint, that individual may be subject to disciplinary action, including verbal and written reprimands, transfers, demotions, and dismissal.

Recommended Corrective Action

The purpose of any recommended corrective action to resolve a complaint will be to correct or remedy the injury, if any, to the complainant and to prevent further harassment. Recommended action may include: a private or public apology, written or oral reprimand of the individual who engaged in sexual harassment, relief from specific duties, suspension, expulsion, transfer, or dismissal of the individual who engaged in sexual harassment.

If complainants are not satisfied with the attempts to resolve the sexual harassment, they may seek resolution through other sources, for example, the [Name of State] Division of Human Rights or the Equal Employment Opportunity Commission or, for students, the Office for Civil Rights.

Policy Review

This policy will be reviewed periodically by [Name of Investigator] and by [Name of President], who welcome comments on the policy, its interpretation or implementation.

For additional information regarding sexual harassment, contact [Name of Investigator] or [Name of President]. They have been trained in complaint resolution and have received additional education about sexual harassment law and its management and psychological applications. Both [Name of Investigator] and [Name of President] will be responsible for a program of information and education concerning this policy and procedures relating to sexual harassment.

Office Numbers and Phone Numbers:

[Of Investigator]

[Of President]

Sample Sexual Harassment Complaint Procedure

Students and employees of [Name of Campus] who have complaints of sexual harassment by anyone at this campus, including any supervisors, are encouraged to report such conduct to [Name of Investigator] so that (s)he may investigate and resolve the problem. Individuals who feel subjected to sexual harassment should report the circumstances orally and/or in writing within 60 days to [Name of Investigator].

[Name of Investigator] will maintain confidentiality in the investigation of complaints of sexual harassment.

Any student or employee pursuing a complaint may do so without fear of reprisal.

Informal Advice and Consultation

Students and employees may seek informal assistance or advice from [Name of Investigator]. All such consultations will be confidential and no action involving any individual beyond [Name of Investigator] and the employee will be taken until a formal complaint has been made.

[Name of Investigator] may, however, take action, within the context of existing policy and procedures, that (s)he deems appropriate on the basis of information received to protect all employees of [Name of Campus].

Resolutions of Informal Complaints

Any student or employee may discuss an informal complaint with [Name of Investigator]. If the employee who discusses an informal complaint is not willing to be identified to the person against whom the informal complaint is made, [Name of Investigator] will make a confidential record of the circumstances and will provide guidance about various ways to resolve the problem.

If the employee bringing the complaint is willing to be identified to the person against whom the complaint is made and wishes to attempt an informal resolution of the problem, [Name of Investigator] will make a confidential record of the circumstances (signed by the complainant) and undertake appropriate discussions with the person complained about.

When a number of people report incidents of sexual harassment that have occurred in a public context (for example, offensive sexual remarks in an office setting) or when [Name of Investigator] receives repeated complaints from different employees that an individual has engaged in sexual harassment, the person complained against will be informed without revealing the identity of the complainants.

Resolutions of Formal Complaints

If a student or employee wishes to pursue the matter through a formal resolution, a written complaint must be submitted to [Name of Investigator], giving details of the alleged harassment, including dates, times, places, name(s) of individual(s) involved, and names of any witnesses. In addition:

- The complaint must be addressed to [Name of Investigator].
- Formal complaints will be investigated in the following manner:
- Upon receipt of a written complaint, [Name of Investigator] will immediately forward a copy of the complaint, along with a copy of [Name of Campus] Sexual Harassment Policy Statement and Procedures, to the individual complained against and request a meeting within three days.
- The investigation will be limited to what is necessary to resolve the complaint or make a recommendation. If it appears necessary for [Name of Investigator] to speak to any individuals other than those involved in the complaint, (s)he will do so only after informing the complainant and person complained against.

[Name of Investigator] will investigate all complaints of sexual harassment expeditiously and professionally. To the extent possible, the investigation will be completed within two weeks from the time the formal investigation is initiated.

[Name of Investigator] will also maintain the information provided in the complaint and investigation process confidential. The only other employee of [Name of Company] who will be informed about the investigation is [Name of President], President of [Name of Campus].

[Name of Campus]'s first priority will be to attempt to resolve the complaint through a mutual agreement of the complainant and the person complained against.

If a student or employee making a formal complaint asks not to be identified until a later date (e.g., until the completion of a course or performance appraisal), [Name of Investigator] will decide whether or not to hold the complaint without further action until the date requested.

If a formal complaint has been preceded by an informal investigation, [Name of Investigator] shall decide whether there are sufficient grounds to warrant a formal investigation.

The names or other identifying information regarding witnesses for either party involved in the complaint will not be made known to the opposing party.

Referrals for therapists and medical personnel for all individuals involved in an investigation will be made available upon request.

Following the completion of an investigation, [Name of Investigator] will make one of the following determinations:

- Sustain the Complaint: A finding of sexual harassment has been made and recommendations for corrective action will be identified. Recommended corrective action may include an apology, written or oral reprimand, relief from specific duties, suspension, dismissal, expulsion, or transfer of the employee found to have engaged in sexual harassment.
- Not Sustain the Complaint: A finding of no sexual harassment has been made.
- Insufficient Information: Insufficient information exists on which to make a determination. [Name of Investigator] will reinvestigate all parties named in the complaint.

Following any determination and recommendations for corrective action, [Name of Investigator] will issue a written decision with findings of fact and reason to [Name of President]. [Name of President] will correspond with the complainant and person complained against of the findings of the investigation and recommendations for corrective action. Appropriate statements of apology will be made to students or employees involved in the complaint by [Name of President].

If complainants are not satisfied with the attempts to resolve their complaint of sexual harassment, they may seek resolution through other sources, for example, the [Name of State] Division of Human Rights or the Equal Employment Opportunity Commission or, for students, the Office for Civil Rights, United States Department of Education.

For additional information regarding [Name of Campus] zero tolerance of sexual harassment, contact

[Name of Investigator]
[Office Number]
[Phone Number]
[Name of President]
[Office Number]
[Phone Number]

Both [Name of Investigator] and [Name of President] are trained in complaint resolution and receive additional education about sexual harassment law and its management and psychological applications.

In addition, [Name of President] and [Name of Investigator] will be responsible for a program of information and education concerning sexual harassment in general and [Name of Campus] policy and procedures.

* * *

SAMPLE POLICY ON WORKPLACE VIOLENCE

Employees of [Name of Campus] must be able to work in an atmosphere of mutual respect and trust. As a place of work, this campus should be free of violence and all forms of intimidation and exploitation. [Name of Campus] is concerned about and committed to our employees' safety and health. We refuse to tolerate violence in our workplace and will make every effort to prevent violent incidents in this workplace. All employees at all levels must not engage in violence in the workplace and will be held responsible for insuring that [Name of Campus] is free from violence. Any employee who engages in such behavior will be subject to disciplinary procedures.

[Name of Campus] has a zero tolerance for workplace violence.

[Name of Campus] has issued a separate policy dealing with domestic violence as a workplace issue.

Definition of Workplace Violence

Workplace violence includes, but is not limited to, verbal threats, nonverbal threats, pushing, shoving, hitting, assault, stalking, murder, and related actions. These behaviors constitute workplace violence whether they are committed by employees who are in a supervisory position or by coworkers, vendors, clients, or visitors. And, these behaviors constitute workplace violence if they occur between employees of the same sex or between employees of the opposite sex.

Threat Assessment Team

[Name of Campus] has established a Threat Assessment Team to assist with dealing with workplace violence. Part of the duties of the Threat Assessment Team is to assess the vulnerability of the company to workplace violence and serve as advocates for victims of workplace violence, as explained below.

Each of these members of the Threat Assessment Team has received specialized training in workplace violence issues, including prevention.

Reporting Workplace Violence

[Name of Campus] requires prompt and accurate reporting of all violent incidents whether or not physical injury has occurred. Any employee who has a complaint of workplace violence is encouraged to report such conduct to the Threat Assessment Team so that the complaint may be investigated and resolved promptly.

All complaints of workplace violence will be investigated by [Name of Investigator] on campus.

Complainants and those against whom complaints have been filed will *not* be expected to meet together to discuss the resolution of the complaint.

Employees who file a complaint of workplace violence may do so orally and/or in writing. A standardized form for filing complaints of workplace violence is included with this policy.

Investigating Complaints of Workplace Violence

[Name of Investigator] will investigate the complaint of workplace violence. The investigation will be limited to what is necessary to resolve the complaint. If it appears necessary for them to speak to any individuals other than those involved in the complaint, they will do so only after informing the complainant and the person against whom the complaint is made.

[Name of Investigator] will endeavor to investigate all complaints of workplace violence expeditiously and professionally. In addition, they will make every attempt to maintain the information provided to them in the complaint and investigation process as confidentially as possible. If warranted, the investigators will work with local police officials in resolving the complaint of workplace violence.

After the investigation of the complaint, the President will institute discipline and corrective action if warranted.

There will be no retaliation against employees for reporting workplace violence or assisting the investigators in the investigation of a complaint. Any retaliation against an employee is subject to disciplinary action.

If after investigating any complaint of workplace violence it is discovered that the complaint is not bona fide or that an employee has provided false information regarding the complaint, the employee may be subject to disciplinary action.

Inspection of Company for Workplace Violence

The Threat Assessment Team will review previous incidents of violence at [Name of Campus]. They will review existing records identifying patterns that may indicate causes and severity of assault incidents as well as identify changes necessary to correct these hazards. In addition, the Threat Assessment Team will inspect [Name of Campus] and evaluate the work tasks of all employees to determine the presence of hazards, conditions, operations, and other situations which might place employees at risk of workplace violence. Periodic inspections will be performed every three months, on the first Friday of the month.

The Threat Assessment Team will also survey employees at [Name of Campus] to identify and confirm the need for improved security measures. These surveys will be conducted once a year.

Training

[Name of Campus] will provide training on workplace violence annually to all employees.

Threat Assessment Team Members:

[Insert names and contact information]

Workplace Violence Complaint Form

Name:
Date:
Date/Time of Incident(s):
Name(s) of Individuals Present:
Employee Who Engaged in Act of Perceived Violence:
Type of Action(s) Employee Engaged in (e.g., verbal threats, pushing, hitting, stalking):
Impact of Actions on You (e.g., on physical health, emotional well-being, work-related consequences):
What Do You Think Will Rectify This Problem?
Additional Information You Would Like to Share:

* * *

SAMPLE RELIGIOUS OBSERVANCES POLICY

[Name of Campus] follows state law concerning the rights and privileges of students unable to attend classes on certain days because of religious beliefs.

No individual shall be expelled from or be refused admission as a student for the reason that he or she is unable, because of his or her religious beliefs, to register or attend classes or to participate in any examination, study, or work requirements on a particular day or days.

Any student who is unable, because of his or her religious beliefs, to attend classes on a particular day or days shall, because of such absence on the particular day or days, be excused from any examination or any study or work requirements.

It shall be the responsibility of the faculty and of the deans to make available to each student who is absent from school because of religious beliefs an equivalent opportunity to register for classes or to make up any examination, study, or work requirements which he or she has missed because of such absence on any particular day or days. No fees of any kind shall be charged for making available to the said student such equivalent opportunity.

If registration, classes, examinations, work or study requirements conflict with religious observations, similar or makeup classes, exams, or the opportunity to register shall be made available on other days, where it is possible and practical to do so. No special fees shall be charged to the student for these classes, exams, or other requirements held on these days.

It is the students' responsibility to inform faculty about classes and/or exams they will miss because of religious observances and to ask for ways to make up the missed work.

* * *

SAMPLE SEXUAL ASSAULT POLICY

[Name of Campus] is committed to creating and maintaining a community in which all individuals can work together in an atmosphere free of all forms of sexual assault. Sexual assault is prohibited by state and federal law and by [Name of Campus].

It is the intention of [Name of Campus] to take whatever action may be needed to prevent, correct, and if necessary, sanction individuals who act in violation of this policy.

[Name of Campus] will also provide and maintain educational programs for all members of its community. The educational aspects of this policy are intended to heighten community awareness and ultimately to prevent sexual offenses.

This policy will outline the procedures that will allow all employees to be effective at providing survivors of assault medical, psychological, educational, and legal resources.

Definitions

The following are definitions for [Name of Campus]. They are not limited to legal definitions. In some cases they expand on legal definitions or put legal concepts in plain English. No matter how carefully worded a definition of sexual assault may be, unforeseen situations may arise that cannot easily be included in any definition.

Consent

The act of willingly and verbally agreeing to engage in specific sexual contact or conduct. If sexual contact and/or conduct is not mutually and simultaneously initiated, then the person who initiates sexual contact/conduct is responsible for getting the verbal consent of the other individual(s) involved.

Obtaining consent is an ongoing process in any sexual interaction. If someone has initially consented but then stops consenting during a sexual interaction, she/he should communicate withdrawal of consent verbally and/or through physical resistance. The other individual must stop immediately.

Lack of consent does not necessarily require physical resistance or verbal refusal; for instance, someone who is asleep or drunk may be considered unable to give consent. To take advantage knowingly of someone who is under the influence of alcohol, drugs, and/or prescribed medication, resulting in an impaired ability to give or withhold consent, is not acceptable behavior at [Name of Campus].

Sexual Assault

Also called *rape*: includes sexual penetration, however slight, by a part of a person's body, or by any object, into the genital, oral, or anal openings that occur when consent is not given. Sexual assault can occur (1) through force, coercion, threat, or intimidation or (2) by virtue of the victim's mental or physical inability to communicate consent to engage in the act, of which the accused is or had reason to be aware.

Rape can occur between members of the same sex, or opposite sex, and either sex could be a victim or a perpetrator.

Reporting the Crime

Students and employees should contact the [Name of City] Police Department and/or [Name of Investigator] on campus as **soon as possible after the offense. Please remember it is most essential to preserve evidence.** Do not bathe, douche, use the toilet, or change clothing. Note everything about the location. If you have been sexually assaulted, it is important to seek medical attention immediately regardless of whether you report the matter to the police. If the survivor will not agree to speak with local law enforcement, the survivor should be advised to contact [Name of Investigator] on campus for assistance.

Campus Responsibility in Dealing with Complaints of Sexual Assault

[Name of State in which Campus is Located] State Law encompasses the offenses identified above; prosecution may take place independently of charges under [Name of Campus]'s regulations. There are differences between the campus and the court process. The campus proceeding determines whether the accused's status as a student or employee will be altered, whereas the criminal process determines if there will be limitations on the accused's liberty. As there are different standards of proof and the purpose of each proceeding is different, [Name of Campus] encourages students and employees who are survivors of sexual assault to go forward with the campus's proceedings, in addition to pursuing possible redress through criminal and civil actions.

[Name of Campus]'s process for hearing a complaint of sexual assault will be initiated by [Name of Investigator], having received a written complaint from a survivor, who will interview parties to determine whether it is reasonable to believe that an offense may have occurred.

If at any time the President becomes aware of an individual who through alleged sexual assault may pose a threat to the campus, the President may bring formal charges on behalf of the campus.

The parties do not have to meet together during the complaint resolution. Both the individual bringing forward the sexual assault allegation and the accused individual are entitled to have someone present during any stage of the process if this will help make them feel more comfortable. This person may not, however, speak in place of the party to the complaint.

If the complaint is sustained, the recommended disciplinary action is dismissal.

The role of [Name of Investigator] is to hear all accounts; to investigate as appropriate; to determine if a violation of this policy has occurred; to develop an appropriate remedy; and to prepare a written report setting forth its findings and recommendations for sanctions and apologies. The report will be forwarded to the President.

If the complainant or the respondent, or a witness for either party, experiences retaliation for the bringing of a case, or for the fact of being a party in the case, that person will inform [Name of Investigator]. Discipline will be issued to the individual who engaged in retaliation.

Education

[Name of Campus]'s President is responsible for education programs regarding sexual assault, including orientation for incoming employees and mandatory workshops for all students and staff. All members of this campus will attend a training workshop on this policy. Each year students and employees will receive a packet with up-to-date materials on these issues.

An information packet will be distributed to each employee at the beginning of each year. Included will be:

- A copy of this policy.
- A listing of sexual assault myths and facts.
- A description of support services.
- A description of safety measures.
- Self-defense tips.
- Information on how to report sexual assault.

There may be instances in which the campus's sexual harassment policy applies to conduct also covered by this policy. Accordingly, the sexual harassment policy should be consulted by the complainant, in each instance for possible applicability.

* * *

SAMPLE POLICY ON MAINTENANCE OF PUBLIC ORDER ON CAMPUS: RULES AND REGULATIONS

[Name of Campus] honors the tradition of the university as a sanctuary of academic freedom and center of informed discussion. The basic significance of that sanctuary lies in the protection of intellectual freedoms: the right of students to learn and to express their views, of faculty to teach, of researchers to engage in the advancement of knowledge, all without external pressures or interference.

[Name of Campus] recognizes that these freedoms can flourish only in an atmosphere of mutual respect, civility, and trust among faculty, students, and employees, only when members of the [Name of Campus] community are willing to accept self-restraint and reciprocity as the condition upon which they share in its intellectual autonomy.

The following rules shall govern the conduct of students and all persons, whether or not their presence is authorized upon all property under the control of [Name of Campus] to which such rules are applicable.

Prohibited Conduct

No person, either singly or in concert with others, shall:

- Obstruct the free movement of persons and vehicles in any place to which these rules apply;
- Deliberately disrupt or prevent the peaceful and orderly conduct of classes, lectures, and meetings or deliberately interfere with the freedom of any persons to express their views, including invited speakers;
- Enter upon and remain in any building or facility for any purpose other than its authorized uses or such manner as to obstruct its authorized use by others, remain (without authorization) in any building or facility after it is normally closed, or refuse to leave any building or facility after being asked to do so by an authorized administrative officer;
- Violate any rules or regulations, or willfully incite others to commit any of the acts herein prohibited with specific intent to encourage them to do so;
- Take any action, create or participate in the creating of any situation which recklessly or intentionally endangers mental or physical health which involves the forced consumption of liquor or drugs for the purpose of initiation into, or affiliation with, any organization.

Penalties

A person who shall violate any provisions of these rules shall:

- If a trespasser or visitor without specific license or invitation, be subject to ejection;
- If a licensee or invitee, have authorization to remain upon the campus or other property withdrawn and be directed to leave the premises. In the event of a failure or refusal to do so, the licensee or invitee shall be subject to ejection;
- If a student, be subject to expulsion or such lesser disciplinary action as the facts of the case may warrant, including suspension, probation, loss of privileges, reprimand, or warning;

- In the case of any other member of [Name of Campus] community who shall violate any provision of these rules, that person shall be dismissed, suspended, or censured by the President.

Procedures

Pending adjudication of the matter by the appropriate authorities, members of [Name of Campus] deemed to have violated these rules will be subject to immediate suspension, as determined by the President.

In the case of a trespasser or visitor who shall violate any provisions of these rules, the President shall inform the trespasser or visitor of violation and direct the violator to leave such premises. In the event of a failure or refusal to do so, the President shall cause the violator's ejection from such property under the control of [Name of Campus].

In the case of a licensee or invitee, the President shall inform the licensee or invitee that the license or invitation is withdrawn and direct the violator to leave the campus. In the event of a failure or refusal to do so, the President shall cause the ejection of the violator from property under the control of [Name of Campus].

In the case of a student, charges for violation of any of these rules shall be presented, heard, and determined by the President.

Enforcement

The President of [Name of Campus] shall be responsible for the interpretation and enforcement of these rules and shall designate the other administrative officers who are authorized to take action in accordance with such rules when required or appropriate to carry them into effect.

It is not intended by any provision to curtail the rights of students, employees, administrators, or faculty to be heard upon any matter affecting them in the relations with [Name of Campus]. In the case of any apparent violation of these rules by such persons who, in the judgment of the President do not pose any immediate threat of injury to person or property, the President may make a reasonable effort to learn the cause of the conduct in question and to persuade those engaged therein to desist and to resort to permissible methods for the resolution of any issues which may be presented. In doing so, the President shall warn such persons of the consequences of persistence in the prohibited conduct including their ejection from any premises of [Name of Campus] where their continued presence and conduct is in violation of these rules.

In any case where violation of these rules does not cease after such warning and in other cases of willful violation of such rules, the President shall cause the ejection of the violator from the campus and shall initiate disciplinary action as herein before provided.

The President may apply to the public authorities for any aid, which is deemed necessary to ease the ejection of any violator of these rules.

* * *

SAMPLE DISABILITY NONDISCRIMINATION POLICY

[Name of Campus] does not discriminate on the basis of disability in the recruitment, admission, or retention of students and employees.

Defining "Disability"

An individual with a disability is defined by law as someone who:

- Has a physical or mental impairment that substantially limits one or more major life activities;
- Has a record of having such an impairment; or
- Is regarded as having such an impairment.

Learning disabilities is a general term that refers to a heterogeneous group of disorders manifested by significant difficulties in the acquisition and use of listening, speaking, reading, writing, reasoning, or mathematical abilities. These disorders are intrinsic to the individual, presumed to be due to central nervous system dysfunction, and may occur across the life span.

Reasonable Accommodation

[Name of Campus] will make an accommodation to the known disability of a qualified applicant or student or employee if it would not impose an "undue hardship" on the campus. Undue hardship is defined by law as an action requiring significant difficulty or expense when considered in light of factors such as size, financial resources, and the nature and structure of its operation.

Reasonable accommodation may include, but is not limited to:

- Making existing facilities used by employees readily accessible to and usable by employees with disabilities
- Acquiring or modifying equipment and/or devices, adjusting training materials and policies, including providing qualified readers or interpreters

A modification or adjustment is "reasonable" by law if it "seems reasonable on its face, i.e., ordinarily or in the run of cases." Thus, the request is reasonable if it appears to be plausible or feasible. A reasonable accommodation enables an applicant with a disability to have an equal opportunity to participate in the application process and to be considered for hire in [Name of Campus]. In addition, a reasonable accommodation permits an employee with a disability an equal opportunity to enjoy the benefits and privileges of employment that employees without disabilities enjoy.

Requesting a Reasonable Accommodation

An individual with a disability must request a reasonable accommodation when she or he knows that there is a barrier that is preventing her or him, due to a disability, from effectively performing studies or duties. [Name of Campus] recommends that an individual request a reasonable accommodation before performance suffers or conduct problems occur.

[Name of Campus] requests that students or employees with a physical disability, psychiatric disability, or learning disability provide professional verification by a licensed health care provider who is qualified to diagnosis the disability. This verification must reflect the student's or employee's present level of functioning of major life activity affected by the disability. The verification must also provide detailed data that support the requests for any reasonable accommodation.

Applicants or employees must pay the cost of obtaining the professional verification. The campus has the discretion to require supplemental assessment of a disability. The cost of the supplemental assessment shall be borne by the employee or applicant. If the campus requires an additional assessment for purposes of obtaining a second professional opinion, then the campus shall bear any cost not covered by any third party.

Students or employees who are recuperating from temporary injuries or illnesses may request interventions during this stage of recovery. Verification of the temporary impairment must be obtained by students or employees. The cost of obtaining the professional verification shall be borne by the student or employee.

An applicant or employee must request a reasonable accommodation by contacting [Name of Person Responsible for Dealing with Reasonable Accommodations] at any time. Written notification of the decision will be mailed to the individual. The decision can be appealed within 10 days by submitting a written request to [Name of President]. This decision will be communicated to the individual. There will be no further appeal.

[Name of Campus] will not coerce, intimidate, threaten, harass, or interfere with any individual exercising or enjoying her/his rights under the Americans with Disabilities Act or because that individual aided or encouraged another employee in the exercise of rights granted or protected by this Act.

Someone other than the individual with a disability may request a reasonable accommodation on behalf of the individual. Thus, a family member, friend, health professional, or other representative may request a reasonable accommodation on behalf of an applicant or student or employee.

Requests for reasonable accommodation do not need to be in writing.

All requests for reasonable accommodation will be dealt with expeditiously by [Name of Campus].

Applicants and employees may be asked about their ability to perform specific functions. [Name of Campus] will not ask applicants or employees about the existence, nature, or severity of a disability.

For additional information, contact: [Insert]

* * *

SAMPLE NONDISCRIMINATION POLICY

[Name of Campus] is committed to maintaining a learning and working environment that supports equal rights for all students and employees. Academic and employment decisions will be based only on merit, performance, and legitimate professional criteria. [Name of Campus] prohibits discrimination on the basis of race, sex, religion, age, color, creed, national origin, disability, or sexual orientation, and discrimination against disabled and Vietnam era veterans, in the recruitment or treatment of students and employees, and in the operation of its activities and programs, as specified by federal and state laws.

Application to [Name of Campus]

With respect to recruitment, recruitment sources will be advised in writing of [Name of Campus]'s policy, and commitment to equal opportunity and must acknowledge their compliance with the program. Applicants are considered with regard to their skills, education, performance, and other bona fide qualifications. Non-meritorious factors, such as age, race, color, religion, sex, national origin, ancestry, veteran status, sexual orientation, or the presence of a disability may not be considered.

Right to Redress

All students and employees have the right to redress possible injustices or wrongs done to them. Employees who believe they have been discriminated against may file an oral and/or written complaint with [Name of Investigator], stating the nature of the perceived discrimination, the alleged perpetrator, witnesses, and recommended remedy needed to correct the situation. A complaint form to use is presented at the end of this policy.

Investigation of Complaints

Complaints will be investigated in the following manner:

1. Upon receipt of a written complaint, the investigator will ask the individual if there are any witnesses the complainant would like to be interviewed. Individuals will complete a form providing names of witnesses as well as the issues to which the witnesses may address. Complainants will provide a signed statement giving permission to contact these witnesses.

2. The investigator will immediately forward a copy of the complaint, along with a copy of [Name of Campus]'s discrimination Policy Statement and Procedures, to the individual complained against, and request a meeting with this individual within three business days.

3. During the meeting with the respondent, the investigator will ask the individual if he or she has any witnesses to be interviewed. Individuals will complete a form providing names of witnesses as well as the issues to which the witnesses may address. Complainants will provide a signed statement giving permission to contact these witnesses.

4. Names or other identifying features of witnesses on behalf of the complainant and respondent will not be made known to the opposing party. This will help ensure participation by witnesses in the investigation.

5. All complaints of discrimination will be investigated expeditiously and professionally. To the maximum extent possible, the investigation will be completed within two weeks from the time the formal investigation is initiated.

   All information provided during the investigation will be treated in a confidential manner. Parties to the complaint will be asked to sign a confidentiality form in which they state they will keep the complaint and complaint resolution confidential. They will also be asked to sign a form indicating they will not retaliate against any party to the complaint.

6. A safe environment will be set up for the complainant, respondent, and witnesses to discuss their perspectives without the fear of being ridiculed or judged.

7. No conclusions about the veracity of the complaint will be made until the investigation is completed.

8. All documents presented by the parties to the complaint will be reviewed. Documents include, but are not limited to: letters and notes.

9. Following the completion of an investigation, one of the following determinations will be made:

   - Sustain the Complaint: A finding of discrimination has been made and recommendations for corrective action will be identified, including reprimands, relief from specific duties, transfer, expulsion, or dismissal.

- Not Sustain the Complaint: A finding of no discrimination has been made.
- Insufficient Information: Insufficient information exists on which to make a determination. All parties will be reinvestigated.

10. Following any determination and recommendations for corrective action, the investigator will issue a written decision with findings to [Name of President]. [Name of President] will correspond with the complainant and person complained against of the findings of the investigation and recommendations for corrective action. [Name of President] will make appropriate statements of apology to individuals involved in the complaint.

11. If employees are not satisfied with the attempts to resolve the complaint of discrimination, they may submit a grievance according to the Collective Bargaining Agreement.

12. If complainants are not satisfied with either internal procedure, they may seek redress through other sources, for example, the Equal Employment Opportunity Commission or the Office for Civil Rights, United States Department of Education.

Any party to a complaint resolution may do so without fear of reprisal.

[Name of Campus]'s first priority will be to attempt to resolve the complaint through a mutual agreement of the complainant and the person against whom the complaint was made.

[Name of President] can, in extreme cases, take whatever action is appropriate to protect the campus community.

Each complaint against the same individual will be handled independently. Similarly, knowledge that the complainant has filed complaints against other individuals in the past will not enter into the investigative process. Such information may be taken in to account in determining sanctions for violation of the nondiscrimination policy.

Referrals for therapists and medical personnel for all individuals involved in an investigation will be made available upon request.

Policy Review

[Name of Campus] will review this policy on equal opportunity annually in order to ensure its completeness and accuracy in light of changing legislation and conditions.

Training

[Name of Campus] will be responsible for facilitating training programs for all administrators and employees on this Equal Opportunity Policy.

Discrimination Complaint Form

> Your Name:
> Date:
> Telephone numbers:
> Description of discrimination problem:
> What was said/done/shown to you?
> Who was the person(s) involved:
> Any witnesses who observed/heard the comments/behaviors, etc.?
> How did you feel when this incident (these incidents) occurred?
> What do you want [Name of Campus] to do to resolve this situation?

* * *

SAMPLE HIV/AIDS NONDISCRIMINATION POLICY

[Name of Campus] does not unlawfully discriminate against applicants, employees, or students living with or affected by the Human Immunodeficiency Virus (HIV) or Acquired Immune Deficiency Syndrome (AIDS).

HIV is a blood-borne virus and is spread only through intimate contact with blood, semen, vaginal secretions, and breast milk. Scientists continue to make new discoveries about HIV infection and AIDS. But one piece of information has never changed—how the disease spreads. Scientists have recognized this fact since 1982. The basic facts about HIV transmission and prevention are sound.

[Name of Campus] is committed to maintaining a safe and healthy learning and work environment for all students and employees. This commitment stands on the recognition that HIV, and therefore AIDS, is not transmitted through any casual contact.

[Name of Campus] recognizes that HIV infection and AIDS, the most serious stage of disease progression resulting from HIV infection, pose significant and delicate issues for the campus. Accordingly, [Name of Campus] has established the following guidelines and principles to serve as the basis for dealing with student and employee situations and concerns related to HIV infection and AIDS.

[Name of Campus] will treat HIV infection and AIDS the same as other illnesses in terms of all of its student and employee policies. Students and employees living with or affected by HIV infection and AIDS will be treated with compassion and understanding, as would individuals with other disabling conditions.

In accordance with the law, [Name of Campus] will provide reasonable accommodations for students, employees, and applicants with disabilities who are qualified to perform the essential functions of their positions. This applies to individuals living with HIV infection and AIDS, and is especially relevant in light of new treatments for HIV infection that may allow people living with AIDS to return to work after periods of disability leave.

Generally, disabled employees have the responsibility to request an accommodation. It is [Name of Campus]'s policy to respond to the changing health status of employees and students by making reasonable accommodations. Students and employees may continue to take classes or work as long as they are able to perform their duties safely and in accordance with performance standards. Employees are asked to contact [Name of Person Responsible for Dealing with Accommodations] in making reasonable accommodations. Students are asked to contact [Name of Person Responsible for Dealing with Accommodations Requested by Students].

Recognizing the need for all students and employees to be accurately informed about HIV infection and AIDS, [Name of Campus] will make information and educational materials available. Individuals who want to obtain information and materials may find them located in the campus library, student center, health center, women's center, counseling center and:

> Individuals are expected to continue working relationships with any student or employee who has HIV infection or AIDS. Individuals who refuse to work with, withhold services from, harass or otherwise discriminate against a student or employee with HIV infection or AIDS will be subject to the same disciplinary procedures that apply to other [Name of Campus] policy violations.

Information about a student's or employee's medical condition is private and must be treated in a confidential manner. In most cases, only administrators directly involved in providing a reasonable accommodation or arranging benefits may need to know an individual's diagnosis. Others who may acquire such information, even if obtained personally from the individual, should respect the confidentiality of the medical information.

If you have questions about this policy, its interpretation, or the information upon which it is based, please contact [Name of Individual Responsible for Dealing with Reasonable Accommodations].

Additional Resources About HIV/AIDS

Centers for Disease Control and Prevention: www.cdc.gov
National AIDS Hotline: 800-342-AIDS
TTY: 800-243-7889
Office of AIDS Research, National Institute of Health: www.nih.gov
U.S. Food and Drug Administration: HIV and AIDS Program
www.fda.gov/oashi/aids/hiv.html

* * *

SAMPLE SUBSTANCE ABUSE POLICY

[Name of Campus] is committed to fostering an environment that promotes the acquisition of knowledge and nurtures the growth of students and employees. In order to create the best possible environment for learning, working, and teaching, [Name of Campus] is committed to being in full compliance with the federal Drug-Free Schools and Communities Act Amendment of 1989 (Public Law 101–226). [Name of Individual Responsible for Assisting Students and Employees with Substance Abuse] is available to assist individuals in the area of substance abuse in seeking corrective help.

Alcohol and other drug abuse adversely affects students and employees on several levels in and out of the campus and requires an ongoing commitment of both attention and resources on the part of [Name of Campus]. There are significant psychological and physiological health risks associated with the use of illicit drugs and alcohol. Physical addiction, loss of control, and withdrawal syndrome as well as serious damage to vital organs of the body result from substance abuse.

[Name of Campus] prohibits unlawful possession, use, or distribution of alcohol or illicit drugs by faculty, employees, administrators, or students on [Name of Campus] property or as part of any [Name of Campus] activity.

Each member of this campus community is responsible for his/her own actions. When making decisions to consume alcohol or to provide alcohol to others, individuals must be mindful of the inherent consequences and risks involved. In addition, students are responsible for understanding and complying with applicable laws. [Name of Campus] will not be responsible for enforcing state and local laws, nor will it shield individuals from the legal consequences of their actions should they violate these laws.

Consequences of Violating the Policy

Any student found to be in violation of the [Name of Campus]'s policy with regard to illegal drugs or alcohol shall be subject to the following range of sanctions: admonition, warning, censure, disciplinary probation, restitution, suspension, expulsion, ejection, and/or arrest and criminal prosecution by civil authorities.

Any visitor, licensee, or invitee found to be in violation of this policy shall be subject to ejection and, if applicable, to arrest by civil authorities.

Any organization that authorizes the violation of this policy shall have its permission to operate on campus rescinded.

Health Risks

There are severe health risks that accompany substance abuse, including: sudden or early death, neurological impairment, convulsions, shallow respiration, heart and liver degeneration, and deterioration of the immune system. There are, in addition, particular risks to pregnant women and infants.

Counseling and Assistance

Students and employees are encouraged to consult with their family and/or their health care provider in making an informed decision on the appropriate type and location of a substance abuse assessment, counseling, or treatment facility. Information may also be obtained from the Campus Counseling Center.

Sanctions

Alcohol Abuse. If students or employees are found in violation of this policy, disciplinary sanctions may range from written warnings, loss of privileges, restitution, suspension, expulsion, or termination. Individuals will also be required to attend a substance abuse course. Repeated violations of this policy will incur increased disciplinary sanctions.

Other Drug Abuse. A student or employee found in illegal possession and/or use of an illegal substance will be subject to the following sanctions at a minimum:

- First Offense: Individuals are subjected to one year disciplinary probation and must attend a substance abuse evaluation session. This includes urinalysis drug screening. If deemed necessary, referral to an outside agency for drug abuse treatment will be required.
- Second Offense: Individuals will be removed from the campus.

Any student or employee who is involved in the illegal sale of any controlled substance will be subject to suspension and/or dismissal from [Name of Campus].

* * *

SAMPLE POLICY ON STALKING

[Name of Campus] prohibits stalking, including cyberstalking, of its students, faculty, administrators, and employees. [Name of Campus] is committed to providing and maintaining a safe and secure working and learning environment that is free from stalking.

Definition of Stalking and Cyberstalking

[Name of Campus] defines stalking and cyberstalking as being comprised of the following behaviors:

- Repeated, unwanted contact, including face-to-face contact, telephone calls, voice messages, text messages, electronic mail, instant messages, and written letters;
- Repeated, unwanted/unsolicited communication on public and college community Internet sites;
- Disturbing messages online;
- Persistent physical approaches and/or requests for dates, meetings, etc.;
- Threats that create fear for one's life or safety, or fear for the safety of one's family, friends, roommates, or others;
- Pursuing or following another person; repeatedly showing up or waiting outside a person's home, classroom, place of employment, or car;
- Trespassing or breaking into a person's car or residence; or
- Vandalism and/or destruction of a person's personal property.

Procedures

If a student or employee wishes to pursue the matter through [Name of Campus], a written complaint must be submitted to [Name of Investigator], giving details of the alleged stalking, including dates, times, places, name(s) of individual(s) involved, and names of any witnesses.

The complaint must be addressed to [Name of Investigator].

Upon receipt of a written complaint, [Name of Investigator] will immediately forward a copy of the complaint, along with a copy of [Name of Campus] Stalking Policy Statement and Procedures, to the individual complained against and request a meeting within three days.

The investigation will be limited to what is necessary to resolve the complaint or make a recommendation. If it appears necessary for [Name of Investigator] to speak to any individuals other than those involved in the complaint, (s)he will do so only after informing the complainant and person complained against.

[Name of Investigator] will investigate all complaints of stalking expeditiously and professionally. To the extent possible, the investigation will be completed within two weeks from the time the formal investigation is initiated.

[Name of Investigator] will also maintain the information provided in the complaint and investigation process confidential. The only other employee of [Name of Company] who will be informed about the investigation is [Name of President], President of [Name of Campus].

[Name of Campus]'s first priority will be to attempt to resolve the complaint through a mutual agreement of the complainant and the person complained against.

The names or other identifying information regarding witnesses for either party involved in the complaint will not be made known to the opposing party.

Referrals for therapists and medical personnel for all individuals involved in an investigation will be made available upon request.

Following the completion of an investigation, [Name of Investigator] will make one of the following determinations:

- Sustain the Complaint: A finding of stalking has been made and recommendations for corrective action will be identified. Recommended corrective action may include an apology, written or oral reprimand, relief from specific duties, suspension, dismissal, expulsion, or transfer of the employee found to have engaged in stalking.
- Not Sustain the Complaint: A finding of no stalking has been made.
- Insufficient Information: Insufficient information exists on which to make a determination. [Name of Investigator] will reinvestigate all parties named in the complaint.

Following any determination and recommendations for corrective action, [Name of Investigator] will issue a written decision with findings of fact and reason to [Name of President]. [Name of President] will correspond with the complainant and person complained against of the findings of the investigation and recommendations for corrective action. Appropriate statements of apology will be made to students or employees involved in the complaint by [Name of President].

For additional information regarding [Name of Campus]'s zero tolerance of stalking, contact:

[Name of Investigator]
[Office Number]
[Phone Number]
[Name of President]
[Office Number]
[Phone Number]

Both [Name of Investigator] and [Name of President] are trained in complaint resolution and receive additional education about stalking law and its management and psychological applications.

In addition, [Name of President] and [Name of Investigator] will be responsible for a program of information and education concerning stalking in general and [Name of Campus] policy and procedures.

* * *

SAMPLE ANTI-BULLYING POLICY

[Name of College] is committed to ensuring a safe, friendly, collegial, and respectful environment, free from offensive behavior in order for all members of the campus community to get the most from their experience at [Name of Campus]. [Name of Campus] does not tolerate bullying of students, employees, faculty, or administrators. We have a zero tolerance for bullying.

Definition of Bullying

Bullying is defined as the abuse of power and the use of aggression with the intention of hurting another individual. Bullying can be direct (face-to-face) or indirect (e.g., via texting or e-mail). Furthermore, bullying can be physical (e.g., pushing, kicking, hitting), emotional (excluding, humiliating, tormenting), and verbal (e.g., name calling, spreading rumors). All forms of bullying are prohibited at [Name of Campus].

Costs of Bullying

There are several symptoms bullied individuals express. For example, they may not want to attend class, become withdrawn, cry, experience nightmares, get failing grades, become aggressive or unreasonable, lack self-confidence, or attempt suicide.

Procedures

[Name of Campus] encourages individuals to report their experiences with bullying to [Name of Investigator]. At all stages of the procedures individuals may bring a friend or anyone of their choosing to support them.

Upon receipt of a written complaint, the investigator will ask the individual if there are any witnesses that should be interviewed. Individuals will complete a form providing names of witnesses as well as the issues to which the witnesses may address. Complainants will provide a signed statement giving permission to contact these witnesses.

The investigator will immediately forward a copy of the complaint, along with a copy of [Name of Campus]'s anti-bullying policy statement and procedures, to the individual complained against and request a meeting with this individual within three business days.

During the meeting with the respondent, the investigator will ask the individual if there are any witnesses that should be interviewed. Individuals will complete a form providing names of witnesses as well as the issues to which the witnesses may address. Complainants will provide a signed statement giving permission to contact these witnesses.

Names or other identifying features of witnesses on behalf of the complainant and respondent will not be made known to the opposing party. This will help ensure participation by witnesses in the investigation.

All complaints will be investigated expeditiously and professionally. To the maximum extent possible, the investigation will be completed within two weeks from the time the formal investigation is initiated. All information provided during the investigation will be treated in a confidential manner. Parties to the complaint will be asked to sign a confidentiality form in which they state they will keep the complaint and complaint resolution confidential. They will also be asked to sign a form indicating they will not retaliate against any party to the complaint.

A safe environment will be set up for the complainant, respondent, and witnesses to discuss their perspectives without the fear of being ridiculed or judged.

No conclusions about the veracity of the complaint will be made until the investigation is completed.

All documents presented by the parties to the complaint will be reviewed. Documents include, but are not limited to: letters and notes.

Following the completion of an investigation, one of the following determinations will be made:

- Sustain the Complaint: A finding of bullying has been made and recommendations for corrective action will be identified, including reprimands, relief from specific duties, transfer, expulsion, or dismissal.
- Not Sustain the Complaint: A finding of no bullying has been made.
- Insufficient Information: Insufficient information exists on which to make a determination. All parties will be reinvestigated.

Following any determination and recommendations for corrective action, the investigator will issue a written decision with findings to [Name of President]. [Name of President] will correspond with the complainant and person complained against of the findings of the investigation and recommendations for corrective action. [Name of President] will make appropriate statements of apology to individuals involved in the complaint.

Any party to a complaint resolution may do so without fear of reprisal.

[Name of Campus]'s first priority will be to attempt to resolve the complaint through a mutual agreement of the complainant and the person against whom the complaint was made.

[Name of President] can, in extreme cases, take whatever action is appropriate to protect the campus community.

Each complaint against the same individual will be handled independently. Similarly, knowledge that the complainant has filed complaints against other individuals in the past will not enter into the investigative process. Such information may be taken in to account in determining sanctions for violation of the bullying policy.

Referrals for therapists and medical personnel for all individuals involved in an investigation will be made available upon request.

Policy Review

[Name of Campus] will review this policy on bullying annually in order to ensure its completeness and accuracy in light of changing legislation and conditions.

Training

[Name of Campus] will be responsible for facilitating training programs for all administrators and employees on this bullying policy.

REFERENCE

Paludi, M., Nydegger, R., & Paludi, C. (2006). *Understanding workplace violence.* Westport, CT: Praeger.

Chapter 12

Security On Campus (SOC): Our Mission Is Safer Campuses for Students

Jonathan M. Kassa

Security On Campus, Inc., is a nonprofit (501(c)(3)) organization whose mission is to prevent violence, substance abuse, and other crimes in college and university campus communities across the United States, and to compassionately assist the victims of these crimes.

Since 1987, Security On Campus, Inc. (SOC) has been the nation's leading force in improving campus safety. Co-founded by Connie and Howard Clery after the brutal rape and murder of their daughter, Jeanne, in her Lehigh University residence hall room, SOC has led the way in making campus crime information public, assisting the victims of campus violence, and improving the level of security offered by colleges and universities across America. SOC has been responsible for more than 30 state and federal campus security laws, including the Jeanne Clery Disclosure of Campus Security Policy and Campus Crime Statistics Act, which Congress named in memory of the Clerys' daughter in 1998. These laws ensure that students and employees receive information about steps being taken to protect them, how much crime is happening on campus, and that they are warned about possible threats to their safety. Campus victimization is now recognized and discussed as a significant problem due to the work of SOC. Between one-fifth and one-quarter of female undergraduates will be the victims of completed or attempted sexual assaults during their time in college, according to the U.S. Department of Justice. Most are victimized by an acquaintance and fewer than 5 percent report it to the police. Every year there are 1,700 alcohol-related deaths of college students. Another 696,000 will be assaulted by a student who has been drinking, according to the National Institute on Alcohol Abuse and Alcoholism. SOC works to empower the victims of this campus violence with a unique victim-assistance program that helps them to navigate the special issues they often face at their college or university. SOC offers innovative educational programming that increases the awareness of campus communities, college-bound students, and the public about critical campus safety issues. SOC also works to ensure that the public has accurate information about campus crime and that, where appropriate, parents are notified when their child is in danger.

MAJOR SOC PROGRAMS AND VICTIM SERVICES

SOC is the only national nonprofit organization providing free advocacy and referral services to the victims of college and university campus crimes including homicide, sexual assault, and hazing. These victims and their families face unique challenges navigating through their school's systems. We are able to leverage our more than two decades of experience with campus violence issues to empower victims to get justice and become survivors.

National Campus Safety Awareness Month

September is National Campus Safety Awareness Month (unanimously passed by Congress in 2005). SOC partners with educational institutions to display banners, promotional posters, and materials throughout their campuses. Our Web site, www.campussafetymonth. org, provides safety topics such as fire safety, sexual assault, alcohol, drugs, hate crimes, and hazing. Each institution creates a program specific to its size and student population in an effort to make its students aware of their safety and the safety of their campus community.

Safe On Campus Peer Education Program

The Safe On Campus Peer Education Program educates high school students on the dangers of high-risk drinking, hazing, drugs, and sexual assault. College-trained peer educators visit high school students and show student-produced videos followed by student-led discussions. Visit our Web site www.safeoncampus.org for more information on this program.

The Clery Act Training Conferences

SOC hosts comprehensive National Jeanne Clery Act Training Conferences—a great opportunity for college and university officials to expand their knowledge about the Jeanne Clery Act's campus crime reporting and victim's rights provisions. SOC's unique training is geared toward developing a collaborative approach to compliance and campus safety.

SIX MAJOR FEDERAL LEGISLATIVE ACCOMPLISHMENTS THAT HAVE BECOME LAW

Crime Awareness and Campus Security Act of 1990 (1990)

This landmark federal law requires colleges and universities to disclose campus crime statistics and security policies in an annual security report. It also requires that timely warnings be issued about ongoing threats.

Buckley Amendment Clarification (1992)

This law ensures that campus police and security records about crimes are not improperly hidden among confidential student educational records. It amended a federal law known as the "Buckley Amendment," which provides that student records, such as grades, are generally confidential.

Campus Sexual Assault Victims' Bill of Rights (1992)

These provisions exist as a part of the "Campus Security Act" and require colleges to have sexual assault policies that guarantee certain basic rights for all sexual assault survivors. These provisions also expanded the scope of sexual assault statistics that colleges report.

Campus Courts Disclosure Provision (1998)

These provisions within the Buckley Amendment provide that the final disciplinary action taken by a college or university against a student accused of a crime of violence may be publicly disclosed. Previously this information had been considered confidential.

Jeanne Clery Disclosure of Campus Security Policy and Campus Crime Statistics Act (1998)

This law, commonly referred to as the Jeanne Clery Act, renamed the original Campus Security Act and expanded its crime reporting requirements to include more geographic areas and crime categories. It also added a public crime log requirement for institutions with a police or security department.

Campus Sex Crimes Prevention Act (2000)

This law, an amendment to the federal Jacob Wetterling Act, provides for the collection and disclosure of information about convicted, registered sex offenders either enrolled in or employed at institutions of higher education.

All of SOC's activities, including helping with legislation such as these, are for the purpose that we state on our Web site: "Lest We Forget The Meaning of Her [Jeanne Clery's] Death, That We Must Protect One Another, So That Her Life Will Not Have Been In Vain."

Chapter 13

College Campus Violence Prevention: How Background Investigations Can Have a Direct Impact

Mario Pecoraro, Jr.

In the summer of 2003, Pennsylvania State University received national attention when it became known to them for the first time that a faculty member had been convicted of murdering three individuals in the mid-1960s. This event ushered in national attention to the use of background checks for faculty as well as employees on college and university campuses, something that had only been previously recommended for job applicants in businesses.

College and university campuses must protect the safety and welfare of their employees as well as students. Campus violence is a form of workplace violence for employees (Paludi, Nydegger, & Paludi, 2006). Traditionally, most campuses have relied solely on their perception of a candidate's character before hiring. Today, that is not enough.

There are many more objective factors to take into consideration that can be uncovered through a thorough background investigation. The campus's human resource department must play a significant role in its interaction with the candidate throughout the entire recruitment and selection process. HR staffers must be cognizant of the potential areas where a candidate may be less than truthful. At the same time, they must be cautious and be sure to exhibit the necessary due diligence in the process.

While many crimes cannot be prevented, there are steps campuses can take to prevent violence by employees. This chapter examines the methods of conducting proper and effective background investigations and how implementing a due-diligence-based hiring process can complement any existing campus violence prevention initiative. The recommendations offered in this chapter may be applied to all new faculty and employees on campus. Doing background checks is especially important for anyone being offered a "critical position" like those involving master key access, finance, or security.

BACKGROUND INVESTIGATIONS

A background investigation is an inquiry into the history and behavior patterns of an individual, usually for the purposes of making a hiring decision. While such investigations have usually been used for employment purposes, more and more campuses now employ background investigations for many other purposes, including reducing negligent hiring claims, and to ensure the safety and security of staff and students. Campuses using background investigations for all employees include the University of Mississippi, Frostburg State University, and Fairleigh Dickinson University. The following campuses are among those that use background checks for new employees except faculty: Emory University, Johns Hopkins University, and Notre Dame University. Among those campuses that use background investigations for critical positions are the University of Maine, the University of California, and University of Texas.

For any background investigation to be effective, it must be part of a due-diligence process. A due-diligence-based process consists of a methodology that uncovers all possible areas within which pertinent information may be found. Such information in most cases requires a firm starting point to initiate the investigation. This may be as simple as the information found on an employment application. Another starting point could also include a name, date of birth, and last known address. Many times, campuses overlook such a crucial step and commence an investigation without having the proper facts at their disposal. It is common for campuses to make this error as they make a quick decision to fill an open position. This may lead to ineffective research and significant waste in time and resources, not to mention a significant increase in liability to a campus. It is crucial that the process include an effective and consistent process for all background investigations.

There are many types of investigations that are available to campuses, including: identity verification and subsequent verification of personal history, criminal convictions history, civil litigations history, credit history, educational attainment, employment history, references, bankruptcies, judgments, liens, government debarment lists, terrorist watch lists, sex offender registries, and driving records.

Once the proper information has been provided, the initial step in any background investigation is to verify the identity and also confirm the validity of the information provided. While the resources used may vary from provider to provider, a background investigative expert should always commence an investigation by confirming the identity of the applicant, as well as identifying any and all addresses that an applicant may have maintained, both personally and professionally. Conducting such research will reveal all possible names that an applicant may have utilized, as well as identify all areas within which an applicant may have resided.

There is a common misconception that an applicant's criminal record is indexed by name and/or Social Security number. While this would be the most preferred method, unfortunately criminal records in the United States are indexed by name and date of birth only. There may be some instances whereby a Social Security number may be on file with a corresponding court/agency, but as a rule the only methods used by investigative firms to confirm the existence of a criminal record are name and date of birth.

CRIMINAL RECORDS INVESTIGATIONS

While these searches are crucial in an effective due-diligence-based search, the most valuable is the criminal records investigation. A criminal records investigation can be time-consuming. It can also be ineffective if not done diligently. As previously mentioned, a criminal records court file is indexed by subject name and date of birth only; therefore, searching the proper name and respective geographic area is the most crucial aspect of an effective investigation. There are two types of criminal conviction searches available: felonies and misdemeanors. While the methods utilized to search the records may vary by location, campuses must be prudent when selecting a background investigations process to ensure that it encompasses all available searches and that there are no searches left incomplete.

Among the factors to consider are not only the types of searches being conducted but also the extent of the searches available. It is important for campuses to recognize the levels of searches available— county as well as state and federal court records, for example—and the importance of avoiding inaccurate searches.

Once criminal convictions research has been completed, and all levels have been identified and searched, the next step would be to identify the remaining searches to be conducted in the screening process. Depending on the nature and level of the background investigation, the efforts would continue with confirming the information provided by the applicant. While some investigations are more in depth than others, ultimately all information researched is gathered in order for the campus to make a hiring decision.

Campuses benefit immensely from the background investigations process in that they bring safety and security to the institution. Conducting

198 Understanding and Preventing Campus Violence

proper and effective screening can ensure that a campus's liability for the wrongful acts of an employee is limited as long as the campus demonstrates that proper due diligence has been exhibited. Campuses may be held liable for acts conducted by employees if it can be proven that the campus could have or should have exhausted necessary due diligence in the screening process. Negligent hiring is deemed as the failure of a campus to use reasonable care in the employee recruiting and selection process. Campuses have a legal duty to not hire individuals who could pose a threat or potentially cause harm to the campus community. "Reasonable care" is discretionary based upon the campus and may vary based upon a number of factors.

Campuses should consult with legal counsel before implementing a background investigation process to ensure that it is not only due-diligence based but avoids potential negligent-hiring claims and stays within the law in all regards.

REFERENCES

Hinton, D. (2004). *The criminal records manual.* Tempe, AZ: Facts on Demand Press.

Paludi, M., Nydegger, R., & Paludi, C. (2006). *Understanding workplace violence: A guide for managers and employees.* Westport, CT: Praeger.

Rosen, L. S. (2005). *The safe hiring manual: The complete guide to keeping criminals, terrorists and imposters out of your workplace.* Tempe, AZ: Facts on Demand Press.

Chapter 14

Responding to Sexually Victimized College Students

Connie Kirkland
Howard Kallem

ORIGINS OF CAMPUS SECURITY THROUGH FEDERAL LEGISLATION

Though sexual assault and related acts of violence have been common occurrences on college campuses across the nation, recognition of this fact has only received the attention it deserves within the past 20 years. With the rape, burglary, and strangulation of freshman Jeanne Clery in her dormitory on a university in suburban Philadelphia, Pennsylvania, campus security became the new watchwords. Following the trial and the conviction of the perpetrator, the Clery family founded Security on Campus, Inc. in 1989, a nonprofit organization dedicated to improving safety and security on America's college campuses.

It was only then that the nation realized that just a small percentage of colleges reported crime statistics to the FBI. Few, if any, victim services existed on any campus to respond to sexual assault, one of the most frequent crimes committed on college campuses today. The Clery family educated federal authorities and pushed Congress to pass a measure to help ensure student safety on campuses across the country. The Federal Student Right-to-Know and Campus Security Act (Campus Security Act) was passed by the United States Congress in 1990 in large measure due to the efforts of this family. The Clery Act, as it came to be known after the 1998 amendments, requires that all campuses report Part I crimes to the FBI. Crimes covered in the act are homicide, sex offenses, robbery, aggravated assault, burglary, motor vehicle theft, and arson. Statistics of these crimes must now be provided not only to college students, but also to campus employees and prospective students and their parents. In addition, the act requires that each college and university have policies, procedures for intervention, and educational programs to help reduce the risks of college students. Since the Clery Act was enacted, campuses and their constituents have begun to think about safety as they make many of their decisions.

Other important federal legislation followed quickly, to include the Campus Sexual Assault Victims' Bill of Rights in 1992, which became part of the United States Department of Education's Higher Education Reauthorization Act in the same year. In 1994 the Violence Against Women Act (VAWA) was passed and included funding to increase sexual assault programming and victim services on college campuses. Amendments to these and other pieces of legislation have continued through the years to strengthen the original campus security laws.

COMMONWEALTH OF VIRGINIA AWAKENS TO CAMPUS NEEDS

During the early 1990s, the Commonwealth of Virginia was also assessing the problem of sexual assault on its college campuses. The State Council of Higher Education in Virginia (SCHEV) led the way by hiring a statewide campus sexual assault coordinator in 1991. A statewide survey developed by SCHEV underscored the need for ongoing education on the issue of sexual assault. As a result of this report, SCHEV recommended that all Virginia colleges and universities create or review their existing policies on sexual assault and rape and distribute the policy to all members of the campus community.

SCHEV along with then-governor L. Douglas Wilder made recommendations that included the designation of a "sexual assault coordinator" at each institution, incorporation of personal safety and security considerations into campus master plans, the creation of campus-wide educational programs related to sexual assault, the establishment of free treatment and support services for victims, and, of course, compliance with all aspects of the Clery Act.

GEORGE MASON UNIVERSITY'S MODEL PROGRAM

George Mason University, a state university of over 28,000 students at that time, located just across the Potomac River from Washington, D.C., in Fairfax, Virginia, was already beginning to incorporate new processes and policies to address the issue of campus sexual assault. In 1992, the university's sexual assault task force had written a thorough policy on sexual assault and was developing a complete sexual assault response protocol, whose goal was to provide a responsive, sensitive, fair, and comprehensive system to assist and support individuals affected by sexual assault. This system was developed to address the requirements of the Higher Education Reauthorization Act, which had recently been passed. In 1993, the university created a new office to respond to the issue of campus sexual assault and hired a director to develop this new office—George Mason University Sexual Assault Services.

Eighteen years later and with a growing population of now more than 30,000 students spread across five campuses, the Sexual Assault Services (SAS) director continues to be the focal point of the university's response to sexual assault on its campus. This position, which I have held for the entire 18 years, provides university-wide coordination of the education/ prevention, treatment, and response policies, procedures, and programs in the area of sexual assault. The position is housed in the Dean of Students Office and maintains close working relationships with the university and local police; campus counseling and local sexual assault centers; campus health services and neighboring hospitals; housing and residence life; and academic departments. The principal responsibilities of this innovative office are to oversee the development, delivery, coordination, and evaluation of the response system on campus. The director of SAS was deemed a "campus security authority" pursuant to the Clery Act and is the collection agency for all unofficial reports of campus sexual assault, which will be enumerated, in the yearly Clery Report, which is prepared by our University Police Department and submitted to the United States Department of Education. The advantage is clear … at George Mason University, we value student victims/survivors, whether or not they choose to make an official police report.

THE STARTING POINT: 1994

Since administrators at George Mason University and other colleagues around the state have shown great support for the principle of addressing sexual assault on our campus, there have been few barriers to contend with as this program unfolded. George Mason University Sexual Assault Services has been recognized over the years by the United States Department of Justice, the National Crime Prevention Council, the United States Department of Education, and the Virginia Department of Education, among others, as an extremely successful program that continues to address the needs of college students and the offices and agencies that serve them.

There is an old adage that goes something like "If you lead a horse to water, he will drink." In campus sexual assault terms, it goes more like this: "If you develop a program and market it successfully, students will come for services." Indeed, that is exactly what happened in the first few years of this new office. The year 1994, the first full year the office existed, was devoted to getting name recognition and educating the campus community about the services available for them. Sexual Assault

Services offered campus-wide prevention and intervention services, and it provided outreach and training to students, faculty, and allied professionals. The director provided crisis and supportive counseling as well as advocacy to students who disclosed incidents of sexual assault. Within just two years, it became evident that one person could not manage the workload that was resulting from this very needed office on campus. I did have one graduate level student working a few hours a week in the office, mainly to help with process rather than substance.

Then, the most wonderful thing happened ... the Violence Against Women Act was passed by the United States Congress and funding became available not only for community victim services agencies, but also for campus offices devoted to the issues of sexual assault, dating/domestic violence, and/or stalking. Though the office name has not changed in its 18-year history, it has enveloped these other two issues within its service delivery. There is ample anecdotal evidence to show the interrelated qualities of these three separate crimes. I began to offer assistance to dating violence victims and stalking victims. Sometimes these victims were also sexual assault victims; sometimes they were not, but the advocacy needed by all three types of victims is essentially the same.

Victims of such personal violence have great areas of loss—physical, financial, emotional, and social—even as college students. Victims must resolve issues caused or exacerbated by the criminal act, the legal system, and the response by their family and friends. Decision making for victims is often difficult because of the feelings associated with victimization—those of self-blame, fear, anger, and heightened vulnerability. My ultimate mission was to assist student victims in order to maintain their student status at George Mason University. Intervening with faculty to salvage academic careers and help administrators understand the tolls of trauma became a major reason for the office to exist.

NEED FOR VICTIM ADVOCACY

There is a great need for victim advocacy through all steps taken by the victim in order to facilitate the reorganization and recovery process following a crime. This is exactly what the Office of Sexual Assault Services proposed to do for those student victims who disclosed behind their closed doors. This is what we do today. Advocacy takes concentration, time, and effort. It also requires great collaboration that can only occur as a result of consistent attention to the needs of the students and the availability of institutional services.

It may be important here to note the use of terms and the need to use more than one to include as many perspectives as possible. Both the term *victim* and *survivor* are used in popular and social science literature on sexual assault. The use of the term *sexual assault survivor* is sometimes used as a way to indicate the therapeutic stage in which an individual began recovery and healing. Those seeking to empower people who have experienced sexual assault broadened the usage further to include anyone who has been sexually assaulted whether or not they disclose the assault at all. Others, however, favor the term *victim* as a way to convey the violence intrinsic to sexual assault. Most would agree that sexual assault causes victimization and that victims then become survivors during their healing and restorative process.

Some victims/survivors experience physical injury; some experience the threat of physical harm; some experience financial loss. And nearly all victims/survivors experience some emotional distress. Emotional suffering may be the most common response and also the least often addressed ... either by the victim/survivor or by the system. The pain of being violated, and of feeling violated, confronts every victim of personal crime.

> You feel stripped naked. You feel as if someone has exposed you totally.... You are powerless. Violation is an adult way to explain that, but it isn't an adult response. It's reminiscent of the kind of helplessness that goes back to early childhood. And I think that's what makes it so crucially painful. Because you can't fight back.
>
> (Bard & Sangrey, 1979)

A victim's sense of trust and sense of control have been permeated in a way that is difficult to understand or even to acknowledge. Thus begins the crime victim's process of recovery and, indeed, the individual's development as a result of the initial impact of victimization.

Crime is a crisis, and a crisis is a time for a person to either grow or deteriorate, depending on how she or he chooses to respond. The influence of personal and social values, as well as society's norms and pressures, are central to any victim's recovery. No matter what the perpetrator's motive or intent, he or she disrupts the victim's way of life. The incident presents a somewhat chaotic interruption to life, confusing most victims and leaving them with many decisions and conflicts to resolve. The conflicts that emerge in a crime victim's response are multifaceted. Conflict is natural and an inevitable fact of life that becomes unhealthy only when it is left unresolved. It is crucial, then, for the victim to attempt to resolve the conflicts that result from the crime in order to regain the power and stability that was taken away during the violation.

The struggle of sexual assault victims is so intense; victims want a resolution, but some are unsure how to reach it. Thoughts of costs, resources, friend and family response, time involved, reliving the event, all are involved in this decision. Most important, though, is probably the person's own feelings and thoughts about such a victimization. The emotional effect—the psychological impact—creates a roadblock to behavior, such as reporting the crime that might hold the perpetrator accountable. The violation deepens. The victim begins, in many cases, to blame herself or himself—directing inward the anger that more appropriately should be directed toward the perpetrator.

- My roommate does not treat the situation with the degree of seriousness that I believe it calls for. She was unsure that the incident was harmful or his fault.
- My mother said that's what happens when you have a party.
- I thought I had been to blame because I left the door unlocked.
- I felt that it was my fault it happened. I had a party and he came. (Kirkland files)

THE GROWING PROBLEM

Legitimizing the issue of sexual assault on our campus by creating an office to respond to it allowed our students, faculty, and staff to understand more and more about this prevalent campus crime. Taking the issue seriously, not minimizing and not overlooking the more difficult non-stranger sexual assaults, sent a signal to our students that Sexual Assault Services was a safe place, a confidential space to disclose such traumas, whether they were recent or had occurred long in the past. Sexual Assault Services did not blame victims who were intoxicated, did not blame victims who went to fraternity parties and "should have known better," and did not blame victims who got into cars with a person they met that night at a party.

Sexual Assault Services (SAS) provided crisis intervention to victims as well as comprehensive support services and supportive counseling for as long as the student victim/survivor needed. As director, I was the liaison between the student and the criminal justice system, between the student and the health and counseling services received, between the student and the academic setting. SAS provided thorough advocacy while allowing the student to regain as normal a routine as possible and remain a college student.

Information given and guidance offered take time. As the word spread that such services were available through my office, more and more student victims came to seek their own services following incidents of victimization. Whether they were pursuing legal, judicial, medical, or academic intervention, they knew I would offer kind and intense assistance. Soon victims of dating violence, domestic violence, and stalking began seeking services as well. There really was nowhere else on campus for these victims to go since many did not actually recognize their situations as crimes. They didn't go to the police and they didn't go to the counseling center, but they did want some sort of vindication and some means to recovery.

AND THE RESPONSE TO GROWTH

By 1997, it was time that SAS expanded its personnel. Though the university continued to be steadfast in its support of our mission, additional funding was not possible at that point. But due to VAWA being passed, I knew where available funds were and I began to write grant applications for some of the VAWA funding. The funding stream that suited our office best was STOP funding. STOP stands for Services, Training, Officers, and Prosecution. Virginia Department of Criminal Justice Services is the agency in Virginia designated for the pass-through of these federal funds. I submitted my application, requesting funds for two part-time assistants, the coordination of a regional sexual assault council, and the creation of a three-tiered peer support program to assist SAS on a volunteer basis.

I received the STOP funds in 1997 and have received continuation funding for the next 12 years. Though this funding has not been extensive (no more than $50,000 per year), SAS has expanded exponentially and has risen to be a recognized full-service victim services program not only on our campus, but also in our entire Northern Virginia region. SAS is often looked to for its innovations, its methods to retain students, and its restorative qualities for student survivors of campus sexual assault, dating/domestic violence, and stalking. We, and I love to use that word, assist all students who come to us, whether their victimization occurred on or off campus.

The two part-time staff members are instrumental in our ability to produce major educational initiatives and serve an ever-growing population of victims/survivors. The education coordinator works on the Fairfax Campus with me where we have the vast majority of students located. The education coordinator's basic responsibilities include supervision of all volunteers, interns, and members of the Peer Support Program (more about that a little later). She also serves as the administrative head of several community councils for which SAS is the leader. These include our own George Mason University Campus-Community Coordinating Council (similar to a SART) and the Metro Washington Coalition Against Sexual Assault, which is composed of other sexual assault providers in the metro region. Both of these groups meet quarterly to discuss emerging issues, campus crime trends, and collaboration issues with other service providers.

In addition, I serve as one of the three agency heads that coordinate an innovative council composed of police leaders from the seven police departments that exist within our county. Fairfax County is a community of over 1 million persons and George Mason University sits within it. Since the majority of the sexual assaults that are reported to SAS occur off-campus, it is imperative that we collaborate with all the differing police departments with which our students may come into contact. This Sexual Assault Council, as we call it, brings differing viewpoints together and allows police and advocates to be trained together on emerging issues and response trends. This council is a direct result of STOP funding as well provided to SAS, the Fairfax County Police Victim Services Unit, and the Fairfax County Victim Assistance Network (our county-wide rape crisis center).

The second staff member funded by VAWA is the SAS Outreach Specialist who provides outreach and services at two of our smaller campuses in neighboring counties. Without STOP funding, this would be impossible and students who take classes only on those campuses would be without services. The role is vital for the entire campus community to be served. This specialist collaborated with staff on these campuses as well as with service providers in the communities of Arlington and Prince William Counties where these campuses are located.

OUR COORDINATING COUNCIL

Necessary in order to receive funding through STOP, the George Mason University Campus-Community Coordinating Council is similar to an advisory board but it has become so well-established on our campus that its members are acknowledged for their participation in it and the members choose to take a very active part in the progress of Sexual Assault Services. When in 1999 I realized that our stalking disclosures were nearly one-fourth of all disclosures to the office of SAS, I discussed this alarming new trend with the Coordinating Council. The most comprehensive to date university stalking policy was soon created by a subcommittee of this council and approved through the university's legal office and signed into effect by our President. This stalking policy is published annually in the university's Campus Safety Report, the university student handbook, and the university catalogue. Students soon came to realize that there was something that could actually be done to address stalking on campus. Since 1999, the federal funds received by SAS are to provide intervention and education for both campus sexual assault and campus stalking. The Coordinating Council has the responsibility of reviewing and revising both the university stalking and university sexual assault policies. Revisions have occurred as laws and perpetrator methods have changed through the intervening years.

SAS offers free training to Coordinating Council members on a yearly basis, both to update their own knowledge and also to expand their views and perceptions. Examples of such training include stalking, cyberstalking, sex trafficking, and civil legal remedies. Because of our university's nearness to Washington, D.C., and because SAS maintains connections with national groups, it is not difficult to attract highly effective and expert trainers to our campus. Members of this council are representatives from local and campus women's centers, police departments, health centers and hospitals, athletic and Greek life offices, advocates, and other administrators who often receive disclosures from students. The collaboration works well for all of us.

SEXUAL ASSAULT SERVICES PEER SUPPORT PROGRAM

The other aspect of the growth of George Mason University's Sexual Assault Services office that began in 1997 is the Peer Support Program. While many universities have peer educators to assist with programming, notably on the issues of sexual assault and substance abuse, we decided to go a couple steps further. With the university's legal office blessing, I developed a program that, on a voluntary basis, would provide extensive assistance to the staff of SAS, to the victims/survivors who disclose incidents to SAS, and to the university as a whole. STOP funds originally funded this initiative; now it is sustained via university funds solely.

Created as a three-tiered program, peer support begins before victimization occurs and is offered as long as a student wants/requests such support. The three components of this system and their responsibilities are as follows:

- *Peer Educators* provide outreach to the campus community via kiosks/tabling events, presentations to classes and organizations, orientation and housing programs, and major SAS initiatives.

- *Peer Companions* provide one-on-one intervention services to students who have disclosed their victimizations to SAS staff. Student victims/survivors are informed by SAS staff of the availability of students trained in crisis intervention and sexual assault/stalking issues who can serve as extra support. SAS staff then links the student victim/survivor with a trained Peer Companion to meet regularly to discuss the minor process needs and to be a sounding board. This is simply an adjunct to SAS staff services and that of any therapist the student may have.

- *Peer Advocates* are the highest trained members of the Peer Support Program and are graduate students or university staff members. They provide advocacy at the point of disclosure and provide on-call services in lieu of the SAS director. This necessitates carrying the SAS cell phone to respond to emergencies or other immediate needs, which can mean response to any police department where a student might be, response to the hospital to support a student about to undergo a SANE (forensic) exam, response to on-campus housing, student health center, faculty office, or Dean of Students/Judicial Affairs office. Or it might mean simply providing telephone crisis intervention to a student victim/survivor or friend or family member.

All members of the Peer Support Program complete a 20-hour training program and attend monthly in-service trainings; all are provided by the SAS staff and other campus authorities. Peers receive no compensation and no credit for their volunteer efforts. Peers normally stay with the program until graduation; thus, enabling continuity of services, continuity of personnel, and greater visibility to the larger campus community.

All Peers are involved in the major initiatives sponsored by SAS each academic year. These include Turn Off the Violence Week/Sexual Assault Awareness Month activities in October, Healthy Relationships Week/*The Vagina Monologues* production in February, and Victims' Right Week in April each year.

Probably the most notable and most visible event that SAS sponsors each year is The Clothesline Project during the first week of October (Turn Off the Violence Week). This event has grown exponentially since its inception at George Mason University in 1997. We provide the T-shirts, the creative supplies, and the clothesline, which hangs outside among trees in the most widely trespassed part of our main campus. We, along with our co-sponsors Women's Center and Alcohol, Drug and Health Education Services, hang all the created T-shirts by 9 a.m. and take down all the created T-shirts by 5 p.m. each day for a week to generate interest in both sexual and domestic violence and to market our services. That first year in 1997 approximately 50 T-shirts were created by George Mason University students. Every year since approximately 50 more T-shirts have been created; thus, this past year in 2007 we hung and displayed over 500 shirts, which evoked an amazing understanding to passersby about the trauma of violence and that the campus community has not been overlooked by this phenomenon.

ON WE GO

George Mason University Sexual Assault Services is growing. It is growing in its own knowledge and expertise. It is growing in its reputation. It is growing in its utilization. And it is growing in its ability to collaborate and connect with other agencies both on and off-campus. We hope it continues to grow and expand its services because we know that it is both viable and vital to the energy of our campus. It helps with the retention of students. It helps students graduate, and it helps them become the productive citizens of our society that we all want them to be.

PREVENTING AND RESPONDING TO GENDERED VIOLENCE ON CAMPUS: AN INSTITUTIONAL APPROACH

There are a number of departments, offices, and programs at a college or university that touch on the issue of gendered violence, including sexual assault, rape, stalking, at least certain forms of sexual harassment, and other types of violence directed toward women based on gender. They include the equity office, sexual assault services, student life, judicial affairs, housing, health services, campus police, and human resources. Each can play an essential role in preventing, recognizing, and/or responding to gendered violence on campus. Some of these units deal with education and prevention. Others provide support and advocacy for students and employees who have been the victims of harassment or violence. Yet others are involved with investigating possible incidents and redressing them. Some may even have responsibilities in all these areas. It is critical that the university coordinate the work of these units to provide a consistent, systematic approach. Only in this way can the university demonstrate an institutional commitment to ensuring a safe environment in which to work and learn.

Of course, the best approach to dealing with gendered violence is to take steps to prevent it from occurring in the first place. A key element to this is education. This is important so that all segments of the university community—administrative employees, blue-collar workers, faculty, and students—can recognize gendered violence so that they refrain from engaging in it, recognize it when they see it, and know how to respond when they do. At George Mason University, as at many colleges and universities, all new employees are required to participate in sexual harassment training conducted by the staff from the university's Office of Equity and Diversity Services in conjunction with the Human Resources Department. Student Life and Housing offers similar training for all new students as part of orientation, and to residential advisors and other student housing staff.

The training generally includes the legal and practical definitions of sexual harassment, the university's legal obligations, and what an individual should do if he or she has been harassed or has observed harassment. For supervisors, managers, and residential advisors, the training provides additional explanation of their responsibilities as agents of the university. In all cases, the training includes real-life examples and an explanation of the university's procedures for responding to incidents of possible harassment.

It is important to consider the format of the training so that it is designed for the specific audience. A lecture to a large group is not likely to be effective. The most effective training will be to small groups, with plenty of opportunity for discussion and interaction. Similarly, the training should be designed to meet the interests and needs of each audience—the training that will work for maintenance staff will not be effective with faculty. Examples should be tailored to the types of situations likely to be encountered by each group.

For example, training for maintenance staff should include how gendered violence may occur among their coworkers as well as between them and students; it should also include examples of the types of harassment and gendered violence they might observe within their work environment among other members of the university community. George Mason hires students as Residential Technicians to provide computer support in the dormitories. The training for them focuses in part on the types of situations they might encounter working in dorm rooms—both as to what might happen to them and what they might observe, and what they should do about either instance.

Training for faculty may be most effective if it includes an academic focus as well as practical instruction. Professors in the sociology department might be interested in discussing the causes of harassment and gendered violence; law faculty might want to delve into the case law. If these suggest a seminar-like format, that is not by accident—if that is the format in which faculty members are most likely to be receptive to the training, then that is the format to use. This should not distract from the primary purpose of the training—the prevention and recognition of harassment and violence at the university and how to respond—but it can enrich the training and make it seem less like just one more requirement for new hires.

Again, it is critical that all new members of the university community receive this training. Training for new students should not only reach first years, but should include transfer students. If the training takes place primarily through the housing program, the university should take additional measures to reach commuter students—a particularly challenging issue at schools like George Mason, where the majority of students do not live on campus. On a campus as diverse as George Mason, training for students and employees should be designed to recognize language and cultural issues. Training for employees should include full-time as well as part-time workers, including student workers.

Particular note should be given to adjunct faculty members. In 2005, the National Education Association estimated that adjunct faculty comprised 43–48% of faculty, depending on the measures employed to define adjunct faculty (Maitland & Rhoades, 2005). This figure has likely only increased since then. Adjuncts are less likely to be familiar with a university's policies on harassment, assault, stalking, and other forms of gendered violence and the procedures for reporting incidents. They are likely to be on campus when many of the university officials responsible for these policies and procedures are not, and when at least certain types of gendered violence may be more likely to occur. Therefore, it is critical that special efforts be made to train new adjunct faculty (e.g., by scheduling training sessions at night or on the weekend or through online or Web-based training). Indeed, well-designed Web-based training can be an effective way to train all elements of the university community, and particularly to follow up on and reinforce in-person training.

Follow-up is, indeed, critical. One-time training, while important, will only be effective if periodically reinforced. All faculty members at George Mason are required to repeat the training when selected for tenure; similarly, it is a part of the required training for all new supervisors and managers throughout the university. Of course, should an incident of sexual harassment or gendered violence take place, there would be additional training for those involved as a remedial measure, tailored to the specifics of what happened (responding to incidents will be discussed further below).

However, these requirements alone will not be enough to reach the majority of the university community. Thus, George Mason, as well as other colleges and universities, puts considerable effort into ongoing programs to remind the community of the importance of these issues. George Mason's Sexual Assault Services plays a particularly active role, providing training and sponsoring programs and activities to alert the community to the many ways that gendered violence can interfere with a safe learning environment. (The program has been recognized nationally as a model and is therefore discussed in detail below.) Campus health services can also help educate students and faculty on how to recognize gendered violence and its impact on students. The Women's Studies program at Mason sponsors courses and seminars on harassment and violence, with an emphasis on recognizing that these are not problems unique to women. The Law School offers courses on gender discrimination and sexual harassment, the School of Social Work has offered courses discussing gendered violence in society, and the English Department has had courses that explored the literature of gendered violence. The Office of Equity and Diversity Services and the Human Resources Department offer annual training to all the employment units within the University. *The Broadside*, the university's student newspaper, periodically carries articles on the university's efforts to prevent and deal with sexual harassment and gendered violence. The university president periodically sends out e-mail messages to the entire community, reminding them of the university's policies and procedures. Student Life and Human Resources conduct climate surveys to gauge the level of comfort students and employees have on campus and their perceptions about the prevalence of sexual harassment and gendered violence. They share this information with the Equity Office, department chairs, and managers so that they can take measures to ensure a safe environment. The university makes special efforts to reach out to athletes, leaders of the Greek organizations, student government representatives, and other student leaders to make them aware of the importance of preventing sexual harassment and gendered violence. These are all part of an ongoing effort to keep the issue alive for the various members of the university community.

Another important step to prevent sexual harassment and gendered violence is to have strong and widely disseminated policies prohibiting such conduct and effective grievance or complaint procedures. George Mason has policies and procedures prohibiting sex discrimination, sexual harassment, sexual assault, and stalking. These policies and procedures let the university community know that the university does not condone and will not tolerate harassment and gendered violence. Title IX of the Education Amendments of 1972 prohibits sex discrimination by and at colleges and universities that receive federal funds, including sexual harassment and violence directed toward women based on their gender. Regulations issued by the Office for Civil Rights (OCR) of the U.S. Department of Education to implement Title IX require each educational institution to have a policy prohibiting sex discrimination and a grievance procedure providing for the prompt and equitable resolution of student and employee complaints (34 C.F.R. §§ Sec. 106.8 and 9). Moreover, such a procedure can help a college meet its responsibilities under Title VII of the Civil Rights Act of 1964, regarding employment discrimination. By encouraging employees to let the employer know about possible sex discrimination, the employer can take quick action to respond. Indeed, the Supreme Court has held that, in certain circumstances, if an employer has an effective procedure by which employees can complain about sexual harassment and an employee who believes he or she was harassed unreasonably fails to use it, then the employer will not be liable (*Faragher v. Boca Raton*, 524 U.S. 775 (1998); *Burlington Industries v. Ellerth*, 524 U.S. 742 (1998); see *also Enforcement Guidance: Vicarious Employer Liability for Unlawful Harassment by Supervisors*, issued by the U.S. Equal Employment Opportunity Commission). However, perhaps more importantly from an educational and human relations perspective, an effective grievance procedure is essential to ensuring a safe and welcoming environment in which employees and students feel comfortable working and learning.

To meet OCR's "prompt and equitable" requirement, the university must provide notice of the procedures to students and employees, including where to file grievances or complaints. The procedures may include a voluntary, informal stage but, where that is not successful, must provide for an adequate, reliable, and impartial investigation, including the opportunity to present witnesses and other evidence. The procedures must include reasonably prompt time frames for the major stages of the process and provide for notice to the parties of the outcome (i.e., whether or not the alleged harassment or violence was found to have occurred). They must also provide an assurance that the university will take steps to prevent recurrence of any harassment and to correct its effects.

Much can be written about how to ensure that policies and grievance procedures are effective. This chapter will highlight a number of areas in which universities commonly slip up, with additional resources cited at the end. One common problem is not adequately publicizing the university's policies and procedures. Students and employees must know that the university prohibits gendered violence and sexual harassment. OCR's regulation at 34 C.F.R. § 106.9 states that notice of the required policy against sex discrimination should be published in local newspapers; newspapers and magazines put out by the university, students, and alumni groups; and in each announcement, bulletin, catalogue, or application form.

Similarly, a grievance procedure cannot be effective unless students and employees know it exists, how it works, and how to file a complaint. Thus, the procedures should be written in clear language, easily understood and, again, widely disseminated. While an important first step, distributing the procedures to administrators or including them in the university's administrative or policy manual will not be enough, as these publications are not widely circulated to and understood by all members of the university community. The procedures should be available at various locations throughout the campus. The procedures, or a summary of them, can be published as a separate document, perhaps in a pamphlet form. A summary can be included in the faculty, staff, and student handbooks, the course catalogue, and other major university publications. Very importantly, the nondiscrimination policy and the procedures should be easy to find on the university's Web site. A student or employee should be able to type into the site's search engine "sex discrimination" or "sexual harassment" and the policy and procedures should be one of the first selections (*Revised sexual harassment guidance: Harassment of students by school employees, other students, or third parties*, Office for Civil Rights, U.S. Department of Education, January 2001, http://www.ed.gov/ocr/publications.html, last accessed November 2007).

Under OCR's regulations, the university can have a procedure that covers all forms of student and/or employee concerns and complaints, or one limited to discrimination. For the latter, the procedure could include a variety of types of discrimination—sex, national origin, disability, race, and age (all prohibited by the laws enforced by OCR)— and perhaps other bases such as sexual orientation, veteran's status, political orientation, and religion. Regardless, the procedures must clearly state that it covers sex discrimination, including sexual harassment, and it should be easy to find, for example, through references in the nondiscrimination policy and on the Equity Office and other university Web sites.

However, because of the complex and sensitive issues associated with sexual harassment and gendered violence, most universities have separate polices and procedures for such conduct. This enables the individual(s) responsible for investigating and resolving such complaints to develop the sensitivity and expertise that will encourage students and employees to have confidence in the procedures. Some universities that take this approach have a single procedure dedicated to all forms of gendered violence while others have separate procedures for sexual harassment and for sexual assault or other forms of gendered violation. On the one hand, too many procedures could create confusion as to which procedure applies in a particular circumstance. On the other hand, a general procedure might not fit all types of complaints. Does it make sense to have the same procedure for students as for employees? For harassment of a student by an employee as for harassment by another student? For harassment consisting of unwelcome jokes or comments of a sexual nature as for sexual or other gender-based assault? A university might well decide that each of these requires different knowledge and considerations—of academic standards, the university's code of conduct, medical issues—and therefore different procedures.

Regardless of the number of procedures, all those involved in applying them must be trained in and knowledgeable of the type of issue as well as the applicable legal standards. If the university does have multiple procedures, there must be a clear "road map" so that the students and employees know the circumstances under which each procedure applies and any differences in how complaints or grievances will be processed. As a good practice, in addition to written explanations, the university should have one or more "portals"—individuals designated as contact points who can then help the individual identify which procedure to use. In part for this reason, OCR's regulations require colleges and universities to have at least one individual designated to coordinate its efforts to comply with Title IX 34 C.F.R. § 106.8. The college or university must notify all its students and employees of the name or position title, office address, and telephone number of this "Title IX Coordinator" in its nondiscrimination policy.

Before leaving the issue of grievance procedures, it is important to note that OCR has cautioned against using the student code of conduct as the vehicle by which students can complain of sexual harassment. Many such codes have provisions prohibiting harassment by one student against another and/or prohibiting assault, including sexual assault. In *California State University Bakersfield*, OCR Case No. 09042067 (2004), OCR noted that procedures for enforcing student discipline codes tend to focus on the alleged harasser without allowing for the participation of or remedies for the complainant. Some university procedures require the victim of the alleged harassment or violence to essentially act as a prosecuting attorney and prove his or her case by gathering evidence, questioning witnesses, and making arguments. Student codes of conduct focus on discipline for the offender, and generally do not contain provisions for correcting the effects of the conduct on the student who had been harassed or otherwise subjected to gendered violence.

Some student codes of conduct require that the alleged violation be proven by "clear and convincing evidence," which OCR has stated does not meet the "equitable" requirement in its regulations. In *Evergreen College*, OCR Case No. 10922064 (1995), *George Washington University*, OCR Case No. 11042004 (2004), and *Georgetown University*, OCR Case No. 11032017 (2004), OCR stated that the appropriate standard is the easier-to-prove "preponderance of the evidence," the same standard used by OCR and the courts in resolving Title IX matters. Another problem with student discipline codes is that they generally do not include references to the Title IX coordinator. Finally, those charged with adjudicating alleged violations of the student code of conduct—often other students—may not have the sensitivity and expertise to effectively deal with sexual harassment, sexual assault, and other forms of gendered violence. If the university makes it unnecessarily hard for students to bring complaints or grievances—if the students believe the university's process for complaining is not effective—they will be discouraged from bringing such concerns to the university's attention in the future.

Of course, effective implementation of a grievance process can only encourage students and employees to bring concerns to the university's attention. There may be a concern that making it too easy to file will encourage frivolous grievances or complaints. Most universities have not found this to be the case, with many taking steps at intake to ensure that the complainant has a valid basis for believing that he or she has been harassed or the victim of other forms of gendered violence. Certainly, George Mason's Sexual Assault Services program demonstrates that an effective policy and procedures will encourage students to raise valid concerns.

Again, coordination is essential in this regard. If a student or employee reports an incident of sexual harassment or sexual assault to campus police, the police should inform the student or employee of the relevant grievance process (or even contact the office administering that process directly) as well as of the advocacy and support services offered by the university's sexual assault services program. Similarly, if a student or employee reports an incident of sexual assault or other possible criminal conduct to the equity office, campus health services, or sexual assault services, the contacted office should take appropriate steps to involve campus police and the other offices. The complaint or grievance should be investigated thoroughly and promptly, with all parties given the opportunity to identify witnesses and other evidence and otherwise present their sides of the matter. This can be through an administrative investigation, as done at George Mason, or through some sort of hearing process. Again, if a hearing process is used, care should be taken to not put too much of a burden on the grievant to prove his or her case. The members of the hearing panel should review any administrative investigation that was done, ask their own questions, and identify and obtain any additional witnesses or other evidence that they feel is necessary to resolve the matter. George Mason and many other universities also provide an opportunity for the grievant, and perhaps the individual accused of violating the university policy at issue, to appeal the results of the investigation or hearing. As explained in OCR's Revised Guidance, a procedure that ensures the rights of the grievant, while at the same time according due process to both parties involved, will lead to sound and supportable decisions.

Issues of confidentiality should also be considered. Under George Mason's complaint procedures, every effort is made to preserve the confidentiality of the parties and the witnesses during the investigation, but it is recognized that this may not be possible in order to provide the parties with due process or where the alleged conduct is particularly serious or could affect other members of the university community.

Where a violation of university policy is found, the university must take steps reasonably calculated to end the harassment or other forms of gendered violence. This involves balancing the university's role as an educational institution with its responsibility to ensure a safe learning and working environment. Thus, steps can range from counseling to discipline to temporary or even permanent removal from the university. The university should also monitor the situation, to ensure that the conduct does not recur; a series of escalating steps may be necessary if the initial steps are not effective. It may be necessary to separate the individuals involved (e.g., by changing housing or working arrangements or directing the accused to have no further contact with the grievant). The university must also correct the effects of the conduct on the grievant and any others affected by the conduct. This can include professional counseling; correction of any effects on grades or performance evaluations; tuition adjustments, restoration of leave, or back pay; and, in appropriate cases, more systematic measures like campus-wide training and other steps designed to clearly communicate that the university does not tolerate such conduct and will effectively address any such conduct that does occur.

Finally, George Mason's sexual harassment policy charges all employees with reporting possible incidents of harassment to the Equity Office. This message is reinforced in training, which also encourages employees who witness possible harassment or other forms of gendered violence to not only report the matter but to inform the student or other employee of the process he or she can use to complain—even to the point of accompanying the individual to the Equity Office and/or Sexual Assault Services. This recognizes the role each employee has in maintaining a safe environment on campus and takes us back to the importance of education—of making sure that all members of the university community know that the university will not tolerate sexual harassment or other forms of gendered violence and what to do about it.

REFERENCES

Bard, M., & Sangrey, D. (1979). *The crime victim's book.* New York: Basic Books.

Enforcement Guidance: Vicarious Employer Liability for Unlawful Harassment by Supervisors, U.S. Equal Employment Opportunity Commission, 1999, http://www.eeoc.gov/policy/docs/harassment.html (last accessed November 2007).

Kirkland, C. J. (2004). Program case study: Campus-based sexual assault services—on the cutting edge. In D. Karm & T. Allena (Eds.), *Restorative justice on the college campus* (pp. 239–256). Springfield, IL: Charles C. Thomas.

Maitland, C., & Rhoades, G. (2005). Bargaining for contingent faculty. *The NEA Almanac of Higher Education.*

National Crime Prevention Council (2005). *Preventing violence against women: Not just a woman's Issue.* Washington, DC.

Notice of Nondiscrimination, Office for Civil Rights, U.S. Department of Education, 1999, http://www.ed.gov/ocr/publications.html (last accessed November 2007).

Paludi, M., & Paludi, C. (Eds.). (2003). *Academic and workplace sexual harassment: A handbook of cultural, social science, management, and legal perspectives,* Westport, CT: Praeger Publishers.

Regulations implementing Title IX of the Education Amendments of 1973, 34 C.F.R. Part 106, http://www.ed.gov/ocr/publications.html (last accessed November 2007).

Revised Sexual Harassment Guidance: Harassment of Students by School Employees, Other Students, or Third Parties, Office for Civil Rights, U.S. Department of Education, 2001, http://www.ed.gov/ocr/publications.html (last accessed November 2007).

Sandler, B., & Shoop, R. (Eds.). (1997) *Sexual harassment on campus: A guide for administrators, faculty and students.* Boston: Allyn and Bacon.

Title IX grievance procedures: An introductory manual, Office for Civil Rights, U.S. Department of Education, 1987, www.eric.ed.gov (search by ERIC # ED396455).

Epilogue
Michele A. Paludi

During the final stages of preparation for this book, our nation experienced another tragic campus violence incident. On February 14, 2008, six students were killed and 15 students were wounded when Steven Kazmierczak entered a large lecture hall at Northern Illinois University with a shotgun (concealed in a guitar case) and three handguns (hidden under his coat) and began shooting into the classroom. He later killed himself.

Within a few minutes of the shootings, the campus police responded; four minutes later, the campus was put in a lockdown situation. Within 20 minutes of the shootings, the university instituted additional responses, which included the following components (Johnson, 2008; Northern Illinois University, 2008):

- Placing an announcement on the Web site, including the following warning to students:

  There has been a report of a possible gunman on campus. Get to a safe area and take precautions until given the all clear. Avoid the King Commons and all buildings in that vicinity.

- Canceling classes
- Closing the campus
- Informing students to contact their parents
- Canceling all sporting events
- Providing counseling services for campus recovery (which lasted throughout the semester)

Illinois governor Blagojevich and Northern Illinois University President John Peters subsequently proposed that Cole Hall, the building in which the shootings occurred, be demolished because of the tragic memories it holds for the campus. In its place, "Memorial Hall" will be built, in remembrance of the victims of the campus violence.

These responses by Northern Illinois University, which take into account physical as well as psychological impacts of violence, were part of Northern Illinois University's new security plan that was developed following the campus violence incident at Virginia Tech (Johnson, 2008). Furthermore, neighboring universities notified their campus about the violence at Northern Illinois University. For example, Illinois State University President Bowman released the following statement:

> We learned of the shootings just moments after the incident happened, and I immediately sent an e-mail message to all students, faculty and staff and placed the same message on this homepage.... Meanwhile, our counselors remain fully prepared to help students, particularly those who may have friends attending NIU. Our police department data tells us we live in a safe University environment–but we continue our work to keep our campus as safe as possible. As always, we welcome your input in that effort ... (Illinois State University home page).

Northern Illinois University's response suggests colleges and universities conduct a campus safety audit to ensure they will be as well prepared to deal with violence should a similar event happen at their campus. Northern Illinois University implemented effective campus violence interventions that focused on prevention as well as response to campus violence. As recommended by the Higher Education Center (Langford, 2006), campus violence interventions should be:

- Prevention-focused
- Comprehensive, including all forms of campus violence on and off the campus itself
- Planned and evaluated
- Strategic and targeted, using results from a risk assessment of the vulnerability of the campus
- Research-based
- Multicomponent
- Coordinated and synergistic, ensuring all prevention and response efforts complement and reinforce each other
- Multisectoral and collaborative, involving campus stakeholders, including counselors and advisors
- Supported by infrastructure and institutional commitment (p. 5)

A campus safety audit is an in-depth review of the policies, procedures, and practices in place at the college or university, for example, a review of residence hall security, how visitors are permitted to enter the campus, how the campus deals with roommate conflicts, the availability of surveillance cameras, escort services, and bicycle patrols, and the availability of health services, including a rape crisis center, wellness center, women's center, and alcohol and other drug counseling.

The campus safety audit addresses legal must-haves to ensure that the campus is compliant with federal and state legislation (e.g., the Family Educational Rights and Privacy Act and Campus Crime Statistics; see Howard, this volume). The audit first determines the legal conditions that must be met by the campus and then determines whether the campus is meeting these conditions. Once the audit is completed, the campus will know exactly what needs to be done to ensure compliance and appropriate responses to campus violence. A sample campus safety audit is provided by Security on Campus, Inc. (see Kassa, this volume, for a description of this organization), and covers the following major issues:

- Residence hall security (e.g., automatic locked doors? guards on duty 24 hours? dead bolt on room door? secure windows? panic alarms in rooms?)
- Visitors (e.g., guest passes with guard? sign in guests with guard?)
- Security patrols in residence halls (e.g., by security nightly? by students?)
- Roommate conflicts (e.g., offending roommate quickly transferred for using illegal drugs? hate speech? physical abuse or violence?)
- Health services (e.g., rape crisis center? support groups for depression, eating disorders?)
- Campus security (e.g., sworn police? arrest power? emergency phones in working condition?)
- Parental notification (e.g., for suicide attempts? for stalking? for sexual assault? for hate crimes or speech?)

Given the incidence of various types of campus violence (e.g., stalking, hate crimes, rape, bullying, intimate partner violence, sexual harassment, murder; see Martin and also Denmark and Baron, this volume), campus safety audits are needed more than ever. The audit will uncover disconnects between the campus's policies, procedures, and practices and what the campus wants to achieve in terms of campus safety.

Following the audit, findings and recommendations can be prioritized based upon the risk level assigned to each item: high (requires immediate attention), medium (requires to be dealt with in a short time frame), and low (suggestions to make the campus safety practices more efficient). From this risk matrix, a campus safety plan can be developed to address the most pressing issues first (Crouhy, Galai, & Mark, 2005).

Rosabeth Moss Kanter has said: "Leaders are more powerful role models when they learn than when they teach." Northern Illinois University's courage in changing its campus safety responses after the

Epilogue

tragic events at Virginia Tech spoke volumes to the entire nation. The school recognized that campus violence is a complex problem that demands complex solutions. It is my hope that other campuses will follow Northern Illinois University's lead.

The recommendations in this book will help campuses achieve this goal.

REFERENCES

Crouhy, M., Galai, D., & Mark, R. (2005). *The essentials of risk management.* New York: McGraw Hill.

Illinois State University (2008). Illinois State University home page. Retrieved March 1, 2008, from http://www.mediarelations.ilstu.edu/isuhome/niu.asp

Johnson, C. (2008). *NIU shooting tests new security plan.* Retrieved March 1, 2008, from http:/en.wikipedia.org/wiki/Northern_Illinois_University_shooting

Langford, L. (2006). *Preventing violence and promoting safety in higher education settings: Overview of a comprehensive approach.* Newton, MA: Higher Education Center for Alcohol and Other Drug Abuse and Violence Prevention. Retrieved March 2, 2008, from www.higheredcenter.org/pubs/violence.html

Northern Illinois University (2008). Northern Illinois University Web site. Retrieved from http://www.niu.edu/tragedy/updates.shtml

APPENDICES

Dealing with and Preventing Campus Violence: Resources for Administrators, Students, Employees, and Faculty

Appendix A: Advocacy Resources Dealing with Campus Violence

Michele A. Paludi
Christa White

Abusive Men Exploring New Directions
http://www.amendinc.org
Acquaintance Rape of College Students
http://www.cops.usdoj.gov/mime/open/pdy?Item=269
American Psychological Association, Presidential Task Force on Violence and the Family
http://www.apa.org/pi/pii/issues/homepage.html
Antistalking Web Site
http://www.antistalking.com
Asian and Pacific Islander Institute on Domestic Violence
http://www.apiahf.org/apidvinstitute
Battered Women's Justice Project
http://www.Bwjp.org/
Campus Outreach Services
http://www.campusoutreachservices.com
Center for Women Policy Studies
http://www.centerwomenpolicy.org
College Violence
http://youthviolence.edschool.virginia.edu/violence-in-schools/college campus.html
Commission on Domestic Violence-American Bar Association
www.abanet.org/domviol
Criminal Justice Information Services Division-National Crime Information Center, Federal Bureau of Investigation
www.fbi.gov/hq/cjisd/cjis.htm

Division of Violence Prevention
http://eee.cdc.gov/ncipe/dvp/dvp.htm
Faith Trust Institute
http://www.faithtrustinstitute.org
Family Violence Prevention Fund
http://endabuse.org/
Feminist Majority Foundation
http://www.feminist.org
Indicators of School Crime and Safety
http://www.ojp.usdoj.gov/bjs/abstract/iscs03.htm
Institute on Domestic Violence in the African American Community
http://www.dvinstitute.org
International Society for Research on Aggression
http://www.israsociety.com/
Men Can Stop Rape
http://www.mencanstoprape.org/
National Center for Missing and Exploited Children
http://www.missingkids.com/
National Center for Victims of Crime
http://www.ncvc.org/ncvc/Main.aspx
National Center for Victims of Rape
http://www.nevc.org
National Center on Domestic and Sexual Violence
http://www.ncdsv.org/
National Coalition Against Domestic Violence
http://www.ncadv.org/
National Domestic Violence Hotline
1-800-799-SAFE (7233)
http://www.nnedv.org/
National Latino Alliance for the Elimination of Domestic Violence
http://www.dvalianza.org
National Organization for Men Against Sexism
http://www.nomas.org
National Organization for Women
http://www.now.org/index.html
National Sexual Violence Resource Center
http://www.nsvrc.org
National Tribal Justice Resource Center
http://www.tribalresourcescenter.org
New York Model for Batterer Programs
http://www.nymbp.org
Office of Violence Against Women of the U.S. Department of Justice
http://www.ojp.usdoj.gov/vawo/
Partnerships Against Violence Network
http://www.pavnet.org/
Psychological Abuse
http://psychabuse.info/
Raising Voices
http://www.raisingvoices.org

Rape, Abuse and Incest National Network
http://www.rainn.org/
Rape and Sexual Assault: Reporting to Police and Medical Attention
http://www.Ojp.usdoj.gov/bjs/pub/pdf/rsarp00.pdf
Rape Myths and Fact
http://www.ccasa.org/documents/Rape_Myths_&Facts.pdf
Resource Center on Domestic Violence: Child Protection and Custody
http://www.dvlawsearch.com/res_center
Security on Campus
http://www.securityoncampus.org
Sexual Assault and Rape Crisis Resources List
http://www.feminist.org/911/resources.html
StopFamilyViolence
http://www.stopfamilyviolence.org/
United Nations Fourth World Conference on Women: Platform for Action: Violence Against Women
http://www.un.org/womenwatch/daw/beijing/platform/violence.htm
United States Department of Health and Human Services
http://www.4women.gov/violence/index/cfm
United States Department of Justice's Victims of Crime
http://www.usdoj.gov/crimevictims.htm
Violence Against Women
http://www.vaw.umn.edu
Violence Against Women in American Indian/Native American and Alaska Native Communities
http://www.vawnet.org
VioLit: Violence Literature Database
http://ibs.colorado.edu/cspv/infohouse/violit/
Violence on Campus: Defining the Problems, Strategies for Action
http://jama.ama-assn.org/cgi/content/extract/284/5/620
Young Women's Christian Association
http://www.ywca.org

Appendix B: Campus-Wide Educational Techniques

Betty Jean Uebrick
Gennette Hollander
Carrie Turco
Christa White
Michele A. Paludi

FOR STUDENTS

- Ask students to identify behaviors they believe illustrate "flirting." Then ask them to indicate how they feel when they are being flirted with as well as flirting themselves. Next, ask students to list examples of behaviors they believe illustrate sexual harassment on the part of a peer. They can then indicate how they believe they would feel if being sexually harassed. Ask students to discuss the distinctions between the lists they have generated.

- Facilitate a "campus violence awareness" week and schedule programs around the issues of stalking, hazing, hate crimes, sexual harassment, rape, and murder.

- Facilitate discussions on campus violence within sororities and fraternities. Encourage students to co-facilitate the training.

- Ask students to help write a public service announcement about types of campus violence that can be broadcast throughout the campus.

- Ask students to assist in putting issues of campus violence, including the campus's policy and reporting mechanism(s), on the campus's intranet.

- Ask students if they know what to do in the event they are a victim or witness to an incident of campus violence. Do they know the name of the investigator of complaints? The office location? Where to locate this information?

- Ask faculty to discuss campus violence within courses, e.g.:

  - Psychology/Sociology: Interaction of gender, race, and power in sexual victimization; attitudes toward victim blame and victim responsibility.
  - Mathematics: Methodology used to obtain incidence rates of sexual violence and reporting sexual violence on college campuses.
  - Political Science: Legal issues in campus violence; social and public policy applications of research on campus violence.
  - History: Sexual violence of women from an historical perspective; history of laws in the United States and other countries regarding campus violence.
  - Literature: Ways sexual violence has been discussed in literature, especially attitudes and attributions for the violence.
  - Business/Management: Strategies for training faculty and staff regarding campus violence.
  - Women's Studies: Conduct an anonymous survey of the incidence of date rape, sexual harassment, stalking, bullying, and intimate partner violence on your campus. Present the results of the survey to the administrators. Collaborate with administrators to ensure safety on your campus.
  - Drama: Ask students to design a play that deals with sexual victimization of a college student by another student. Ask actors to remain in their role as the audience asks questions regarding the issues raised about the play.

- Help begin a support group for victims and witnesses of campus violence. Consider partnering with local police and women's centers in offering programs such as self-defense classes.

FOR EMPLOYEES

- Invite the human resource department to display informational brochures and posters about workplace violence, including intimate partner violence as a workplace issue.
- Invite Campus Security to do informal presentations on how to stay safer on campus, how to report a crime, how to convey concerns, campus-provided security features like emergency phones, escort services, etc.
- Invite the Employees Assistance Program to facilitate brown-bag lunch discussions on workplace violence. Topics to include:

  - Legal definition of workplace violence.
  - Behavioral examples of workplace violence.
  - Organizational and personal factors contributing to workplace violence.
  - Intimate partner violence as a workplace concern.

o Campus policy statement and investigatory procedures on workplace violence and intimate partner violence as a workplace concern.

o Personalized safety plans the employer can set up for victims.

- Ask a local Women's Shelter to facilitate a brown-bag lunch discussion on intimate partner violence, including the impact of battering on children and shelters who offer assistance to women and children in the community. The following topics are helpful for victims to learn about: cycle of battering; long-term consequences of battering; and the relationship between workplace violence and intimate partner violence.

  o Require management staff training to help identify employees who are at risk to become violent in the workplace.

  o Require training to help management identify employees who are victims of domestic or intimate violence that could become a threat in the workplace.

- Train managers in the appropriate steps to assist employees who are victims to get needed help and assistance.

- Ensure the human resource department updates its policies on sexual harassment, workplace violence, and other forms of violence on campus/in the workplace, taking into account case law and social science research.

- Ensure the human resource department facilitates training programs on an annual basis on sexual harassment and other forms of victimization, fostering a preventative and proactive approach to educate employees.

- Ensure the procedures for reporting sexual harassment and other forms of violence are confidential, free of retaliatory actions, and perceived by employees as "safe" and effective.

- Provide training for investigators of complaints of sexual harassment and other forms of violence that include the following at a minimum:

Psychological issues involved in dealing with sexual harassment
Physical and emotional reactions to being sexually harassed
The complainant's perspective
Psychology of the victimization process
Internally and externally focused strategies
The accused's perspective
Differential evaluations of identical behavior
Interviewing techniques

Appendix C: Campus Security Recommendations for Administrators to Help Prevent and Deal with Violence

Jesse Middelkoop
John Gilhooley
Nicholas Ruepp
Raymond Polikoski
Michele A. Paludi

FOR ADMINISTRATORS, FACULTY, AND STAFF

- Ensure faculty and staff have access to employee assistance programs to discuss incidents of workplace violence and other forms of violence on campus. Offer EAP services for family members of employees.
- Ensure effective background checks as part of the employment process.
- Provide annual training to employees on campus violence policies and procedures. Clearly communicate and ensure understanding of acceptable vs. non-acceptable behavior on campus.
- Train faculty to detect the beginnings of potential problems, such as unnatural stress, preoccupation with violence as indicated in term papers or class discussions.
- Establish a Threat Assessment Team to assist with dealing with workplace violence. Make part of the duties of this team to assess the vulnerability of the campus to intimate partner violence and serve as advocates for victims of workplace violence and domestic violence as a workplace issue.

- For victims of domestic violence, offer the following services:
  - Provide receptionists and building security with a photograph of the batterer and a description of the batterer
  - Screen employee's calls
  - Screen employee's visitors
  - Permit the employee to park close to the office building
  - Accompany the employee to his/her car
  - When there is a restraining order, the campus President should send a formal notification to the assailant that indicates that he/she cannot be present on campus; failure to comply will result in arrest
  - Provide referrals for individual counseling
  - Permit time off for counselor and attorney visits
- Provide escort and/or shuttle services for employees and faculty who request them at any time of the day or night.
- Coordinate electronic surveillance, campus security, vehicle global positioning, communications, etc., with local law enforcement to provide quicker response times.
- Install voice activated and Braille security call boxes.
- Provide access to policies and procedures on the campus Web site.
- Develop a risk-reduction plan to prevent repeat victimization.
- Offer rape aggression defense training.
- Ensure emergency medical care immediately following any campus violence.
- Ensure a campus-wide emergency notification system in the event of violence.

FOR STUDENTS

- Ensure students have access to the counseling center to discuss incidents of campus violence, including sexual victimization.
- Ensure effective background checks as part of the admissions process.
- Provide annual training to students on campus violence policies and procedures.
- Provide escort and/or shuttle services for students who request them at any time of the day or night.
- Enforce electronic surveillance, campus security vehicle global positioning, communications, etc., with local law enforcement to provide quicker response times.
- Install voice activated and Braille security call boxes.
- Provide access to policies and procedures on the campus Web site.
- Develop a risk reduction plan to prevent repeat victimization.
- Offer rape aggression defense training.

- Ensure emergency medical care immediately following any campus violence.
- Ensure a campus-wide emergency notification system in the event of violence.
- Ensure students have safe and adequate transportation to parts of campus.
- Ensure commuter students are appraised of their rights and responsibilities with respect to campus violence policies and procedures.

GENERAL

- Utilize a "Lessons-Learned" symposium to exchange, or pass down, knowledge on judgment errors, regrettable actions made under the influence of alcohol/drugs, misunderstandings, regrets, and/or close calls.
- Establish a campus security-exchange program designed to help campuses learn from each other instead of developing plans in a vacuum.
- Ensure all members of the campus community have proper identification carried with them at all times.
- Post unobtrusive no trespassing signs around the campus perimeter.
- Increase lighting on campus, especially in limited vision areas.
- Increase security patrols on campus, including foot patrols.
- Establish an anonymous "tip line" for reporting threats, suspicious behavior or persons.
- Identify local criminal authorities for campus community, e.g., publish telephone numbers of police department.
- Ensure campus security frequently stops suspicious individuals on campus, i.e., those individuals who have no campus identification and no legitimate reason for being on campus.
- Security alarm systems should have security alarm systems.
- Establish a bike patrol for the campus that is pedestrian-based.
- Establish a fire and general evacuation plan.
- Provide all campus crime statistics as reported to the United States Department of Education to prospective students as well as current students, employees, faculty, and staff.
- Provide campus safety procedures at various sites on campus, e.g., library, campus center, dorm, sororities, fraternities, health center, counseling center.
- Ensure the counseling center has a therapist trained in sexual victimization to assist individuals in healing from the victimization.
- Establish a student and employee auxiliary force to assist campus security (similar to a neighborhood watch).

Appendix D: Keeping Safe on College Campuses: Recommendations for Students

Michele A. Paludi

- Familiarize yourself with legislation on campus violence, e.g., Jeanne Clery Act, Title IX of the 1972 Education Amendments, Campus Sex Crimes Prevention Act.
- Take courses that focus on campus violence, abuse of power in dating relationships, etc.,: psychology of women, women's studies, gender studies.
- Have the following phone numbers available at all times:

  Campus Security
  City Police
  Rape Crisis Center
  Dean of Students
  Walking Escort Service
  Any Additional Security Services Offered by Your Campus
  Counseling Center
  Health Services
  Fire Department
  Local Hospitals
  Emergency Medical Transportation Services
  Individual(s) Charged with Hearing Complaints, e.g., Sexual Harassment Investigator
  Campus Ministry

- Familiarize yourself with your campus's policies dealing with campus violence, including: sexual harassment, sexual assault, hazing, hate crimes, and stalking.

- Know your rights and responsibilities with respect to filing a complaint, how your confidentiality will be maintained, how you won't be retaliated against for filing a complaint, the role of witnesses, etc.

- Participate in training programs on campus violence. If there are no programs in place, talk with your Dean of Students about the importance of students knowing their rights with respect to campus violence.

- Familiarize yourself with voice activated and Braille security call boxes on your campus.

- Know your campus-wide emergency notification system in the event of violence.

- Know your campus's fire and general evacuation plan.

- Trust your discomfort in relationships. Listen to your instincts if you sense potential danger.

- If a classmate confides in you about being a victim of campus violence:

  Listen to them discuss the violence;
  Let them know their feelings are valid;
  Help provide information, e.g., hotline, shelter, individual on campus to report the violence, therapeutic support, medical attention.

- Be aware of your surroundings while on and off campus. Be vigilant about people present, lighting, accessible exits, etc.

- Take stairs and elevators in well-trafficked areas on campus, including classroom buildings, laboratories and the library.

- Yell, scream, and make a scene if you are feeling threatened or frightened. Tell people. Do not feel ashamed or blame yourself.

- Know the impact of alcohol and other drugs on your judgment and of others.

- Participate in self-defense classes.

- If your dorm has doors that lock automatically, do not prop them open.

- If your campus requires a card to get into buildings, don't lend out your card.

- Be sure your cell phone is on when you are not in classes.

- If you are bicycling at night, use a light and wear light-colored clothing.

- Let someone know where you are and when you will be leaving or arriving at a destination.

- Report suspicious incidents and persons to your campus security immediately. Be as accurate and complete as possible in your descriptions.

- If you witness or are the victim of a violent crime, seek help. Advocacy, medical care, and counseling assistance are available.

- If you live in a residence hall, ask your resident hall advisor to schedule safety programs.

- Secure your possessions in your dorm or residence hall.

- Escort guests in your dorm/residence hall at all times.

- Report suspicious nonresidents to a resident assistant.
- If you hear gunshots or witness an armed person, isolate yourself and those you are with from the suspect. Lock and barricade doors if you can and lie on the ground. If you are in an open space, hide to the maximum extent possible. If it is safe to do so, call 911 and provide as much detail as you can. Do not assume the danger is over until you are notified by police that the danger has passed. Assist those individuals with disabilities as much as you can. Notify 911 that a disabled person is in potential danger.

For additional information, contact Security on Campus at: www.securityoncampus.org

Index

About the Editor and Contributors

EDITOR

Michele A. Paludi, Ph.D., is the author/editor of 27 college textbooks, and more than 140 scholarly articles and conference presentations on sexual harassment, psychology of women, gender, and sexual harassment and victimization. Her book, *Ivory Power: Sexual Harassment on Campus* (1990, SUNY Press), received the 1992 Myers Center Award for Outstanding Book on Human Rights in the United States. Dr. Paludi served as Chair of the U.S. Department of Education's Subpanel on the Prevention of Violence, Sexual Harassment, and Alcohol and Other Drug Problems in Higher Education. She was one of six scholars in the United States to be selected for this subpanel. She also was a consultant to and a member of former New York State Governor Mario Cuomo's Task Force on Sexual Harassment. She is the series editor for Praeger's Women and Psychology Series.

Dr. Paludi serves as an expert witness for court proceedings and administrative hearings on sexual harassment. She has had extensive experience in conducting training programs and investigations of sexual harassment and other EEO issues for businesses and educational institutions. In addition, Dr. Paludi has held faculty positions at Franklin & Marshall College, Kent State University, Hunter College, Union College, and Union Graduate College, where she directs the human resource management certificate program. She teaches courses in the School of Management: Foundations of Human Resource Management, Managing Human Resources, and International Human Resource Management.

CONTRIBUTORS

Erika M. Baron received her B.A. in psychology from the University of Michigan. She is pursuing her Psy.D. in school-clinical child psychology at Pace University in New York City. Her research interests include the effects of body image on female adolescent personality development as well as gender issues in a cross-cultural perspective. She has co-authored several writings that focus on women, violence, and leadership.

Joan C. Chrisler, Ph.D., is professor of psychology at Connecticut College. She has published extensively on the psychology of women and gender, and is especially known for her work on women's health, menstruation, weight, and body image. She has served as President of the Society for Menstrual Cycle Research, the Society for the Psychology of Women (APA Division 35), the Association for Women in Psychology, the New England Psychological Association, and the Connecticut State Conference of the American Association of University Professors. She recently completed a five-year term as editor of *Sex Roles: A Journal of Research,* and is editor or co-editor of seven books, including *Women over 50: Psychological Perspectives* (2007), *From Menarche to Menopause: The Female Body in Feminist Therapy* (2004), *Arming Athena: Career Strategies for Women in Academe* (1998), and *Lectures on the Psychology of Women* (4th ed.; 2008).

Darlene C. DeFour, Ph.D., is a social psychologist/community psychologist. She is a graduate of Fisk University and received her doctorate from the University of Illinois at Urbana-Champaign. She is currently an associate professor of psychology at Hunter College of the City University of New York. There she teaches classes including social psychology, personal adjustment, psychology of women, theories of ethnic identity development and issues in black psychology. She is currently a member of the board of directors of the New York Association of Black Psychologists and has served on the board of directors of the national association. She is also active in several divisions of the American Psychological Association. The theme of her current research is the exploration of the various ways that violence in the form of racism and sexism as well as physical violence affects the everyday lives of adolescent and adult black females.

Florence L. Denmark is an internationally recognized scholar, researcher, and policy maker. She received her Ph.D. from the University of Pennsylvania in social psychology and has five honorary degrees. Denmark is the Robert Scott Pace Distinguished Research Professor of Psychology at Pace University in New York. A past president of the American Psychological Association (APA) and the International Council of Psychologists (ICP), Denmark holds fellowship status in the APA and the American Psychological Society. She is also a member of the Society for Experimental Social Psychology (SESP) and a Fellow of the New York Academy of Sciences. She has received numerous national and international awards for her contributions to psychology. She received the 2004 American Psychological Foundation Gold Medal for Lifetime Achievement in the Public Interest. In 2005, she received the Ernest R. Hilgard Award for her Career Contribution to General Psychology. She was the recipient in 2007 of the Raymond Fowler Award for Outstanding Service to APA. Also in 2007, Denmark was elected to the National Academies of Practice as a distinguished scholar member. Denmark's most significant research and extensive publications have emphasized women's leadership and leadership styles, the interaction of status and gender, aging women in cross-cultural perspective, and the contributions of women to psychology. Denmark is the main NGO representative to the United Nations for the International Council of Psychologists and is also the main NGO representative for the American Psychological Association. She is currently Chair of the New York NGO Committee on Aging and a member of APA's Committee on Aging.

John Gilhooley earned his MBA from Union Graduate College. He also earned certificates in leadership and management and financial management. He has been a supply accounts manager for Xerox's Northeast Quarter of New York State. He has previously worked for Chase Manhattan Bank, Sterling National Bank, Irving Trust, and Livingston Police Department.

Gennette Hollander is a personnel administrator covering the areas of recruiting, staffing, health benefits, leaves and separations, and workers' compensation. She has been a child protective, adult protective, and child preventative services case worker. In addition, she worked for the Office for the Aging. She also was a paralegal/legal assistant in a private law firm. She earned her certificate in Human Resource Management from Union Graduate College in spring 2008. Her undergraduate degree is in communications from the State University of New York at Plattsburgh.

Linda Gordon Howard is an attorney and consultant in workplace diversity issues, including sexual harassment. She has spent the last 30 years successfully practicing, advising, counseling, and teaching in the areas of employment discrimination and sexual harassment law. Ms. Howard has trained thousands of employees in how to understand and to comply with the difficult and confusing law of sexual harassment. Her original and proven methods communicate the logic behind the law and illustrate how to deal with sexual harassment as it happens. Her book, *The Sexual Harassment Handbook* (Career Press, February 2007) is a practical, street smart guide for working men and women. Ms. Howard received her law degree from the University of Virginia Law School and her undergraduate degree from Reed College. She is a former law professor at the Ohio State University, member of the White House Staff, college legal counsel, and senior attorney for the City of New York. She serves as a Trustee of Reed College and a director of the not-for-profit, A More Perfect Union, Inc., and leads transformational programs for Landmark Education. She practices law in New York City.

Howard Kallem is a senior equal opportunity specialist with George Mason University's Office of Equity and Diversity Services. Previously, he was the chief regional attorney for the Office for Civil Rights, U.S. Department of Education's D.C. Enforcement Office for 10 years and in OCR's policy office for four years. Before that, he was with the U.S. Equal Employment Opportunity Commission for 14 years. He has worked extensively with issues such as sexual and racial harassment, testing, and meeting the needs of students with disabilities. He has served as a commissioner and vice chair of the Arlington County, Virginia, Human Rights Commission. He received his law degree from Catholic University of America.

Jonathan M. Kassa is executive director of Security on Campus. He brings a dynamic 13-year nonprofit experience to SOC, having worked for an entrepreneurial nonprofit agency serving at-risk youth and their families in the Mid-Atlantic (starting as an intern and rising to senior executive, as regional director of operations). Over his career, Mr. Kassa developed a reputation for facilitating effective public-private partnerships and cross-systems collaboration. Mr. Kassa played a crucial role in the strategy, development, and delivery of a broad array of quality community-based programs serving juvenile justice, social services, and school systems. He helped expansion from a single-county agency to a statewide, and then multi-state organization, with national partners and interests. Besides typical operational duties, Mr. Kassa was the lead agency writer and focused on the start-up and implementation of outcomes-based, award-winning youth development programs. Some accomplishments include a unique governor's earmark in Maryland, more than a dozen successful grants totaling over $3 million, the successful proposal, negotiation, and completion of Maryland's first multi-county alternative education contract with a private services provider, the development of significant State of Delaware contracts, creation of a groundbreaking mentor/tutoring program selected by the State of Maryland as a site-visit to highlight successful federally funded programs, the design of two other county-wide Programs of the Year (casework, community service). Mr. Kassa also received the *Dare to Soar Award* from the Cecil County Local Management Board; honoring "dedication and vision" toward improving the lives of youth and families in the region. Jonathan is proud to be a member of the SOC team and excited to help expand upon a solid foundation of programs, resources, and services. He is a graduate of Penn State University (B.A., History) and is enrolled in Villanova University's Masters in Public Administration Program.

Connie Kirkland, M.A., is currently the director of sexual assault services at George Mason University, Fairfax, Virginia, where she provides university-wide education and training, as well as crisis intervention for victims of campus sexual assault, stalking, and relationship violence. She is also a George Mason University faculty member in the New Century College and the departments of women's studies and the administration of justice. Ms. Kirkland has worked for over 30 years in crime victim advocacy, as a college instructor, and as a criminal justice researcher and trainer. She is an ATSS Certified Trauma Specialist (CTS), a National Certified Counselor (NCC), and a Certified Law Enforcement Instructor. She has authored legislative bills, training manuals, and materials related to crime victim issues, specializing in violence against women. From 2005 to present, Ms. Kirkland has been a member of the curriculum committee as well as a faculty member for the Jeanne Clery Act Compliance Training, a project sponsored by Security on Campus, Inc., and the U.S. Department of Justice Office for Victims of Crime. This training has been provided to over 2,000 college and university officials to date. In 2004, Ms. Kirkland authored a chapter titled "Program Case Study: Campus-Based Sexual Assault Services—On the Cutting Edge," in *Restorative Justice on the College Campus* by David R. Karp and Thom Allena (Charles C. Thomas publisher). In 2003, Ms. Kirkland partnered with the U.S. Department of Justice National Drug Intelligence Center to co-author a manual designed for law enforcement and medical investigators, titled "Drug-Facilitated Sexual Assault Resource Guide." She was recognized in 2002 in several ways for her expertise in sexual assault and stalking. She was appointed to the Virginia Attorney General's Advisory Council on Domestic Violence and Sexual Assault. She was also appointed to the Virginia Sexual Violence Strategic Planning Team. In addition she authored "Campus Stalking," a bulletin for the U.S. Department of Justice Violence Against Women Office. The recent releases of *Net Crimes and Misdemeanors* (2002 and 2006), a book on cyber-stalking by J. A. Hitchcock featured the advocacy of Ms. Kirkland with victims of campus cyber-stalking. She has served as the consulting editor of *Campus Safety*

& Security: Forms, Checklists & Guidelines from 2001 to present. She served as chair of the Northern Virginia Turn Off the Violence Coalition, a major community violence prevention initiative from 1993 through 2001. In February, 2001, Ms. Kirkland's research and advocacy in the field of campus stalking was highlighted in the *Chronicle of Higher Education* and in September 2000, she was a featured speaker at the U.S. Capitol Hill "Rally to Re-authorize the Violence Against Women Act." In June 2000, the Giraffe Project, a national organization that honors those who "stick their necks out" for the common good, chose Connie Kirkland as one of 10 yearly honorees for her victim advocacy and community violence prevention work. The U.S. Department of Justice, Violence Against Women Office, and the National Crime Prevention Council have recognized Ms. Kirkland's sexual assault research and innovative programming as a promising practices resource. She has also been recognized by the U.S. Department of Justice for her work in the area of sexual assault and stalking protocols, serving as expert resource, national speaker, and federal grant peer reviewer. She is a consultant for workplace crisis management, campus security initiatives, and public policy development.

Maria D. Klara received her B.A. from Boston College in 1999 and then her M.S. in counseling psychology from Northeastern University in 2003. She is currently pursuing her Psy.D. in school-clinical child psychology at Pace University. Her academic interests include women and gender issues, psychological assessment, and clinical work with adolescents.

Paula Lundberg-Love is a professor of psychology at the University of Texas at Tyler (UTT) and the Ben R. Fisch Endowed Professor in Humanitarian Affairs for 2001–2004. Her undergraduate degree was in chemistry and her doctorate was in physiological psychology with an emphasis in psychopharmacology. After a three-year postdoctoral fellowship in nutrition and behavior in the Department of Preventive Medicine at Washington University School of Medicine in St. Louis, she assumed her academic position at UTT where she teaches classes in psychopharmacology, behavioral neuroscience, physiological psychology, sexual victimization, and family violence. Subsequent to her academic appointment, Dr. Lundberg-Love pursued postgraduate training and is a licensed professional counselor. She is a member of Tyler Counseling and Assessment Center, where she provides therapeutic services for victims of sexual assault, child sexual abuse, and domestic violence. She has conducted a long-term research study on women who were victims of childhood incestuous abuse, constructed a therapeutic program for their recovery, and documented its effectiveness upon their recovery. She is the author of nearly 100 publications and presentations and is co-editor of *Violence and Sexual Abuse at Home: Current Issues in Spousal Battering and Child Maltreatment.* As a result of her training in psychopharmacology and child maltreatment, her expertise has been sought as a consultant on various death penalty appellate cases in the state of Texas.

Jennifer L. Martin is department head of English at a public alternative high school for at-risk students in Michigan and holds a Ph.D. in educational leadership. Dr. Martin is also a lecturer at Oakland University where she teaches in the departments of educational leadership and women's studies. She is a past co-chair of the Girls' Studies Interest Group for the National Women's Studies Association. Her research interests include peer sexual harassment, feminist identification, teaching for social justice, service learning, and the at-risk student.

Jesse Middelkoop holds a Masters of Business Administration degree from Union Graduate College and currently resides in upstate New York. He is an avid outdoorsman, father of two, and currently employed in the defense industry.

Presha E. Neidermeyer, Ph.D., CPA, is an associate professor of accounting at West Virginia University's College of Business and Economics. She has published numerous articles in behavioral accounting focusing on the way that gender and culture affect decision making. She has co-edited the book *Work, Life, and Family Imbalance* (Praeger, 2007) and is presently working on a book investigating the effect of the HIV/AIDS Pandemic on women's issues in Africa. Her non-research activities include involving business students in philanthropic activities harnessing the students' unique skill set to assist various African charities in their quest to resolve the AIDS pandemic.

Carmen Paludi, Jr., holds advanced degrees in electrical engineering from Clarkson University and Syracuse University, and has conducted graduate studies in applied physics and electronics engineering at the University of Massachusetts, and engineering management at Kennedy Western University. His 32-year career spans work for the Department of Defense in Federal Civil Service as well as the private sector. He has held positions as Senior Principal Engineer, Member of the Technical Staff, and Senior Scientific Advisor for the United States Air Force, Sanders Associates, The MITRE Corporation, Titan Corporation, and L-3 Communications, Inc. He has over 20 technical publications in refereed journals, and presentations at international symposia and conferences. Mr. Paludi was an adjunct faculty at New Hampshire Technical College, a guest lecturer at the Advanced Electronics Technology Center at the University of Massachusetts, is a frequently lecturer at the

Union Graduate College, and a consultant to Human Resources Management Solutions. He is a Capability Maturity Model Integration (CMMI) trained and certified Appraisal Team Member by the Software Engineering Institute at Carnegie Mellon University. He has developed and presented in-house training programs in requirements management, requirements development, and risk management. He has over 30 years of program management experience.

Mario Pecoraro, Jr., is president/CEO of Alliance Worldwide Investigative Group in Albany, New York. This is a full-service investigative firm dedicated to serving the needs of employers of all sizes. Mr. Pecoraro has extensive experience in assessing potential workplace violence, theft, and risk mitigation.

Raymond Polikoski is the director of finance for Amsterdam Memorial Hospital in Amsterdam, New York. He is also completing his graduate studies towards his MBA from Union Graduate College.

Amy J. Ramson has been an assistant professor in the Public Administration & Criminal Justice Unit of Hostos Community College (CUNY) since September 1990. She is an attorney licensed to practice in New York State since 1983 and the state of Georgia since 1987. Ms. Ramson has worked as an attorney for Patterson, Belknap, Webb & Tyler, a large law firm in New York City; an international law boutique in New York City; a law firm in Geneva, Switzerland; and at a non-profit organization in Newark. Her areas of expertise are immigration and international law. Since 1990, Ms. Ramson has practiced law on a part-time basis. At Hostos Community College, Ms. Ramson has been the education chair of the currently named Sexual Harassment Awareness and Intake Committee since 1997. In this capacity, she has devised the curriculum for a workshop with a multimedia approach; created a myriad of printed materials including posters, a brochure, a summary of the CUNY Policy and Procedures; and has conducted hundreds of workshops and assemblies to educate the academic community. Her areas of academic expertise along with sexual harassment include women and policing, instructional technology and paralegal studies. Her latest scholarship is an article which was published in May 2006 as editor's choice in *The Community College Review*, entitled, "Sexual Harassment Education on Campus: Communication Using Media."

Nicholas Ruepp is a 2007 graduate of the Union Graduate College in Schenectady, NY, where he obtained an MBA. He is a 2001 graduate of the George Washington University in Washington, D.C., where he obtained a B.S. in criminal justice. Nicholas is currently a retirement specialist for Employer Services at Fidelity Management and Research Corporation in

Cary, NC. He is a former officer of the Metropolitan Police Department in Washington, DC, and a former intern of the University Police Department at the George Washington University in Washington, DC.

Maritza Santos is working towards her MBA at Union Graduate College in Schenectady, NY, and will graduate in March 2008. She is a 2006 graduate of Siena College in Loudonville, NY, where she obtained a B.S. in marketing management. Maritza is currently a marketing intern for the Health Care Benefits and Delivery Team at General Electric in Schenectady. Maritza is native Spanish speaker and spent a semester abroad in Seville, Spain. Upon graduation she hopes to secure a position in brand management or international marketing.

Mab Segrest currently holds the Fuller-Maathai Chair in Gender and Women's Studies at Connecticut College. She is author of three books: *My Mama's Dead Squirrel: Lesbian Essays on Southern Culture, Memoir of a Race Traitor*, and *Born to Belonging: Writings on Spirit and Justice*.

Janet Sigal is a professor of psychology at Fairleigh Dickinson University. She received her Ph.D. in social psychology from Northwestern University. Her major research interests include sexual harassment, domestic violence, and other issues relevant to women. In addition, she has conducted cross-cultural research in several countries. She has several publications and over 100 conference presentations. She is a fellow in Divisions 35 and 52 of the American Psychological Association.

Siri Terjesen, Ph.D., is an assistant professor in the department of management at Texas Christian University. Concurrently, she is a Visiting Research Fellow at the Max Planck Institute of Economics in Jena, Germany. Previously, she was a lecturer at the London School of Economics and Political Science and a senior lecturer at the Brisbane Graduate School of Business at Queensland University of Technology. She has published in journals including *Strategic Management Journal, Small Business Economics, Journal of Business Ethics, Entrepreneurship Theory & Practice*, and *Venture Capital* and is co-author (with Anne Huff, Steve Floyd, and Hugh Sherman) of *Strategic Management* (Wiley, 2008).

Carrie Turco is currently completing her MBA and certificate in human resource management at Union Graduate College. Her career goals include becoming a director/vice president of human resources in the private sector. She enjoys photography, tennis, and volunteering for the St. Jude's Children's Hospital.

Betty Jean Uebrick received an MBA and human resource certificate in 2007 from Union Graduate College in Schenectady, NY. She is a 2001 graduate of Siena College in Loudonville, NY, where she obtained a B.S. in finance. As a non-traditional student she has worked full-time in the field of finance while attaining her degrees. She is currently seeking a position in the field of employee benefits.

Bethany L. Waits is a graduate student in clinical psychology at the University of Texas at Tyler. She anticipates graduation in May of 2009 and plans to pursue the Licensed Professional Counselor designation upon completion of her degree. Ultimately, she would like to work as a therapist for a nonprofit community organization, such as a crisis center. In May 2007, she obtained her B.A. in psychology from UT-Tyler graduating summa cum laude. She was accepted as a lifetime member of Psi Chi, the national honor society in psychology, and Alpha Chi, a national college honor society. While an undergraduate, she participated in a student panel addressing issues related to sexual assault on campus. Additionally, she has worked with several professors on various research projects.

Christa White is majoring in psychology at Union College and is expected to graduate in June 2008. She has conducted research in work/life integration, especially the impact of maternal employment on children and elder care responsibilities for women.